The Christian Counselor's Commentary

Romans
Philippians
I Thessalonians
II Thessalonians

Jay E. Adams

Institute for Nouthetic Studies, a ministry of Mid-America Baptist Theological Seminary, 5640 Airline Road, Arlington, TN 38002
mabts.edu / nouthetic.org / INSBookstore.com

Romans, Philippians, I & II Thessalonians:
The Christian Counselor's Commentary
by Jay E. Adams
Copyright © 2025 by the Institute for Nouthetic Studies,
© 1995 by Jay E. Adams

ISBN: 978-1-970445-05-3 (Paper)
ISBN: 978-1-970445-06-0 (eBook)
Old ISBN: 0-889032-09-3

Editor: Donn R. Arms

Library of Congress Cataloging-in-Publication Data
Names: Adams, Jay E., 1929-2020
Title: *Romans, Philippians, I & II Thessalonians:*
The Christian Counselor's Commentary
by Jay E. Adams
Description: Arlington, TN: Institute for Nouthetic Studies, 2025
Identifiers: ISBN 978-1-970445-05-3 (paper) | OCLC: 33193291
Classification: LCC BS2665.3 .A438 | DDC 227

All rights reserved. No part of this publication may be reproduced, stored in a retrieval system, or transmitted in any form or by any means – electronic, mechanical, photocopy, recording, or any other – except for brief quotations in printed reviews, without prior permission of the publisher.

Published in the United States of America

Introduction to ROMANS

Paul was headed for Spain. Whether or not he made it is uncertain, but many commentators think he did. In Spain you can visit places where he is said to have planted churches. But of importance for us is the fact that on his way to Spain he planned at long last to visit the church at Rome. For many years, and in various ways, he had attempted to do so before, but always, for some reason or other, he found it impossible. Now, it seemed that he would have his long-standing wish fulfilled. It was not only because he was headed to Spain that he was going to stop off at Rome (perhaps to establish a base for a western ministry); he had longed to become acquainted with the members of the Roman church for quite some time. But, specifically, why write a letter like this? That is the critical question.

Paul did not plant the church at Rome. That, of course, makes this letter unique; all of his other letters are to individuals, or to churches he began and with which, therefore, he was familiar. He planned to visit a Roman congregation (or perhaps several congregations by now) that probably had been begun by some of those who were converted under the Pentecostal preaching of Peter (cf. Acts 2:10). Doubtless, many who had become Christians elsewhere visited Rome from time to time and spent some years fellowshipping with the congregation. Others, moving to this metropolitan center—the capital of the empire—became permanent residents and members of the church. Paul knew a few persons from the church, whom he had met in other locations (see chapter 16), but the majority of the individuals at Rome were unknown to him. The names mentioned in the last chapter of Romans show that Jews, Greeks and Latins were a part of this cosmopolitan church. He hoped to receive support for his trip to Spain from the Roman church, but as a prelude to that he wanted to let them know what he preached, so that if they concurred with his message they would have good reason to support his new missionary endeavor (cf. 15:24).

With one possible exception (the issue raised in chapter 14) there are no references to problems in the church, but only brief references to the good things that he had heard. The bulk of the book, therefore, deals with the gospel that he preached and the implications of this gospel for the sanctification of the believer. Though a letter, Romans is more than a letter. It is a sophisticated theological treatise.

Christian Counselor's Commentary

The church was largely gentile in composition, though there were Jews among its members. Perhaps, as in Paul's ministry elsewhere, there were a number of the God-fearing Gentiles (also called "proselytes of the gate") who made up the bulk of the membership. These God-fearers were Gentiles who had come to believe in Jehovah as the true God and had forsaken heathen worship, but had not been circumcised and did not observe all of the dietary laws or attend all of the feasts. The book of Acts shows how receptive they were to the preaching of the gospel.

During the early spring of A.D. 58, Paul penned this letter which he wrote in Corinth (see the introduction to Romans by James M. Stifler). Paul was planning to come soon, but Phoebe was about to take a trip to Rome before him. Paul sent the letter by her (16:1).

Romans is a systematic statement of Paul's teaching. By the time he arrived, they would have been able to peruse it, discuss it at length and be ready to ask any questions that came to their minds. It was an interesting and powerful way to introduce himself to the church. While not every counselor can spend the time to detail all his beliefs to those whom he counsels, it behooves him to give something of a statement of where he stands either in a written form (a booklet, a page or two, or something) that would identify his position theologically and his beliefs about the sufficiency of the Scriptures in counseling. Counselors are of such a varied sort (except for truly biblical counselors) that counselees need to be given some idea of what they are getting into when they apply for help. To call oneself a "Christian counselor" or even a "biblical" one, today, means very little since integrationists of every sort have distorted those terms beyond all meaning. Obviously statements need not be as long as the book of Romans, but they ought the cover the crucial points. Do you have such a statement available for your counselees? Why not draft one right now so that, like Paul, you will be able to introduce yourself and your beliefs to any who have not previously known you. Of course, many members in your congregation will need no such statement. But, even there, if they are new to the church, or if they are weak in their understanding of biblical counseling, the statement would be of great benefit to them and to you.

In this extraordinary book, excelling all others that came from his hand, Paul provides so much help for Christian counselors that it is difficult to decide which elements to access. Much will be mentioned suggestively, presupposing that you will be able to get the idea and run with it yourself. It is my prayer that what you read here will be of the utmost benefit to you.

Chapter 1

> 1 Paul, a slave of Jesus Christ, called to be an apostle, set apart to tell God's good news,

In this first chapter, Paul first greets the Roman church and then begins his theological discourse about the condition of the gentile world and the judgment of God upon it. The introduction is not unusual in that **Paul,** as he was accustomed to do, styles himself **a slave of Jesus Christ**. A slave was bought with a price and was owned by another whose will he was charged to follow. In this case, that Owner is Jesus Christ, Whose slavery is slavery to righteousness, which is perfect freedom. Counselees who complain that the commandments of God are too strict or "binding," fail to realize that freedom comes in conforming to the rules of God. Slavery to Christ means the freedom to do all that you were intended to do, to be all that God intended you to be. The train is free to run smoothly, as it was designed to, only when it is "confined" to the tracks. It is not free bouncing over the countryside where it will damage itself and everything in its path. The same is true of a person. He is truly free only when he conforms to the biblical principles according to which his Creator designed him to live. But more of this in later chapters.

Paul's slavery, then, was freedom to serve Christ. The peculiar service to which he was **called** was to be **an apostle.** An apostle (lit., a "sent off one") was an emissary of another, who went forth in his name on a mission authorized by him. He spoke and acted not for himself, but for the one who sent him. As Christ's apostles, there is authority and power in the apostolic *message*. Counselees may ignore the Scriptures (the recorded message that apostles and prophets proclaimed) only at their own peril. When you counsel biblically—that is to say, according to principles enjoined in the Bible—unlike other forms of counseling, you counsel in the Name of Jesus Christ and with all His authority. Never forget that; and when necessary, remind your counselee as well. You, too, have the same apostolic message which still carries the same apostolic authority.

Paul was **set apart to tell the good news**. That is the message of salvation, along with all that accompanied it. The good news is that Christ died for our sins and that He rose again on the third day (see I Corinthians 15:1ff.). Those who believe that gospel are saved. Any elements added to or subtracted from the message distort the gospel. It is good news about

Christian Counselor's Commentary

2   that He promised beforehand by His prophets in the holy Scriptures,
3   about His Son Who, according to the flesh, was born as a descendant of David
4   and Who, according to the Spirit of holiness, was constituted the Son of God by His resurrection from the dead: Jesus Christ, our Lord.

---

an event that has already transpired, not good deeds yet to be accomplished.

To be **set apart** means to "have a line drawn between you and something else." In this instance, Paul was marked out for his special task; he was separated, isolated from all others. Being set apart, then, is both unto and from. And that is precisely what Paul did: he devoted himself entirely to proclaiming the gospel of God. Counselors must not consider counseling a mere job. Rather, they must understand it as a calling that sets them apart to it and from other things; it is a ministry to which God **calls** His slaves.

This good news, as I indicated above, is to be found in the Scriptures. It is important to note that though the apostles and the prophets recorded it in the books that we call the New Testament, the gospel is also **promised** in the **Scriptures** of the Old Testament (v. 2). It is important for counselors, therefore, to be fully acquainted with the Old Testament. They may not counsel from the New Testament alone. One strong assurance of the truth of the message of the New was that it was a fulfillment of the Old. This, counselors must be able to show counselees whose faith may be weak, and who may be wondering about the message. After all, the commands to which you are calling them may have momentous impact upon their future and the lives of others as well. They need, then, to be thoroughly assured of the basis for their beliefs and actions so that they may make a wholehearted commitment to the will of God. Paul is certifying the message by showing that it is in complete harmony with the predictions of the prophets—what they said would happen *did*. Jesus is the **promised** Messiah Who has every right to make claims on counselees' lives.

The gospel concerned God's **Son Who, according to the flesh,** came from the line of **David**, as the Old Testament predicted. And **according to the Spirit, Who sets apart**, He was **constituted** officially to be **the Son of God** as well. The humanity and the deity of Christ are thus both affirmed. **Constituted** does not mean "made to be", but *made to be in the sight of others* who did not know it before. That is to say, the

5   Through Him, and for His name's sake, we have received grace and apostleship to bring about obedience, that comes from faith, among all the Gentiles,
6   including you who have been called by Jesus Christ.
7   To all God's loved ones in Rome, called to be saints: May help and peace from God our Father and the Lord Jesus Christ be yours,

---

Spirit **of holiness** (the One Who sets apart) set Him apart from others *as such*. And He did this by the **resurrection**. Thus He has come to be known as **Jesus Christ,** *our Lord*. The resurrection was the confirming act that made all of this clear.

Now, in verse 5, Paul continues, identifying himself as one who had **received grace (unmerited favor and help) and apostleship for the purpose of bringing about the obedience of faith (that comes from faith) among all the Gentiles**. His task is not limited to some Gentiles, but extends to all—even those in Rome. One is not saved by obedience, but faith in the gospel leads to obedience on the part of those who believe. It is the fruit of belief. A tree is planted not for its root, its trunk or its leaves. All these are necessary; but it is planted for its fruit. Gentiles, believing the preaching of the Word, for the first time are able to love God and their neighbors in ways that please God. Prior to that they could do nothing to please Him (cf. 8:8). If the object of preaching is to lead to faith that, in turn, leads to works, then you, counselor, are intimately involved in the second half of that process. Your task is to help those who have believed, but struggle with obedience, to succeed in that struggle. Counseling is an integral part of sanctification as Paul will describe it later on in this chapter. The gentile world was in a sorry state. Paul knew what his ministry involved, what he was up against. Do you? Have you read lately about what sin can do? Reread this chapter then. Then ask yourself, "How would I describe my counselees?" Do you see them having many of the same difficulties as the unsaved world? Would you call them Christians with much of the past clinging to them? Do you have a realistic picture of the effects of sin upon a human being? This chapter, should be read again and again by Christian counselors.

As we said, Paul's ministry was to **all the Gentiles**—including those in the church at Rome. Apparently Paul was thinking of ways in which he could contribute to the obedience of those called by Christ who had answered by faith. Accordingly, he wishes **help and peace for all those in Rome who are God's loved ones** (v. 7).

Christian Counselor's Commentary

8 First, I thank my God through Jesus Christ for all of you, because word about your faith is being spread throughout the world.
9 God, Whom I serve with my spirit by preaching the good news about His Son, is my Witness that I regularly mention you
10 in my prayers, asking that somehow now at last I may succeed in coming to you by God's will.
11 I long to see you so that I may give you some spiritual gift to strengthen you,

---

Next comes a thanksgiving and an explanation (vv. 8-17). Paul had heard good things about the Roman church (v. 8). Wherever he went, the word was the same. And for that he was thankful. After all, the church was in a pivotal location. How its members lived had a lot to do with what the Roman emperors and other high officials might think of the church. And, as we said in the introduction, people were constantly coming and going so that there was the possibility of a witness to many travelers who, coming to know Christ there, would carry the gospel back to their own communities throughout the world.

Then, Paul calls on God to testify to the truth of the next statement: **I regularly mention you in my prayers**. Paul prayed for all the churches—even for those he did not plant. He **served God**, he declared, not only outwardly, but from the heart (**in my spirit**). That is, genuinely. That is the kind of service God requires of His workers. They may not simply "go to work" in order "to make money;" they are to serve God in all they do. And, in His service, they are to do so from an internal conviction that He has called them and that He is to be pleased regardless of what people say. Prayer that God will use your ministry is also in order.

Among his prayers for the Roman church, Paul asked God to make it possible for him to come to Rome (v. 9). He didn't know if it was possible, or how he would be able to do so, but he implored God to let it happen. Why? Because he **longed to see [them] in order to strengthen [them] by imparting some spiritual gift, and to mutually encourage one another.** This would happen as they spoke of the faith that they held in common and what it had done for them. In counseling, as in all true ministry, it is not just those who minister who bless others; they, in turn, receive blessings from those to whom they minister. How many times have I been brought up short in counseling as I heard some word from a counselee that reminded me of some failure in my own life! How often, just the way a counselee words something—even his statement of a problem—leads to a new insight into Scripture. Or, as he is perplexed over a

12 that is to say, that we may be mutually encouraged by each other's faith, both yours and mine.

13 I don't want you to be ignorant, brothers, of the fact that I have often determined to come to you (but was prevented until now) so that I may have some fruit also among you just as I have among the rest of the Gentiles.

---

counseling situation, the counselor is driven more deeply into the Bible in search of help. When he finds the biblical solution, it is a source not only of bringing help to the counselee, but also of providing further understanding of the Bible for himself and others in days to come.

The biblical counselor alone enjoys the opportunity of discovering more and more about God's will simply by faithfully carrying on a ministry that is entrenched in and based solely on the Scriptures. No wonder Paul looked forward to talking to the Roman Christians and anticipated mutual **encouragement** as the result! Counselor, do you **long** to see your counselees? Now wait; I know many of them can be exasperating. But if you have problems doing so, think of counseling as an opportunity not only to help, but to *be* helped as well. Some of the most aggravating cases, in the long run, may prove most fruitful all around.

The **spiritual gift** that Paul wanted to **give** in order **to strengthen** the Romans, doubtless, was one of those extraordinary gifts that were conveyed to members of the churches by the laying on of the apostles' hands (cf. Acts 19:6), gifts that were confined to the first generation church. Today, the extraordinary gifts cannot be conveyed to another by counselors, but the ordinary gifts that they possess may be used for the benefit of their counselees. Indeed, those who possess them are obligated to use them. No gifts were given for the sake of an individual alone; they were for the **strengthening** of the whole body. And counselors can help counselees to discover, develop and deploy their gifts for that same purpose.

Often Paul had attempted to find his way to Rome, but heretofore had always been hindered (v. 13). This time, it looked as if he might actually fulfill that desire. He wants to gather among them the same sort of spiritual fruit that God had given him in other places across the Mediterranean world. And, by the introductory phrase, **I don't want you to be ignorant, brothers...** (a favorite phrase of his for the stronger idea, "I want you to know...") Paul expressed his concern that they know for sure how he felt—he **longed** to see them.

Paul also considered himself **a debtor both to Greeks and barbar-**

> 14 I am a debtor both to Greeks and barbarians, to the educated and to the ignorant,
> 15 so, as far as it depends upon me, I am eager to announce the message of good news to you who are in Rome also.
> 16 I am not ashamed of the good news since it is God's power for saving all who believe (Jews first, but also Greeks),
> 17 because by it God's righteousness is revealed from faith to faith, as it is written: **The just person lives because of faith.**

ians: to those of the civilized world (the *oikoumene)* and those beyond it. To the educated and to the ignorant. He knew that he owed everything to Jesus Christ; even though he deserved nothing. He was like a person to whom great wealth had been loaned, who would work off the debt by serving the one who made the loan to him. Actually, Paul knew that the debt was greater than anyone could ever repay, but he was endeavoring to do what he could. So, since he had never had the opportunity to work in Rome, he longed to visit to serve Christ there too. And, as far as he was concerned, he was ready—indeed, eager—to do so at any time (v. 15).

Paul had no reason to be ashamed of the gospel. Writing to a people who appreciated power, he said, **it is God's power for saving all who believe (Jews first, but also Greeks)**. Paul was eager to preach to everyone: not only if you slice the world as the Greek-speaking people did (between Greeks and barbarians) but also if you divided it as the Jews did (between Jews and Greeks [Gentiles]). Divide as you might, it made no difference; he wanted to declare this saving message, that was powerful enough to transform anyone, no matter where he lived or whatever his background might be. God's power in saving all who believe springs out of His **righteousness** provided in Christ for all who believe the gospel. It is a righteousness procured by faith and promoted by faith (v. 17). The good news reveals this righteousness of God by which, as Habakkuk wrote, **those who are justified by faith live** (Habakkuk 2:4), the great message that the next few chapters will explicate.

It is helpful to realize that Paul cautiously sets up the rest of the letter by these seventeen important verses in which he lays out the purpose and the major topic he wishes to discuss. As in all his letters, the frontispiece is not mere formality, nor is it detached from what follows. Counselors need to think more deeply about how to open counseling sessions. The first session can be all-important. Either it prepares the counselee for what follows or it fails to do so. If it does not, it actually detracts. A preacher knows the importance of a good introduction. The word introduce means

Romans 1

18 God's wrath from heaven is being revealed against all sorts of godlessness and unrighteousness among people who suppress the truth by their unrighteousness,

---

"to lead into." And that is precisely what Paul's letters always do. The first few paragraphs of spoken discourse in counseling are your introduction to the course of sessions that will follow. Do they lead the counselee into what follows? Do they help bridge the gap between where he is and where you want him to be? Do they involve him, give him hope, intrigue him sufficiently so that he is anxious to continue? Those are the sorts of questions you might ask yourself. These introductory words are every bit as important as an introduction to a sermon is.

In verse 18, the letter actually begins as Paul sets forth the course of human history in relationship to God. It is a sad picture. But your counselee—as do you—has a part in it. It is a picture not of evolution from primitive to more refined faith, as anthropologists sometimes like to theorize. No, it is a picture of sharp decline. Mankind has moved from true knowledge to ignorance and a lifestyle that grows out of it and is appropriate to it. What is surprising to those who read this for the first time is the fact that this decline is the result of deliberately bad choices.

That the tendency to make bad choices—in which God is removed farther and farther from the decision-making milieu—is a problem not only with mankind in its history, but with many counselees as well. The tendency does not disappear once one has trusted Christ as Savior. There are still old patterns that drive Christian counselees to try to make it on their own apart from God. They too tend to exchange God for creatures and things. Perhaps there is no more powerful way of exposing this tendency during counseling than to read portions of this chapter of Romans and point out to the counselee that he, too, like an unbeliever, is making the same sort of poor, sinful choices. Much of the book has to do with this matter.

God's **wrath** will be **revealed** at the coming of Christ (cf. II Thessalonians 1), in all its everlasting fullness. But it is also true that it is being revealed in this life as well. He now reveals it **against all sorts of godlessness and unrighteousness in people who suppress the truth by their unrighteousness** (v. 18). That people actually suppress the truth when they know it for what it is, in order to go their own ways, is an important insight. Counselors, the feeling-oriented era is still upon you. But there will, inevitably, come a swing of the pendulum to more cognitive theories

19 since what can be known about God is apparent to them because God has made it so.
20 Ever since the creation of the world His invisible attributes, His eternal power and deity, have been clearly perceived, being understood by the things that He has made, so that they are without excuse,

---

of counseling. Don't fall for the idea that if only people come to know the truth, they will do it. If dispelling ignorance is the sum of all people need to change, then counseling would be simple. But education alone—even in the truth—will not do it. People don't like truth; they are born that way. Therefore, even when they receive it, they often suppress it. There is more to counseling than merely imparting truth. Truth must be accompanied by conviction, often brought about by rebuke, exhortation—or whatever it takes to make the truth penetrate to the heart of the individual (cf. II Timothy 4:2). Otherwise, people will suppress it so that others are unaware that they possess it, or in such a way that they deceive themselves. Both of these tendencies will be seen in your counselees as well. Understand clearly that it is **by their unrighteousness** that people suppress the truth. That is, because they love unrighteous ways, they develop patterns by which they learn to do so. Often these patterns of suppressing the truth become habitual and are carried over into the Christian's life. You must help them to replace them with patterns that are characterized by love of the truth. Such poor patterns include lying, deception, evasion, selectivity of data, the ignoring of facts and prejudice against truth.

How does God reveal His wrath in this life? We must wait a bit to discover what Paul has in mind. For now, he says, **what can be known about God is apparent to them because God has made it so.** They cannot blame God for their ignorance; such ignorance is *willful*. How has God made His presence known? Verse 20 says, that **ever since the creation the invisible attributes of God have been clearly perceived.** In what way? They may be **understood by the things that are made.** The creation implies a Creator; he who fails to make the inference is a fool (cf. v. 22). The existence of the invisible God is clear from the things He brought into being. Therefore, God says, **they are without excuse.** God accepts no excuses from the heathen world. There is enough known of God to set any heathen seeking—if he only will. "Are the heathen lost?" Absolutely, you must tell your inquiring counselee; that is exactly what Paul is saying in these verses. General revelation, contrary to the thinking of many integrationists, is quite limited. It is designed to tell us only that

Romans 1

21 because although people knew God, they didn't glorify Him as God or thank Him. Instead they became involved in futile rationalizations and their senseless hearts were darkened.
22 Claiming that they were wise, they became fools,
23 and for the glory of the incorruptible God they substituted images bearing the likeness of corruptible human beings and birds and animals and reptiles.

---

there is a God and that He made and judges the world. It provides no information about redemption, either with reference to justification or sanctification.

Paul explicates (vv. 21-23): because **although people knew God**, they failed to **glorify Him or thank Him** for all that He has done for them. Rather, they became **involved in futile speculation about God and their senseless hearts were darkened** (cf. Ephesians 4:17ff.). God does not want people speculating about Him. All we can know of God must be known by revelation. Speculation, philosophizing, and the like, are useless—indeed, harmful. Never allow speculation in counseling. When counselees speculate about what God is like or what He will do ("Oh, I don't think God will mind so much if I tell a few lies now and then"), drive them to prove their statements biblically ("Can you substantiate your view from Scripture?"). When they fail, warn them from this passage about the dangers of speculating about God. One's doctrine of God in relation to sanctification must come from special revelation, not from sinful, human imagination.

Because of this **senseless** activity, they wandered farther and farther away from the truth, so that, eventually, they wandered into total **darkness** (ignorance) about God. At the same time, the farther they went the more self-satisfied they became: **claiming to be wise, they became fools** (v. 22). That is God's estimate of such speculations and those who engage in them. What a clear description of many that you face in counseling! In what ways are they fools? The rest of the chapter tells you. In verse 23, he notes that **they became fools** by **exchanging the glory of the incorruptible God for images bearing the likeness of corruptible human beings and birds and animals and reptiles**. What stupidity! The Greeks and Romans, with their pantheons of gods and goddesses exemplify the first sort of fools. What they worshiped were blown-up people, beings with greater power, but with all the failings and sins of human beings. The latter sort of fools were represented by Egyptian crocodile worship and Dagon, the fish-god of the Philistines. When people **suppress truth**, their

Christian Counselor's Commentary

> **24** Therefore, God handed them over to the uncleanness that was involved in the desires of their hearts, to dishonor their bodies among themselves;
> 25 this was because they exchanged the truth of God for a lie and worshiped and served the creature rather than the Creator, Who is blessed forever. Amen!

unrighteous acts bring the **wrath** of God upon them. In this life, that heavenly wrath is evidenced by God **handing them over** to such foolheartedess and all that goes along with it (v. 24). False worship, bad doctrine, speculative theology are not neutral; they lead to **unclean** living: the **uncleanness that was involved in** following **the desires of their hearts.** That uncleanness will be articulated presently as Paul continues. People are saved while involved in such things. Often, they bring much of this past into their Christian lives. Uncleanness must be dealt with in counseling. It is not always pleasant to counsel such people. Yet the work must be done. Counselors must not shy away from those whose lives are despicable. They cannot counsel only "clean" (white collar) sinners!

People want to remove God from their lives. They don't like His "absolutes." They prefer relative morality, fluid standards, partial "truth." God will have none of that. He will hand them over to their wrongful desires if they refuse to listen to His revelation from heaven. That is what has happened to our society. The strongest sort of judgment short of hell is to be handed over to one's self; it is the most horrible punishment possible in this life. When sinful man is allowed to act unrestrained, he will always destroy himself and all around him. If you want to know whether our society is under God's judgment or not, ask yourself: is it restrained by the absolutes of Scripture or is wide open, people doing as they please with no regard to God? You know the answer. And, of course, the other evidence is that all the behavioral consequences that Paul is about to list in the remainder of this chapter are prevalent among us as well. Many Christians, coming from years of this sort of sinful living, find it difficult to abandon the continuum thinking that supports it. To teach absolutes and the antithetical thinking of Scripture is a major counseling task.

From time to time you will meet counselees who insist on going their own way, suppressing God's truth. Warn them of the frightful consequence of this: "God may hand you over to yourself to follow your desires." They may think that this is a crazy warning; to them, nothing could be better. "That's exactly what I want," one may say. "Oh?" you

> **26** For this reason, God handed them over to dishonorable passions, so that even their women exchanged natural sexual relations for unnatural ones.
> 27 Similarly, men also, giving up natural sexual relations with women, burned in their desire for one another, men performing shameful acts with men, and getting back for themselves the full penalty that their error deserves.

may reply, "and with it all of the consequences of Romans 1? Let me read some of them to you..."

They **dishonored their bodies among themselves,** says Paul (v. 24), and **exchanged the truth of God for a lie, worshiping the creature rather than the Creator** (v. 25). That is the direction in which one who is abandoned by God to his own desires soon finds himself headed. New Age thinking today is a clear example of this as it puts man in the place of God. If Paul had said no more, that would be a devastating fact: continue to suppress the truth and God will abandon you to perversion, falsehood, error and the worship of created beings! "Never," says a counselee. But the next thing you see is all three beginning to happen; he becomes loose sexually, he starts believing all sorts of falsehoods (perhaps even wandering into liberalism or New Age thinking) and finds himself adoring people (to his utter frustration) rather than God. The ingrained worship of created beings rather than their Creator is reflected in the propensities of counselees (and counselors), though saved, to follow the ideas of men rather than God (see Psalm 1:1, 2).

What about those desires of the heart? Paul continues. **God handed them over to dishonorable passions** (v. 26). What are they? In verses 26 and 27 he mentions lesbianism and homosexuality. Notice that quite contrary to all that some avant-garde "Christians" maintain, lesbianism and homosexuality are **dishonorable** (Paul will described them in harsher terms later on). There is no way that they can be described as genetic dispositions or alternative lifestyles. Any counselor who attempts to fit either of these perversions of sexuality into the picture as biblically allowable either is suppressing the truth himself or is an ignoramus. And don't miss the fact: it is the **passion** as well as the act that is dishonorable. Don't let people convince your counselee that the desires are OK so long as they are not fulfilled by the act.

These are sexual perversions, Paul notes, because they are **unnatural**. People may tell you that homosexuality is genetic, but this passage teaches otherwise (as does I Corinthians 6, and the experience of every

> **28** Now just as they disapproved of retaining God in their knowledge, so God handed them over to a disapproved mind, to do those things that are not proper,

counselor worth his salt): it is against nature. What God calls unnatural, let no one call natural. The homosexual life is a chosen lifestyle. Doubtless, older persons can early enlist younger ones in it so that it is something that they grow up with. But, in the discussion, every time anatomy will win out!

Don't allow anyone to distinguish between the act (as sin) and the desire (as not). Notice, Paul says that the act (as in adultery) is the outworking of unclean desires of the heart. Homosexual lust of the heart is every bit the sin that heterosexual lust is. Paul does not suddenly abandon Christ's clear linkage of heart sin with body sin when he come to homosexuality. To do so is but a modern dodge, attempting to make the Bible say things it doesn't say at all.

And as we have come to see (though the Romans were familiar enough with the fact), VD, AIDS, syphilis, etc., are the inevitable consequences of such activities (v. 27). It is as if in thus playing the game of life, one who transgresses the rules receives the **full penalty** for doing so (27^b).

They **disapproved** of God. They did not want to **retain a knowledge** of Him and what He is like. Can you imagine that? People disapproving of God! What unmitigated gall that is. Man sets up his own standard of right and wrong and judges God by it. In the process, they weigh God and find Him wanting. That is a description of our times, if there ever was one. And, to some extent, such attitudes rub off even on Christian counselees. When people don't like what God tells them in the Bible, they protest, "That's not fair," or words to that effect. By words like these they have told you in no uncertain terms that they have adopted a standard by which they are willing to judge God! Even counselors who reject biblical principles in favor of the world's thereby unwittingly disapprove of God. Warn them of the arrogance and the consequent dangers of this. And be sure to uncover, challenge and replace unbiblical standards whenever you encounter them in counselees.

So, God **disapproved** of them and **handed them over to do things that are not proper** (another description of homosexuality, etc.). Verses 29-31 describe the sorts of things that you can expect to find in the lives of those who have been **handed over** to do as they please. It is a formidable

29 filled with every sort of unrighteousness, wickedness, greed, maliciousness. They are full of envy, murder, strife, deceit, malignity.
30 They are gossips, slanderers, God-haters, insolent, arrogant, boasters, inventors of evil practices, disobedient to parents,
31 senseless, faithless, without family affection or pity.
32 They know God's ordinance, that those who practice such things deserve death, yet they not only do them but heartily approve of those who practice them.

---

and disgusting list. When you find such things in the lives of counselees, as you often will, point out to them that these are the very things that occur in the lives of those who have been abandoned by God. Ask, "Do you want to be associated with such persons? Have you picked up these ways from associating with them? Or are you still *part* of the crowd and not really a Christian after all?" A number of the items in this list are those that bring counselees to you in the first place. I do not intend to take space here elucidating the meaning of each of these items in Paul's list of **dishonorable** activities that God considers **improper**; you can find that kind of exposition in the exegetical commentaries. I simply want to urge you to use the list to the full in the way I have suggested.

Again, as with our own society, it is not because of ignorance (v. 32) but out of sheer rebellion against truth and God that people do these things. They **know** full well that they are wrong; indeed, Paul says that they know that **they deserve death** for them! That assessment surely doesn't let the homosexual (or others) off the hook. N.B., God's idea of what these sins deserve is **death**. Yet many **not only do them, but heartily approve of those who practice them.** There is a determining factor: if you find that a counselee not only participates in these forbidden practices—suppressing the truth about God (while believing a lie) and, in addition, encouraging others to follow suit—you may very well have not a Christian counselee at all. He may turn out to be one who has been handed over by God to himself. He will need to be converted, not counseled. And, short of conversion, you must warn others around him of the nefarious influence that he may be exerting on them and their loved ones.

CHAPTER 2

1 Therefore you are without excuse, whoever you are that judge; indeed, in whatever way you judge another you condemn yourself, because you who judge are doing the very same things.

As the first chapter dealt with the declining spiritual history of the Gentiles who turned from the knowledge of God to the worship of idols and the degradation that brought, so now Paul considers the state of the Jews who had been chosen by God to become His people and to whom He gave His holy law. Their plight is no better. Indeed, considering the enormous amount of light they possessed in contrast to the Gentiles, their failures, apostasy and sins loom even larger.

Paul begins by supposing that he is about to speak to a critical Jew who has been listening to the reading of the first chapter with its catalog of sins. Picture him. There he stands in all his self-righteousness shaking his head in utter disapproval. Paul will have none of that. His opening words are penetrating: **you are without excuse, whoever you are that is judging; indeed, in whatsoever you judge another you condemn yourself, because you who judge are doing the very same things.** That should bring him (and any self-satisfied critical counselee) up short! It certainly wasn't what he expected to hear. Paul calls him a hypocrite; he is guilty of committing the very sins of which he accuses another. Counselors will find that similarly unexpected, penetrating remarks often will bring counselees to their senses.

Paul wants to show this Jew the truth that Jesus taught in the Sermon on the Mount: the mere outward keeping of the law is unacceptable. Rather, God also judges the inward intent of the heart. While the Jew may have never murdered another, that anger that wells up in his heart from time to time is, in God's sight, the equivalent to murder. He is guilty, therefore, of breaking the commandment. Paul is about to demonstrate that the Jew with the law is as guilty as the Gentile without it.

Counselees clearly are a part of those upon whom the **condemnation** falls. They sin like Jew and Gentile alike. No one is excluded (as Paul will plainly point out in chapter 3). If, therefore, counselees attempt to establish their basic innocence, these two chapters will prove useful in proving otherwise. So often the critical spirit is present in counseling. One counselee rails against another, as if he considered himself virtually free from

2   But we know that God's judgment on those who practice such things is according to truth.
3   And do you, whoever you may be that judge those who practice such things and do them yourself, suppose that you will escape God's judgment?

---

sin. Surely this first verse says otherwise. It is certain that most persons who judge specific sins in another have themselves been guilty of the same sins. Otherwise Paul's argument would lack force. You will be wise to probe counselees critical of others for such sins. Frequently you will hit pay-dirt. He who casts the first stone must be without sin. You won't find anyone who is. Paul wants all, Jew and Gentile alike, to recognize their basic guilt before a holy God.

And, Paul says (v. 2), **we** (Paul included himself along with his fellow Israelites) **know that God judges truthfully. Those who practice such things** (that is, those who have never been regenerated, and so continue in the old ways of the flesh) are judged by God according to the unerring standard of His Word. It is those he addresses in this chapter, but much that he says also has broader application. God judges with utter impartiality and absolute accuracy according to infinite knowledge. Your judgment cannot be so. Why? You may be harsher than God, or more lenient. That is because you are a fallible creature who cannot know what is going on in another's heart (II Chronicles 6:30), and who is never totally impartial. But God's judgment is free from every such failing. It will do no good then to protest; in the day of judgment God will demonstrate how we all are totally without excuse. There is little room for harsh or haughty criticism of others when one examines his own life.

In verse 3, Paul takes up a common misconception held by many Jews. At that time Jews depended on their inclusion in the Covenant that God made with Abraham for their salvation ("We are children of Abraham," they cried; but Jesus called them children of the devil: John 8:33!). They thought their sins were covered by the sacrificial rituals. But neither membership in the covenant community, nor mere participation in the ceremonies of Judaism cleansed from sin. Those who were saved, like Abraham, all looked forward to the death of the Lamb of God Who alone could take away sins (Galatians 3:8). There had to be genuine faith in the gospel of Christ; short of this they were lost.

There are many modern variations on that mistaken Jewish theme. Church membership, baptism, walking an aisle are all thought by some to save. They do not. That is not to say that either the Old Testament ordi-

Christian Counselor's Commentary

> 4 Or do you despise the wealth of His kindness and tolerance and patience, not realizing that God's kindness should lead you toward repentance?
>
> 5 But by your stubbornness and unrepentant heart, you are storing up wrath that will be yours on the Day of Wrath when God's righteous judgment will be revealed,

nances or the New are wrong. They were prescribed by God, but not to save. They were given to lead one to Christ. Many people think they can ride into heaven on the coattails of their spouses, or their parents, etc. They cannot. All of these misconceptions and more were rampant among the Jews. In this chapter Paul is going to counter every notion of that sort. Notice how he does so and, when necessary, use the same approach yourself.

In verse 4 Paul explains the reason for the **tolerance, patience and kindness of God**. It is not because He doesn't care that He doesn't act immediately against sinners. Nor is it because He is so lenient that He simply bypasses sin. No, God's benevolent attitude is intended to **bring men to repentance**. He gives time, He shows His goodness and care and He endures man's sin, all to indicate to them that He wants them to repent. But people misunderstand. They take His goodness as a lack of concern. It is precisely the opposite.

The Jew, who thought he could get away with sin, was only **storing up wrath** that will be poured out on him in **the day** of Judgment. This will happen when the full **revelation** of **God's righteous judgment** will occur. In that day, **He will repay every person exactly what his deeds deserve** (vv. 5, 6). Salvation is not by works, but judgment is. One is saved by faith, as Paul will go to lengths to observe in the next few chapters. But that faith, and the salvation that it appropriates, should lead to works. There are truly good works, that grow out of saving faith (cf. Eph. 2) and there are "dead works" (Hebrews 6:2) from which one must repent. These dead works are works that result from our efforts unassisted by the Holy Spirit of God. They are works in which this hypothetical Jew trusted for salvation.

It is because of an **unrepentant heart** that wrath comes (v. 5). God's goodness is ignored and people go about trying to establish their own righteousness. But those who are regenerated move in the opposite direction: **they persevere in doing good** according to the power of the Spirit within them, looking forward to the **eternal glory, honor and incorrup-**

Romans 2

6   since He will pay every person exactly what his deeds deserve.
7   To those who by perseverance in doing good deeds seek glory and honor and incorruption, He will give eternal life,
8   but to those who are divisive and disobey the truth and obey unrighteousness, wrath and anger.
9   Affliction and anguish will come upon every human being who is at work doing evil (to the Jew first, and also to the Greek),
10 but glory and honor and peace to everyone who is at work doing good (to the Jew first, and also to the Greek);
11 God shows no partiality.

---

tion that is promised to those who trust in Jesus Christ (v. 7). That is the evidence of their salvation. But to those who disobey God's command to trust in His Son and who obey the command of the devil to serve him in unrighteousness there is nothing to look forward to but wrath and anger (v. 8). This is straight talk. There is no mincing of words, no softening of the facts. It is what the unsaved Jew needed to hear. And, as you talk to Christian counselees about the needs and sins that keep them from glorifying God, can you be any less straightforward? Are your words weak? Do you worry that you may lose counselees or church members if you tell it like it is? Well, perhaps you will lose some. Eventually, you might have lost them anyway. But, more often than not, when you are honest, people will respect you; they will trust you too. And, in times of trouble, they will come to you when they won't darken the door of a namby-pamby counselor up the block. Telling it straight from the shoulder need not be rough, nasty or overly confrontive. It does not exclude compassion. As a matter of fact, if not accompanied by that compassion, it will probably have all the ill-effects that you fear.

Verse 9 indicates that God will not allow unrepentant sinners (Jews or Greeks) commit iniquity unpunished. And, he makes clear to the Jew, as the gospel goes **first to the Jew, then to the Gentile**, so too judgment comes in the same order. Privilege means greater responsibility. And, according to verse 10, **glory and honor and peace come** (once more in the same order) to those whose salvation is judged genuine because they **are at work doing good. God shows no partiality** (v. 11). That is Paul's word of contrast and comparison.

Greater responsibility is required of those counselees who have had greater access to truth and to help. If in the light of light they fail to respond to instruction from God's Word, they must be warned of the greater judgment that will come upon them. Their associations with good

Christian Counselor's Commentary

> **12** All those who have sinned without law will also perish without law, and all those who have sinned with law, will be judged by law;
> **13** since it is not the hearers of law who are just before God; rather the doers of the law will be justified.
> **14** When Gentiles who don't have law by nature do what the law requires, they are a law of their own, even though they don't have law.
> **15** They show the work of the law written on their heart; their conscience also testifies, and their thoughts, in debate with one another, either accuse or defend them.

---

churches, their families who are outstanding Christians, etc., all serve to condemn, not exonerate them. When they plead such associations, warn them of the danger.

All those who have sinned with the law and those who have sinned without law will equally perish in their sins apart from the Savior. And the Jew, who has the law, will be judged by it. **It is not the hearers of the law, but the doers of the law, who will be justified.** And there is only One Who has perfectly fulfilled the law—the Savior, whose righteousness is attributed to Christians by faith. That is the point of the law. James and Paul agree!

Now (vv. 14ff.) Paul indicates that the Gentiles, to whom the law was not given, nevertheless, **by nature do what the law requires.** *Phusis*, the Greek word translated "nature," can refer to the genetic makeup with which one is born, or it can refer to that which is written on the heart by society (in which a bit of knowledge about God's original creation remains). Its exact meaning is "that which is done without any conscious decision." The law written on the heart, then, could mean written at birth or after birth, in the first case by God, in the second by the culture. Either way, directly or indirectly, God's requirements in part are known by all—the Jew with the written law, the Gentile with **the law written on the heart**. And, according to their light, each has failed to keep those requirements.

It is **the *work* of the law** that is written on the heart—not the law itself (according to Jeremiah 31:33 *that* is reserved for believers alone). So, the work of the law probably means some effects of the original law that have been passed down among the Gentiles by which they know from their societal upbringing that it is wrong to steal, murder, etc. Those commandments, in their culture and in their minds, may be grossly distorted, but there are remnants of God's commandments with which they are all familiar. They all have a sense of fairness, or right and wrong. But, even at

Romans 2

16 This, according to my good news, is what will happen on that day when God through Christ Jesus judges what people have kept hidden.

17 But if you go by the name Jew and depend upon law and brag about belonging to God

---

its minimum, they fail to fulfill these commands. They have problems with **conscience,** however seared with a hot iron it may be (v. 15). That, of course, renders them without excuse. Whether it is a good or bad conscience (i.e., one properly informed by Scripture or not) is not the point here. The fact of a *functioning* conscience is what is at stake. The same functioning conscience operates within—accusing or excusing one's self—that takes place within the Jew. It is important, then, to tell counselees that they are not to be excused because of ignorance of the law. They are still in possession of a conscience and the work of the law on their hearts. Don't let them try to put it over on you that they "didn't know" that stealing, lying etc., are wrong. Probe them: "Didn't you have some pangs of conscience over doing this?" There are, according to this verse, no sociopaths (also known as psychopaths)—people without a sense of right or wrong. Because you know this from the passage in hand, you know how to treat people on whom those labels have been wrongly gummed.

Paul says God will judge people in this way on Judgment Day. And, incidentally, he says that this fact is according to (that is, taught by) his **gospel**! How could it be good news to talk about judgment? This way: the good news is only good in the light of the bad news of judgment. It is from this judgment that Christians are saved. That is why in everything in this sinful world that we discuss that is good we must talk in contrast about that which is bad. That is why Christ is central to all good; apart from His gospel there is *nothing* good. So, it is not wrong to talk of that which is bad first when talking about that which is good; indeed, you must do so to rightly understand that which is good.

Now, Paul zeros in on the Jew in a very personal way (v. 17ff.). From this passage you can learn how to counsel in order to bring conviction to a counselee. Listen to *what* he says, and *how* he says it. He has a long introduction summing up what the proud Jew trusting in his privileges thinks of himself (vv. 17-20). **If you go by the name Jew, depend on the law and brag about belonging to God, and, if you know His will (in the Scripture) and approve of those things that really count because you have been instructed from the law, and if you are convinced that you**

18 and know His will and approve the things that really count because you have been instructed from the law,
19 and if you have convinced yourself that you should be a guide to the blind, a light for those in darkness,
20 a disciplinarian of the foolish, and a teacher of children since you have a formulation of knowledge and truth in the law,

should guide the blind (Gentiles), being a light for those in darkness, a disciplinarian of your foolish countrymen, and have a formulation of knowledge and truth in the law, then...

And now he digs in:
you who are teaching another, shouldn't you teach yourself?
you who are preaching "Don't steal," are you stealing?
you who say, "Don't commit adultery," are you committing adultery?
you who find idols an abomination, do you rob temples?
you who brag about the law, do you dishonor God by transgressing its commandments?

What a powerful series of questions! Penetrating, incisive, apropos. He pierces with words to bring conviction leading to repentance. That is Paul's way of addressing the haughty hypocrite. It is not the way to treat everyone. He uses it to convict the braggart, the proud and the self-righteous. In addressing people like that then, it is clear that a barrage of that sort often may be necessary. Are you up to putting it to a counselee in that manner? To do so is clearly biblical, and since God was inspiring the apostle, it is also one of the Holy Spirit's ways. You had better learn how to pierce hard hearts with penetrating questions when necessary (Read Acts 2:37; 7:54). And notice once again, the critic is caught in his own criticism: in the way he condemns another, he also condemns himself.

The items listed in these verses are of interest. The **name** "Jew" by which he went, and was proud to be known, became a stumbling block to him. He equated the possession of it with salvation. How often have you been faced with a similar problem: "Well, I'm a Methodist (Presbyterian, Baptist, or whatever), I want you to know." But that is not what is important, says Paul. He **depends on the law**, but the law does nothing for him if he fails to keep it (and all have failed)! Having the Bible, believing it is the inerrant Word of God is fine, but if that is all...then...I guess that *is* all. Alone, it does nothing. He **brags about belonging to God**: "We are the chosen people." But he does not belong to God unless he is one of those

Romans 2

21 then, you who are teaching another, shouldn't you teach yourself? You who are preaching, "Don't steal," are you stealing?
22 You who say, "Don't commit adultery," are you committing adultery? You who find idols an abomination, do you rob temples?
23 You who brag about the law, do you dishonor God by transgressing its commandments?

---

who is circumcised not only in the flesh but also in the heart. He **knows God's will**. Truth is at his disposal. But does he believe and act on it? He **approves of those things that count**. Good. But mere approval is not enough. He must appropriate them as well. All these things help counselors to identify a person who is trusting in his position, his heritage, his privileges and ultimately in himself. He is not trusting in God. There is some of that in the best of us. And, therefore, there is some (more or less) in most counselees. Sometimes this self-trust, this trust in others, etc., can be the very reason why a counselee is having trouble. He has never learned to trust God as he should. Now that he is experiencing difficult circumstances he hardly knows which way to turn. Those in whom he trusted fail him. He must be taught to look beyond his false security to God. You will find that it is important to expose his error to him; otherwise, you will not be able to extricate him from the problem.

And, as we have seen, turning the tables on the critic, asking him if he is also guilty of the very things that he finds objectionable in another, may bring him to the place where he recognizes his own sin. The very characteristics found in verses 19 and 20 are those that you will discover in innumerable counselees. They want to teach others, lead them from darkness into light, discipline those who do foolish things and straighten out their misconceptions so that they conform to the formulation of truth they hold. It is amazing how many counselees, themselves mired in problems from which they ostensibly have come to find help, nevertheless, take the position of one who is there to instruct others. Often, that instruction may even include directions for the counselor ("Now, what I want you to do first...")! There are times when you wonder why they came. Of course, in some instances, that sort of behavior may indicate that a counselee does not really want to be there. They may have come only at the urging of another, desirous of proving that the counselor is a dolt, unable to help. Others may simply be proud and haughty, supposing that they can actually help the situation by enlightening everyone else around them, thinking, "After all, my problem is their fault, isn't it?"

24 Indeed, **God's name is blasphemed by the Gentiles because of** you, just as it was written.
25 Circumcision is really worthwhile if you practice the law, but if you are a transgressor of law, your circumcision becomes uncircumcision.
26 If, on the other hand, an uncircumcised person keeps the requirements of the law, won't his uncircumcision be considered circumcision?
27 And those who are physically uncircumcised, but keep the law, will judge you who, though you have it written out and have circumcision, are a transgressor of law.

Paul saw clearly the inconsistency of their behavior and the bad effect it had on others (v. 24): **God's name is blasphemed by the Gentiles** because of it. The haughty, self-righteous, critical Jew who held himself superior to all others turned them off. Pointing that out to a counselee of the same temperament may be the first time anyone has had the courage to tell him. But if it is a fact, it is essential for him to hear it.

Of what worth are the rites and ceremonies of Judaism then? They are worth much if one really **practices the law**, discerning and trusting in the Savior of which the law spoke prophetically and typologically (v. 25). But if one fails to do so and is but **a transgressor of the law**, his circumcision is worthless; it is as if he was never circumcised at all. And the Gentile, never physically circumcised at all, is **considered** circumcised if he keeps the law (v. 26). Everything is exactly the opposite of the way the Jew thought. The reason being that he proudly trusted in his own righteousness, failing to recognize that the law condemned him but at the same time pointed to redemption in a coming Messiah who could take away his sins if he only trusted Him instead. And the Gentile who practices the law will judge the Jew who does not! See verse 27.

So (and this is an important New Testament insight) **it isn't the one who outwardly appears to be a circumcised Jew who is, but the one who inwardly is a circumcised Jew,** the one whose heart has been circumcised by the Spirit. He may never be praised by people for this, but **God will praise him** (vv. 28, 29). It is the inner reality that counts, not the external form. All through the Bible that is the problem teachers have to struggle with; people want to settle for form and externals whereas God looks at the heart. Counselees will have this problem too. They will appear to be genuine, but balk when called on to actually do what the Bible tells them to do about their situation. Either they fail to understand perfectly, they fear some consequence or they are in-genuine. After having pursued the first two possibilities (and perhaps others in special

28 You see, it isn't the one who outwardly appears to be a Jew who is, nor the one who outwardly appears to be circumcised because of his fleshly circumcision who is,
29 but he is a Jew who is so inwardly, and circumcision is of the heart, by the Spirit, not by writing. His praise isn't from people but from God.

---

cases), you may fairly conclude that there is only an outwardness about them that initially appeared to be the real thing but is not. If the Spirit has not done a regenerating work in the heart, there can be no change that is pleasing to God.

CHAPTER 3

1 So then, what advantage does the Jew have? Or of what worth is circumcision?
2 Much in every way. But principally that they were entrusted with God's revelatory words.

Now Paul, finished with the Jewish moralist, follows up on the first two chapters in which he asserts that the Gentiles and the Jews (by which he means the entire world) are guilty before God, and need to be saved. This lost condition is strongly emphasized in the chapter. But for the first time he also *explicitly* articulates God's provision for man's salvation in Jesus Christ. It is a powerful chapter to use in leading people to faith in Him.

If the Jew is also guilty, though he possesses the oracles of God, **what advantage** does he have, Paul asks (taking the place of an inquirer who has been listening to the reading of the previous chapter)? **Of what worth is circumcision**? The questions follow naturally from what he had asserted in chapter 2. Doubtless Paul uses this method of raising objections to what he has said because he had heard like objections many times before. Thus he proves himself ready to respond to them by way of anticipation. Counselors, likewise, hear the same objections to biblical advice over and over again. You should not only anticipate questions ("You might wonder 'how can someone handle a trial like that?'"), but also have answers ready at hand. Learn thoroughly this Pauline method used so effectively throughout the Book of Romans.

What are the advantages of this method? There are at least two: first, the counselee recognizes that you understand his thinking. That is important so that he cannot later on protest that you don't; secondly, he realizes that his situation is not unique. Others have faced it previously, or you would not be prepared with a stock question and answer. It is like handing out a previously printed paper that deals step by step with something that the counselee thought no one else ever had to. As a result, he gains confidence in you and in your assurance that this matter has a solution.

What is Paul's stock answer to the question? He replies, **Much in every way.** Then he emphasizes the fact that this meant that the Jews **were entrusted with God's revelatory words**. That is to say, they were given the Old Testament. In Paul's thinking this was a principal advantage. And of course it was. They were able to know the mind of God as it

3   What does that mean? If some of them were unfaithful, their unfaithfulness doesn't nullify God's faithfulness, does it?
4   Of course not! God must be true, even if every person is a liar. As it is written: **so that You may be justified in Your words and will win the case when You are brought to trial**.

5   But if our unrighteousness demonstrates God's righteousness so clearly, what shall we say—that God is unrighteous (I'm speaking in human terms) if He brings down wrath on us?
6   Of course not! If that were true, how would God judge the world?
7   But now, if my lie results in His glory by making God's truthfulness all the more obvious, why am I still going to be judged as a sinner?

---

was expressed by His prophets. They could know precisely what it was that He required of man. They were provided with an objective, infallible, inerrant Standard of faith and practice. On and on we could go, detailing the advantages of having a written revelation from God. The same truth is clear today: those who possess the Scriptures have every advantage over those who do not. But there is one catch—they must believe and submit to God's Word. The same is true of counselors. But, sadly, many to whom God has entrusted His Word seem strangely unwilling to turn to it as the Source for counseling principles and practices.

That, of course, is what Paul goes on to say. Some of those who had the Scriptures of the Old Testament were not faithful to Him. But, he continues, regardless of that, **their unfaithfulness doesn't nullify God's faithfulness, does it?** The answer is **Of course not**. Even if everybody is **a liar, God** still **is true**. What people do or fail to do does not affect the nature of God. He cannot deny Himself. He is always dependable; unlike sinful human beings, whatever He says you can bank on. If anyone could bring Him to **trial**, He would be vindicated (v. 4). And in the process, human **unrighteousness** would only be made all the more manifest. "But," objects someone, "if human unrighteousness **demonstrates God's righteousness so clearly, why should He bring down wrath on us?** Isn't it a good thing to demonstrate God's righteousness in that way?"

The answer to this cavil again is, **Of course not!** One shouldn't sin as a means of glorifying God. If it were otherwise, **God could not judge the world**. But, as you know, He will. The answer is built on the known, agreed-upon fact of judgment to come. But the objector will not be silenced. In verse 7 he comes at it again, putting the question this way: "**if my lie results in His glory, why judge me a sinner?** After all, my lie makes His truthfulness all the more conspicuous, doesn't it?" Paul's

Christian Counselor's Commentary

8   Why not say, "Let us do evil that good may come," as some slanderously claim that we are saying? Their judgment is just.

9   What then? Are we better than others? No, not at all. We have already charged that both Jews and Greeks alike are all under the power of sin.

10   As it is written:
   There isn't anybody who is righteous, not a single one.
11   **There isn't anybody who understands, there isn't anybody who seeks God.**
12   **All have turned aside; one and all have become vile. There isn't anybody who does good: there isn't even one.**
13   **Their throats are like a grave that has been opened; they deceive with their tongues. The poison of cobras is hidden behind their lips;**
14   **their mouths are full of cursing and bitterness.**

---

response: If what you are saying had any merit it would be right to say **"do evil that good may come," as some slanderously claim** we teach. The claim is a boldfaced lie; and those who make it will be judged justly for doing so. Thus Paul deals summarily with those who would argue in that fashion. Never allow a counselee to argue that way; read him these verses if he attempts to do so.

Now the next objection (one that always seems to appear when one's opponent has been bested) is "You must think you are a holier-than-thou." The way Paul phrased it was that from what has been said the accusation will be made that you think **you are better than others**. Paul replies, **"No, not at all**. As I have been saying for two chapters, everyone is **under the power of sin,** Jews and Gentiles alike—which, obviously, includes me!" The personal attack is one to which people have resorted in all ages. To avoid God's penetrating Word (cf. Hebrews 5:12,13) they attack the one who ministers it. Sweep it aside as deftly as Paul does by admitting your sin along with everyone else. The key is don't argue against the attack; simply agree with whatever part of it that you honestly can. The opponent (which a counselee often becomes at certain points in counseling when he refuses to obey God) expects you to defend yourself. If you convenience him by doing so, you can begin a grand irrelevant argument that will serve only to divert attention from the issues at hand. If you diffuse his argument by agreement, you can turn immediately back to the reason why you have met for counseling.

Romans 3

15   Their feet are swift to shed blood;
16   they leave ruin and misery in the paths they have walked,
17   and they don't even know the path of peace.
18   They have lost sight of the fear of God.

19 Now we know that whatever the law says, it speaks to those who are involved with the law, so that every mouth may be closed and the whole world may become accountable to God.

By quoting several passages from the Old Testament in verses 10 through 18 (Psalm 14, Psalm 5, Psalm 10, Isaiah 59 and Psalm 36), Paul overwhelmingly establishes the universality of sin in the human race. It is not our purpose to interpret these verses here. But it is of importance to ask why Paul brings in Scripture at this point. It would seem that he is trying to do two things at once. He wants the listener to know that it is no casual statement that he believes he is a sinner along with the rest of mankind. After all, he is able to marshal a bevy of passages that establish the fact. Because he is able to do so, it is also obvious that he has thought long and hard beforehand about the matter and reached this conclusion on his own. He is not driven to admit to the charge that he is no better than anyone else; he, himself, can prove it from an abundant number of Scriptures. But, secondly, these passages, brought in to speak about himself as a sinner, also speak about the objector as well. If Paul cannot squeeze out from beneath their condemnation, neither can anyone else. And so by further substantiating that he is not taking a holier-than-thou attitude he more firmly nails down the sin of the objector as well. Paul is a skillful debater. As a counselor, who must deal with objections regarding the biblical statements you make, to be faithful to God and to him means you must become as skillful as possible too. Paul uses every objection as a stepping stone to reach his objective. Keep that point in mind and work at learning to do so in similar circumstances.

Having quoted the Bible at length (vv. 10-18), he makes his point: **whatever the law says, it speaks to those who are involved with the law** (here the Jew, from whom these hypothetical objections are arising) **so that every mouth may be closed and the whole world may become accountable to God**. In the light of the Scripture verses quoted, you—along with all Jews and Gentiles—should consider yourself silenced in shame and guilt. You should acknowledge that God has condemned everyone in the world—including you. That means no one has kept the law. So **no one will be justified by works of law**. After all, I have just quoted and used the law for the purpose for which it was given: **it is by**

20 Nobody will be justified by works of law, since it is by law that one becomes fully aware of his sin.

21 But now, without law, God's righteousness has appeared, a fact to which the Law and the Prophets testify;

22 and it is a righteousness from God that is channeled through faith in Jesus Christ to all who believe; there isn't any difference—

23 all have sinned and come short of God's glory

---

law that one becomes fully aware of sin. That means you should humble yourself under the law's universal condemnation of the human race, falling down in repentance rather than maintaining your innocence in haughty pride.

Well, if that is the effect of the law, and you recognize your sin, what can be done about this deplorable condition in which you find yourself? You can do nothing. But God has already done something; indeed, what He has done is totally sufficient to solve the problem and rescue His own from the dilemma in which they, along with the rest of mankind, find themselves.

Without law, God's righteousness has appeared, a fact to which the law and the prophets testify (v. 21). The Old Testament spoke of a righteousness that God gives, one that is not earned by human merit, that is, by keeping the law. This righteousness of which I speak comes **from God and is channeled through faith in Jesus Christ to all who believe; for there isn't any difference**. It is a righteousness that God gives to all (Jew or Greek) who believe the gospel; it really makes no difference whether one is a Jew or not—all must receive it the same way. In other words, the righteousness that God accepts is one that He has provided in Christ for all who believe; not for those who try to become righteous through the keeping of the law.

All (Jews and Gentiles) have sinned and come short of God's glory. That is the miserable, but clearly-substantiated fact. The Scriptures just quoted condemn all: **there isn't anybody who does good; there isn't even one**. That is what the law says. When counselees protest their superiority over others or maintain some sort of basic innocence, it is well to read this list of Bible verses that Paul has culled from the Old Testament, and then to conclude with the words of verse 23. Nothing could be more all-encompassing.

The only way that a person could be saved, then, is by grace, and that means through the grace that was poured out on God's own as He **redeemed** them through the cross of **Christ Jesus** (v. 24). This was no

Romans 3

24 and must be justified without cost, by His grace, through the redemption that has been accomplished by Christ Jesus,
25 Whom God publicly provided (by the shedding of His blood) as an appeasing sacrifice to be appropriated by faith. He did this to demonstrate His righteousness because, in His tolerance, He had passed by sins committed previously
26 in order to demonstrate His righteousness at the present time, so that He Himself might be just and the Justifier of the person who believes in Jesus.
27 Where, then, is bragging? It is shut out. By what sort of law? Of works? No, but rather through a law of faith.

---

private thing, but He **publicly provided** redemption by the **shedding of Christ's blood** right there in the environs of Jerusalem itself. The crucifixion of Christ was **an appeasing sacrifice** (one designed to appease God and stem His wrath toward all those who trust in Him). And the benefits of this sacrifice may be **appropriated by faith**. This way, God **demonstrated His righteousness** as well. In His **tolerant patience, God had passed by sin,** never really atoning for it (temple sacrifices didn't take away sin), while planning to bring to light His righteousness **at the present time**. And what has He done? Well, in one act He has **demonstrated** Himself **just and the Justifier of** those who trust Christ. How, you ask? **Just**, by dealing definitively with the sins of the elect as His Son bore the punishment they deserved; **Justifier**, by counting them righteous since their sins had been definitively done away with in His death.

How can you **brag** then, Paul asks (v. 27)? There is no room for any such thing: **it is shut out. By what sort of law? Of works? No, but rather through a law of faith**. That is Paul's conclusion. The word **law** is used here in a somewhat different manner than it was previously. It refers not to the Scriptures, but to a *basis or rule* from which one operates. Paul asks, "On what basis is bragging excluded?" And he answers, "On the basis of faith." Since God saves by faith, and one who comes by faith must recognize that he has not earned his salvation by works, he should realize too that there is no ground for bragging about what he has done. Salvation by faith is a gift; it is the work of Another to be appropriated by faith. He himself has contributed nothing to it.

The argument here is somewhat tight. But it is irrefutable. Paul has caught his proud objector in his net. There is no way out. People must often be brought to the point where they finally see that there is no escape from Scripture's inevitable **conclusions**. But it often takes a considerable

28 We have come to the conclusion that a person is justified by faith without works of law.
29 Or is God the God of Jews only? Isn't He also the God of Gentiles? Yes, of Gentiles also,
30 since there is one God Who will justify the circumcision by faith and the uncircumcision by faith.

---

amount of argumentation from those Scriptures in order to establish one's point. Ministry of the Word is not merely citation of passages (though certainly there are times when that may suffice) but making the proper applications of them while arguing cogently from them to conclusions that are inevitable. You must be able to use the Bible in counseling as Paul does here to make your case. You may think that it is unnecessary to make a case. Well, of course, at times that may be true. But many counselees are dubious. They may not know the Scriptures well. They often fail to see implications and applications that are obvious to you. And they may be hesitant to act until fully convinced. Their attitudes are not necessarily wrong; their caution may, indeed, be a holy caution kindred to that commended to us in the last verse of Romans 14 (to which we will come in time). It is not only requisite to argue your case from Scripture in those instances where these are the factors hindering progress; it may be the only kindly and charitable thing to do.

In verse 28, Paul states the simple conclusion of all he has been arguing: **a person is justified by faith without the works of law.** That is the gist of the whole matter summed up in a memorable sentence. Again, this is something you might do so that the counselee may carry away a succinct statement of all that you have been discussing. Often, for instance, I write on a homework assignment sheet, as the summary of an extended discussion, "Follow your feelings and you will become depressed; follow God's Word and you won't," or, "Give in to your feelings and you will give up on your responsibilities." Summary statements like Paul's often become slogans that people can carry around in their mind (some write them down and literally carry them in a purse or wallet).

The next conclusion Paul reached was that God is the God of all; not merely the Jews (vv. 29, 30). How did he sum up this argument? He said "This is clearly the case since there is one God with one way (faith) by which he justifies both Jews and others" (v. 30). Does salvation by faith alone **nullify the law** he asks? **On the contrary**, he replies, **by it we are establishing the law.** How is that? Well, if the law's demands had to be

Romans 3

31 So then, do we nullify the law by this faith? Of course not! On the contrary, by it we are establishing the law.

---

satisfied by the appeasing sacrifice of the cross, the law is not only established but honored by God. He refused to ignore the law, but conformed to it so closely that He punished His Son to fulfill its demands. Make it clear that God will never relax His commands; counselees may not bargain with God (they will try it!). He honors and holds firmly to all that He required in the Bible.

CHAPTER 4

1 What then shall we say that Abraham, our forefather according to the flesh, found?
2 Indeed, if Abraham was justified by works, then he had something to brag about; but not before God.
3 What does the Scripture say? "**Abraham believed God and it was counted to him for righteousness.**"
4 Now the pay that a working man receives isn't considered a gift, but something owed to him.
5 But to a person who doesn't work for it, but depends on Him Who justifies the ungodly person, his faith is counted for righteousness.
6 It is just like when David speaks about the happiness of the person that God considers righteous without works:
7   **Happy are those whose lawless acts have been forgiven, and whose sins have been covered;**
8   **happy is the man that the Lord won't ever again consider sinful.**
9 Is this happiness only for the circumcised or is it also for the uncircumcised? Now what we are saying is that Abraham's faith was counted for righteousness.

In this chapter Paul is going to explicate the doctrine of justification by faith alone as, at the same time, he demonstrates and proves his case from the justification of Abraham, the father of the Jewish people. That is the story to which he directs our attention in verse 1. What of Abraham, he asks?

Well, what of Abraham? **If Abraham was justified by works, then he had something to brag about**; but that wasn't the way it was in God's providence (v. 2). Indeed, the Bible tells us something quite different: **Abraham believed God and it was counted to him for righteousness**. That statement is the foundation of all that he will say about Abraham in the verses to come. But what does it mean? That justification is by faith.

Paul illustrates. Take **a working man.** His **pay isn't a gift, it is owed to him**. But if a person doesn't work for something yet receives it (as God's righteousness is received), his righteousness is a gift. He is justified by faith since **his faith is counted for righteousness**. This word, **counted**, is key. David, Paul says, is another case in point. He notes for the reader the happiness of David over receiving a freely-given forgiveness according to which he was counted righteous without works. Then he

Romans 4

10 In which condition, then, was it counted, when he was circumcised or when he was uncircumcised? Not after circumcision; it was before he was circumcised.
11 As a matter of fact, he received circumcision as a sign, a seal of the righteousness that he had when he was uncircumcised, so that he might become the father of all who believe, and thus have righteousness counted to them, even though they are uncircumcised.
12 And, he is also father of the circumcised who are not merely circumcised, but who walk in the steps of our father Abraham by following the example of the faith that he had while uncircumcised.
13 The promise to Abraham and to his descendants that he would be heir of the world didn't come through law but through the righteousness of faith.

---

quotes Psalm 32:1 and 2 to substantiate his argument. And he goes on to ask whether David's happiness over imputed righteousness is for Jews alone.

Well, is it? Go back to the case of Abraham once again (v. 9); we have seen that **his faith was counted for righteousness.** Correct? Correct. Well then let me ask you, **in what condition** was it counted—when he was circumcised or before? **Before** (v. 10). As a matter of fact, the circumcision he received was **a sign, a seal of the righteousness that he already had received when he was still uncircumcised**. It was a token of the righteousness that he had by faith alone. Incidentally, children, on the eighth day, long before they could receive righteousness by faith, were given this sign and seal. That means that a sign could be given before the fact, and automatically eliminates all objections to the contrary when it comes to baptizing children—an act that signifies inclusion in the true church (even before it ever occurs or, as in circumcision as well, if it never does).

Abraham thus becomes **the father of all who believe and** thereby **have righteousness counted to them, even if they are uncircumcised** Gentiles. And among Jews he is father only of those who **walk in the steps of** faithful Abraham. It is not those who are circumcised among the Jews who are his children, but only those who, like him, believe and whose faith is counted for righteousness (v. 12).

And **the promise to Abraham and his descendants that he would become heir to the world was not made because he kept the law but out of pure grace by faith** (v. 13). Everything worthwhile given to father Abraham he did not earn but received out of God's unmerited favor. So,

Christian Counselor's Commentary

> 14 So, if those who are of the law are the heirs, faith is worthless and the promise has been annulled.
>
> 15 Law can only bring about wrath, but where there isn't any law there isn't any transgression.
>
> **16** Because of this it is of faith, that it might be by grace, so that the promise may rest on a solid basis for all his descendants, not only to those who are of the law, but also to those who share Abraham's faith; he is the father of all of us.

---

what is the upshot of all this? Simply this: **if those who trust in righteousness by trying to keep the law are the heirs to the Abrahamic promise, then faith** (including Abraham's) **is worthless and the promise made to him has been annulled** (v. 14). But of course neither of those things is true. Yet that is where any argument contrary to mine leads, says Paul. **All the law can do is bring about wrath** (v. 15), but **where there is no law** to transgress, **there is no transgression** to summon that wrath. By trying to be saved through keeping the law, you only expose yourself to wrath. By receiving righteousness by faith, you avoid doing so.

So **the promise to Abraham rests on a solid foundation**. It is not dependent on sinful human beings trying to keep the law; it is based on God-given faith. And therefore it is to all (Jews and Gentiles as well) who are of faith (v. 16).

Is there anything in all of this for counselors? Yes, there is. Those who insist on going their own way rather than God's biblically-prescribed way (and their number is legion) run terrible risks. They place themselves on the side of the self-helpers rather than on the side of those who depend solely on the gracious work of God in and through them. That is something of significance to anyone trying to help another. You must not allow a counselee to think that his way is as acceptable as God's, no matter how clever it may seem. If God has expressly set forth a way for dealing with problems, there can be no other. Yet, counselees, other counselors and friends (who may mean well, but don't think biblically) may all tempt your counselee to try another route to righteous living. Any solution that fails to call on God through His Spirit, in concert with the Bible, for the solution to a problem falls under God's condemnation. That is what it all amounts to for the counselor. The **solid basis** for all who would be helped is God's gracious promises, not something they must do.

Yet Abraham's faith was an acting faith. He believed that God's promise would be fulfilled in spite of the fact that it seemed impossible (humanly speaking) **since Sarah's womb was dead and he himself was**

Romans 4

17 As it is written, **I have determined for you to become the father of many nations.** Standing in God's presence, Abraham believed that God can give life to the dead and can call into existence things that don't exist.
18 Hoping against hope, Abraham believed that he would become the father of many nations in keeping with what he had been told; **So your descendants will be**.
19 His faith didn't weaken when he considered that his body was as good as dead, now that he was about a hundred years old, or when he considered that Sarah's womb was dead.
20 And he didn't hesitate about God's promise because of unbelief, but fortified by faith, he gave God glory
21 since he was thoroughly convinced that whatever He has promised He is able to do.

---

nearly 100 years old! Yet he believed God, and did not hesitate to glorify Him (vv. 18-20). He was thoroughly convinced that whatever He promised He is able to do (v. 21). Now that is the sort of faith that we are talking about—faith that accepts and follows God's Word for what it is. He did not question; he believed. Many counselees seem to *want* to question the Word of God. They sound like the devil in the garden saying, "Has God said...?" God **is able** to do what He promises. Now there is a reassuring statement that ought to be a regular part of the counselor's repertoire. You may ask your counselee, "If God was able to come through on His promise to give Abraham a child in his old age, don't you think that He can solve your problem too?" The counselee may be thinking at this point, "But that was Abraham. I'm not going to become heir of the world." As he often does (see I Corinthians 10; Romans 15) Paul here stresses the fact that these words were not spoken for Abraham's sake alone; the fact that they were recorded means that they were written down for ours as well (vv. 23, 24). The Scriptures have the church of all time in view. That is an important point to make when counselees tend to throw off the promises of God as something special that happened "in Bible times." The implication is, God's promises aren't for today. You must use the Bible as it if were written to you and to your counselee, not only to those in Rome (or elsewhere) who first received it. Because it *was* written for today. The contemporary use of the Bible is critical to good counseling. It must never be spoken about as if it were for long ago and far away.

What Christ did is for His church of all time. **He was delivered up for our trespasses and raised for our justification.** The death and resurrection of Christ for guilty sinners (the essence of the gospel message) is

Christian Counselor's Commentary

> 22 That is why it was **counted to him for righteousness**.
>
> **23** The words, "it was counted to him," weren't written for his sake alone,
>
> 24 but also for our sake. It is going to be counted to us who depend upon the One Who raised Jesus our Lord from the dead.
>
> 25 He was delivered up for our trespasses and raised for our justification.

as pertinent today as ever, isn't it? Romans 4 may not have much additional to say beyond that, but nothing could be of greater importance to the biblical counselor than to know that what God says applies today. Never forget it. And never let your counselee do so either.

CHAPTER 5

1 Therefore, having been justified by faith, we have peace with God through our Lord Jesus Christ,
2 through Whom also by faith we have been led into this grace in which we stand, and we boast about the hope of God's glory.

Chapter 5 opens with the wonderful assurance that those who are justified by faith have **peace with God.** That is a counseling statement. That peace, of course, is the fundamental peace that was achieved by **Christ's** cross. It means those who are saved are no longer enemies. Ever since they surrendered in faith they have been not only captives of God but have become members of His empire. Peace with God means the cessation of hostilities, the elimination of enmity and access to the *shalom* of God.

Peace (*shalom*), as understood by the Jew, was a condition of prosperity, joy and contentment. It was often described as every person *under his vine and fig tree*. This peace however is never complete in this world of sin in which, because of the sin of others and one's own sin as well, *shalom* is always less than it has potential to be. Therefore one must always keep growing in his love for God and his neighbor, since this is the path to the increase of *shalom*. Fundamentally, *shalom* means satisfaction that comes from satisfying God. While peace is held out as a desirable biblical goal and as a motive for service, it may never become one's primary motive; that always must be to please God. Counselees looking for peace should be shown both sides of the page. On the one side is written "*shalom*" and on the other "Pleasing God." They must not neglect the one for the other; nor may you allow counseling to deteriorate into mere peace-seeking conferences. If you do, they will be as hollow and meaningless, and about as effective, as the peacekeeping efforts of the U.N.

Through Christ **we have been led into this grace in which we stand,** says Paul. That means just about what I have been saying about the access into *shalom* that Jesus has provided for you. The mention of the word **grace,** however, suggests an additional dimension. All that you have—not only your justification, but everything you now have access to as a believer—is the result of God's power, graciously at work in your life. It is unmerited goodness that Christ has loosed into your life; His unearned, undeserved power is at work making you more and more like Himself. And, as a result, there is more and more of the *shalom* that God promises.

Christian Counselor's Commentary

3 But not only that; indeed, we also boast about afflictions, knowing that affliction produces endurance,
4 and endurance approval, and approval hope.

That is our present **standing** or position in relationship to the **grace of God**. But there is much more to come: **we boast about the hope of God's glory**. The word **glory** seems to mean (at least as Paul uses it in Romans) the completion of the *shalom* one receives when he is perfected in heaven (cf. 3:23). We have so much now, but we anticipate so much more in the eternal state. So peace with God means present peace to some extent (growingly so), but it also means perfect peace in the life to come. *Shalom*, therefore, is a large concept. Try to sketch something of its meaning for your counselee so that, with Paul, he will be able to say, **But not only that; indeed, we boast about afflictions**. Now, how was he able to make that boast a reality?

By recognizing that in the realm of the empire of God **affliction produces endurance, and endurance approval, and approval hope,** Paul could actually boast about afflictions. That is the way in which Paul thought *and* actually *experienced* the grace of God at work in his life. What it means is that Paul saw more than the affliction. He was more interested in what lay beyond it; he focused on what affliction produces. Then he wanted not only to know that, but also what the product of endurance would be—and so on. He follows this chain to the end: moving as far as possible in this life, to hope (expectation, anticipation of the things that lay in the future at death). **Affliction**, handled God's way, always strengthens. It produces **endurance**—the ability to hang in there when the going gets tough. The affliction that one endures today is preparation for greater trials tomorrow. If one fails to endure present affliction he will cave in when he must face the greater trials of tomorrow. That is why some affliction today is a good thing. One never knows what may lie ahead. But if he is to endure it, whatever it may be, he must prepare today. When your counselee experiences affliction he will need to be told how important it is to allow affliction to do its job. He is not to flee it if it is at work in his life producing endurance. And the same is true of **endurance**. It leads to **approval**. To know God's approval is everything. And then, **approval** leads to **hope**. How wonderful if, after enduring affliction, God approves of your behavior! Approval comes through knowing that you have done what the Scriptures require. When you have that under your belt you can look forward to the greater hope of the day when you will

Romans 5

5   We need not be ashamed of hope because God's love has been poured into our hearts through the Holy Spirit Who was given to us.
6   Indeed, when we were weak, precisely at that time when it was needed, Christ died for the ungodly.
7   Yet one wouldn't ordinarily die for a righteous person, though perhaps for a good man someone might dare to die,
8   but by this God establishes the fact of His love for us: that while we were still sinners Christ died for us.

---

actually hear him *say,* "Well done, you good and faithful servant."

All of this should assure a beleaguered counselee. If you fail to major on the beneficial results of affliction (rightly borne), you will fail him. In order to endure, he needs to understand and count on the chain of products that are the outcome of endurance of affliction. It is always wrong in counseling to allow a counselee to focus only on the trial. Your task is to enable him to endure it by helping him to see beyond it. Just yesterday I was able to use this Pauline dynamic to help a counselee to face a difficult situation. He had to go to six persons to confess sin. When I explained that doing this would strengthen him for future trials at first he said, "Well, that's not too encouraging." But when I continued to explain that without building assurance through facing affliction today (even when self-inflicted by one's own sin) he would cave in under far more difficult pressures in the future, when more hung in the balance, he replied, "I guess that is encouraging after all."

In verse 5, an interesting observation is made: there is no reason for the believer **to be ashamed of hope**. The expression "be ashamed of" means to be ashamed because the expectation (hope) failed. The Christian hope does not fail. And we know that because we already have the earnest of what is to come: **God's love has been poured into our hearts through the Holy Spirit Who was given to us** at regeneration. Because we can now actually love as Christ loved by His power, since He has given us new desires and capabilities, we have already been experiencing something of the age to come. That is why we know we will never be let down by God; our hope will be realized in all its fullness. And that is a fullness that is greater than we now can anticipate.

The next section is verses 6 through 11. In it, Paul describes the believer's condition before regeneration. It is one that only grace could overcome. He demonstrates that one in that condition has nothing to commend him to God. It must be God's unmerited favor that reaches down to redeem. The three phrases that sum up all he says are **when we were**

Christian Counselor's Commentary

> **9** Having now been justified by His blood, it is all the more certain that we shall be saved from the wrath through Him.
> 10 Indeed, if while we were enemies we were reconciled to God by the death of His Son, how much more—now that we are reconciled—shall we be saved by His life!

---

weak (v. 6), **while we were still sinners** (v. 8) and **while we were enemies** (v. 10). That says it all. The kind of people God saves are incapable of helping themselves because of their weakness (morally, and in every other way); they are lawbreakers, going their own ways, caring nothing for the rules of human society given by God; and they are enemies, who in everything they do (knowingly or unknowingly) show their antipathy toward God and His ways. What counselee, then, has any reason to boast about anything that he is or that he has achieved? These verses should eradicate all such pride in a flash.

Notice that God did things rightly, in *a timely* way (v. 6). Christ's death came at the proper time. What, precisely, that means to a counselor is this: God *cares about* being on time. Too often that is the very thing wrong with a counselee. Unlike the God in Whose image he is made a counselee may be sloppy, do things perfunctorily and late. That can be the prime reason for losing jobs, for losing friends and for losing face before a world that does not know Christ.

The remarkable nature of Christ's death for sinners is described in verse 7. Ordinarily one would not give his life for a person who is **righteous** (here this means someone who lives according to the law), though he might possibly do so for one who was especially **kind (in his goodness)**. But we were neither. It was while we were **sinners**—notorious in God's sight—that He died for us! That unfolds something of the amazing **love** that God determined to set on us. Verses 7 and 8 are designed to elicit amazement and gratitude. If they do not when read to a counselee, try to discover why. Does he not know Christ as Savior? Does this seem like old hat? Does he fail to appreciate what these words mean? Ask. His answer probably will be important.

Back to the theme of verse 1 he writes, **Having now been justified by His blood, it is all the more certain that we shall be saved from wrath through Him. Indeed, if while we were enemies we were reconciled to God by the death of His Son, how much more—now that we are reconciled—shall we be saved by His life!** What is Paul's point? If by dying Christ could accomplish so much, think of what He can do for

Romans 5

11 But that isn't all; we also boast in God through our Lord Jesus Christ, through Whom we have now received reconciliation.

12 Therefore, just as through one person sin entered into the world, and death through this sin, and thus death spread to every human being, because all have sinned—

13 of course sin was in the world before the law, but it isn't counted as such when there is no law.

14 Yet, death reigned from Adam to Moses, even over those who didn't sin in a way that was exactly like the transgression of Adam, who was a type of the One to come.

---

you as a risen, living Person. That is the point Paul wants to make. His **blood** (i.e., His death) sufficed to shield us from the eternal **wrath** of God to come. He **reconciled us to God** by the blood of the cross. God is no longer our Enemy. We are His friends. Now that we have been reconciled to Him think of what He has in store for His friends. If He would do what He did for us when enemies, how much more will He do for us now that we are His friends!

So we can now boast since we have Someone to boast about—the Lord Jesus Christ. Ask your counselee, "Are you proud of your Savior?" To him it may be a new question. His answer will be instructive. It will reveal, perhaps, how much he thinks about himself and how much he thinks about Christ. When you recognize all He has and will do for you, how can you help being proud of Him?

Now comes an interesting section because of its theological import and because it is of significance to counselors. **Death,** Paul says, **came into the world through one person** (Adam), and **it passed to all people** [Christ excepted]. And, as a result, **all have sinned** because all were born sinners by this spiritual death. **Of course sin was in the world before the law**, he writes. But when there is no law one doesn't have the clear knowledge that he has when it is there. The point is that people did not sin as Adam did—in the face of an express commandment. But people died anyway (v. 15). Death, as God told Adam, is the penalty *for sin*. So for whose sin did they die? They died for the representative act of one person—Adam. They died because they were counted sinners in him. So people died **from Adam to Moses** not because of their personal sins but because in Adam they were constituted sinners. That was true even though they didn't sin in the full face of a written law as they did from the time of Moses on. So it is not necessary (Paul is saying) to have broken a *known* law in order to be counted a sinner; because Adam represented the entire

15 But the free gift is different from the trespass: if many died by the trespass of one person, the grace and gift of God (by the grace of the one Person, Jesus Christ) much more abounded to the many.
16 Nor is the gift like the effect of one person's sin. On the one hand, the judgment of the one trespass resulted in condemnation, but, on the other hand, the free gift had to be great enough to result in justification after many trespasses.
17 So if death reigned because of one person's trespass, how much more will those who receive the abundance of grace and of the gift of righteousness reign in life through the one Person Jesus Christ!
18 So then, as one person's trespass resulted in the condemnation of all people, so also one Person's righteous act results in the justification that means life.

---

human race (all were in Adam), all sinned and all died in him. That is the point.

Now in verse 15 Paul begins to talk about the other One, in Whom many are given life. All through this section representative acts of single individuals that affect many others are in view. As bad as the result of Adam's representative act was, its power and effect it does not even begin to compare with the one representative act of Christ on the cross. Jesus' act of obedience in dying is so much fuller, so much more powerful, that its effect goes abundantly beyond Adam's act. Its results have **abounded**. Adam's sin differed from Christ's death in that Adam's one trespass resulted in condemnation, but Christ's free gift of grace by means of the cross was great enough not only to deal with Adam's sin, but all the other sins of His people. That is how great it was (v. 16).

If death reigned through one person, asks Paul rhetorically, **how much more will those who receive the abundance of grace and of the gift of righteousness reign in life through the One Person Jesus Christ!** Previously death reigned; now those in Christ reign in life (v. 17). The act of one person resulted in **death of all people**; the act of One Person **resulted in the justification of many**, a result that for them means life. And the former act constituted many sinners while the latter constituted many righteous. Each of these acts led to a particular relationship to God. The former brought the entire human race into condemnation; God looked upon all men as sinners who deserved His wrath in hell. The latter brought those who are justified by faith into favor with God so that they will spend eternity with Him in heaven. **The law** was given later in order to show the pervasive nature of sin, making it clear what Adam's trespass

Romans 5

19 Just as by one person's disobedience many were constituted sinners, so by one Person's righteousness many will be constituted righteous.

20 Now law came in as an addition to make the trespass abound. But where sin abounded, grace far more abounded,

21 so that as sin reigned by death, so grace also might reign through righteousness resulting in eternal life through Jesus Christ our Lord.

---

did to the human race. But while we see how widely sin permeated the world and the life of every creature in it, we also can see how greatly God's grace in Christ meets sin and overcomes it. **Where sin abounded, grace far more abounded.**

That last statement (from v. 20) is a crucial one for every counselor. Rather than being defeated by sin, it is possible to defeat sin in Christ. The entire hope of the Christian faith is summed up in verse 20^b. Think of it; here is a counselee crushed under the load of some sin wondering whether there is any relief. You tell him, "Yes, I recognize sin's weight, sin's power—truly it **abounds**!" You may not minimize sin and its effects. It is always wrong to do so; people know the devastating effects of sin in their lives. If you minimize it they will not hear you. "But," you continue, "Where sin abounds, grace far more abounds. That means that no matter how sin may affect you, grace can counter its evil effects in your life." While you lost what Adam had through his sin, in Christ you have gained more than he had. The idea is not to minimize sin and its effects, but to magnify Christ. That is what Paul does.

And in all your counseling the goal should be more than redemption (a buying back of what was lost). You should hold out hope of something better in Christ than existed before.

Sin reigned by death, so that grace might reign by righteousness resulting in eternal life through Jesus Christ our Lord (v. 21). In this summary statement, Paul says it all. The reign of sin over the human race that began in the garden led to death; the reign of God's grace that began on the cross resulted in eternal life for all who trust in Christ. All in Adam (that is, the entire human race) died; all in Christ (His elect) live.

This fifth chapter is bedrock for teaching the representative work of Adam and of Christ. Some object to the fact that God could use one man to represent the entire human race, and that through him we should all be condemned to hell. But they rarely object when they are told that by the work of One Person they can have life through faith. Like it or not, the fact is that God does act through representatives. And it is also a fact that

Christian Counselor's Commentary

when one man (the President of the US) declares war on a country, like it or not, if you are in his army you'd better begin to dodge bullets. His one act can put you in jeopardy. That is just how life is in this world.

So every counselee who has been redeemed by the blood of Jesus Christ has spiritual life, is declared righteous, and has eternal life. That is what the one act of the One Person accomplished. Stack that up against anything your counselee can present by way of the evil effects of sin and though the latter may be terrible, the former are far greater in their immediate and ultimate effects on believers. While refusing to minimize sin, never allow the counselee to represent it as greater than the grace of God. Remind him of the truth of this chapter, perhaps in the words of the hymn that rightly declares that God's grace "is greater than all our sin."

Chapter 6

1 What shall we say then? Should we continue in sin so that grace might abound?
2 Of course not! How can we who died to sin still live in it?
3 Or don't you know that as many of us as were baptized into Christ Jesus were baptized into His death?

I should begin by saying that there is not one drop of water in this passage. This is not a Presbyterian/Baptist problem; it is a problem between those who believe that water baptism saves and those who do not. If the chapter speaks of *water* baptism then clearly that baptism is necessary for salvation because Paul writes of baptism **into Christ** (v. 3). But it is plain everywhere in the New Testament that water baptism and salvation are linked only as reality and symbol. That is to say, baptism is but the outward symbol of the inward reality; water baptism is *not* necessary for salvation. Having said that, let us move one stage further: the baptism here mentioned is baptism by the Holy Spirit. That, of course, *is* necessary to salvation. Paul will say that anyone who doesn't have the Spirit doesn't belong to Christ.

The chapter begins by referring back to the discussion in the previous chapter. He had said that where sin abounds, grace far more abounds (v. 5:20). "Now," asks Paul, "if that is true shouldn't we sin as we please so that there can be an abundance of grace to meet the sin (v. 1)?" And then he replies **Of course not!** (v. 2). The very idea is absurd (not to say vicious). It is not necessary to sin more in order to experience more of the grace of God. There is so much sin in our lives already that if we were to receive grace for sin proportionally we would be overwhelmed with grace. As it is, when we realize all that God has provided for us *we indeed are overwhelmed!* Yet from time to time, in spite of the absurdity of the idea, counselees will think, and some will say, much the same thing: "Oh well, does it matter whether I sin a little longer or not? After all, I've been at it this long; could a little longer make any difference? After all, there will only be all the more forgiveness and grace when I stop." People who think this way should not only hear Paul as he writes these first two verses of Romans 6, but you also need to ask them whether they understand what sin is. It is not just some unpleasant thing. It is not alienation. Sin is the violation of the commandments of a holy God; it is saying "no" when He says "yes;" saying "yes" when He says "no." Sin is a heinous affront to

Christian Counselor's Commentary

God. It is well, somewhere early in counseling, to explain the nature of sin. The highest motivation for change is not to get something for one's self, but to avoid displeasing God while learning to do those things that please Him. Unless a proper, biblical view of sin fills the mind of the counselee, not only will his motivation be wrong but he will be likely to come up with some such absurd idea as the one that Paul postulates here.

Paul is shocked at the suggestion. He asks, **How can he who died to sin still live in it?** That is a good question. As a matter of fact, that question sets up the discussion to follow. Paul says that there is a way in which the Christian has died to sin. Obviously that does not mean he can never sin again; both your experience and the two chapters that we will now discuss give the lie to any such notion. What does he mean then? Simply that to have died to sin and then to go on sinning is the height of inconsistency. The two things do not mesh. To sin under that circumstance fails to compute: the buzzer on your computer is making a noise! Paul is saying, then, that there is no reason for Christians to go on sinning as they have in the past and that there is every reason for them not to do so. If that is so, and it is, then *your counselee need not sin as he does* at the present. That is a powerful point to make with him from time to time. When he tells you that he can't help it, you can tell him, "To the contrary, since you have died to sin it is totally inconsistent for you to sin." This inconsistency is the nature of the Christian life in this world. And it is the reason for counseling as well. The task of counseling is to bring the counselee's lifestyle more closely in sync with what has happened to him (his death to sin).

Now, let's ask "What does it mean that the Christian has **died to sin**?" In the verses that follow, Paul explains. In somewhat of an astounded manner he asks, "**Or don't you know**...?" This is not simply an argumentative style in which he is writing. It is that; but it is a style chosen because the question he is asking need never to have been asked. That Paul asks it (along with the various questions that occur throughout this Book) indicates that he encountered ideas among Christians that forced him to do so. Paul was a counselor and he knew the problems, the attitudes, the questions and the ideas with which every counselor must deal. Romans is a practical book; it is not a mere theological treatise. It grows out of the experience of a counselor who had heard everything before.

What is it that every Christian should know, the thing that is inconsistent with sinning and that has caused him to die to sin? It is that he was **baptized into Christ**. That is the seminal statement out of which the rest of the present discussion flows. Notice that he did not say, "baptized into water." Nor, as we so often hear the passage incorrectly quoted, does he

Romans 6

4 Therefore, we were buried with Him by baptism into death so that just as Christ was raised from the dead by the glory of the Father, so also we might walk in newness of life.

5 If we have become united with Him in a death like His, we shall indeed also be united with Him in a resurrection like His,

---

say "baptized into Christ's death, burial and resurrection." He says, baptized *into Christ*. To miss this fact is to miss everything.

It is because one is baptized into Christ that he is—*as a result*—baptized into His death, burial and resurrection. The one depends upon the other. Put a bean in a pot. Where is the bean? "In the pot," you say. Yes, but where is the pot? Let us say that it is on the table. Then, since it is in the pot, the bean is also on the table. Lower the pot on to the floor: the bean is on the floor because the pot is there. Raise it up and place it on a shelf. The bean is on the shelf because that's where the pot is. *Wherever the pot goes the bean goes too because it is in the pot.* That is the point to get hold of. Because the Christian has been baptized into Christ (**united with Him**, as Paul says in v. 5), he is **in** Christ (Paul's favorite expression to describe the condition of the regenerate person). And like the bean in the pot, wherever Christ went, God counts the Christian to have gone also: that is why he can be said to be buried and raised in Christ. It is true, also, that he is reckoned to be circumcised with Him (Colossians 2), crucified with Him (Galatians 2:20), buried and raised with Him (as we read here) and seated in the heavenlies with Him (Colossians 3). The entire life, death and post-resurrection life of Christ is in various parts of the New Testament attributed to the believer since he is reckoned to have experienced all that Christ did. So then, if the Christian has the whole (i.e., if he is baptized into all of Christ's experiences by being **baptized into Christ**) he has the part (the death, burial and resurrection) attributed to him. If you have the whole, then you have the part. Paul selects from the whole that part which will illustrate his point—you are counted dead in Christ to the past, but alive in Him to **newness of life** (v. 4). If that is so, than how can you go on sinning?

In verse 5 Paul argues the point this way: **if you have become united with Him in a death like His,** you will also be **united** in **a resurrection like His**. Death (ours) here is not literal; resurrection likewise is not literal. The body and soul of the believer are raised to new potential for service. The old man is raised a new man. The resurrection after death to sin is to **newness of life**. And that is the point—your lifestyle should be new.

Christian Counselor's Commentary

> 6 knowing this, that our old person was crucified with Him so that the sinful body might be made ineffective, and we might no longer serve sin as its slaves.
> 7 The one who has died has been freed from sin by justification.

We should **walk** in this way to the **glory** of God (v. 4). Justification means that God looks on us as dead to the past, but also alive to the future. By justification the Christian is counted perfectly righteous, as righteous as Jesus Christ Himself. But there is more. Christians are also regenerated: given life to believe the gospel and to live for the Lord. Their natures have been changed; the believer no longer has a heart that is deceitful and desperately wicked. His heart has been filled with the Spirit of God (cf. Romans 5:5) so that he can love God and his neighbor as the Bible requires. He not only is looked upon differently, he *is* different. This regenerative difference provides new desire and new power for living the new life. The Christian needs to "know" (v. 6) that the **old person** he used to be was crucified not only in principle, but in fact. This is the basic motif for all that follows. The death and resurrection of the soul and the freeing of the body for the Lord's service by regeneration enables the believer to live differently. By this regenerative act, based on the work of Christ and communicated to him by the Spirit, the **old person** is rendered **ineffective** so that **the body** that was the slave of **sin** (v. 6) might no longer **serve sin as a slave.** When Paul speaks of **the body of sin,** what he means, according to the rest of the verse and those that follow, is the body that had become sin's **slave**. It is the body that was owned by the slave-master that Paul calls sin. Truly when one is unsaved he has been taken captive by sin which becomes his master. Sin uses him as a slave's body is used. He learns the ways of sin; he becomes proficient in them. He is a faithful and skillful servant of sin. But when regenerated he is given a new outlook, freed from slavery to sin and the ways of sin: the old person need no longer dominate and use his body in the service of sin. That is the image Paul uses to communicate the facts important to sanctification.

The counselee may protest that he is unable to change, that he is enslaved to some habitual lifestyle that God abhors. But you may not allow him to get away with that: the **old person is crucified**. He now has both the status (v. 7) of one who has been emancipated from sin's authority and power and the potential for new life (v. 6). Justified and regenerated! What more could he want? On the positive side: there is hope abundant. This **body** that was in the slavery of sin, habituated to sin's

8   But if we died with Christ, we believe that we also shall live with Him,
9   knowing that since Christ has been raised from the dead He won't ever die again; death no longer holds lordship over Him.
10 The death that He died, He died to sin once, forever, but the life that He lives, He lives for God.
11 So too you must count yourselves to be dead to sin, but living for God in Christ Jesus.
12 Therefore, don't let sin reign in your mortal body, with the result that you obey its desires;

---

ways, need no longer be **effectively** pursuing them.

Dying **with Christ** means living **with Him** (v. 8); the two go together. They may not be separated. Indeed, they are but two sides of one door. Looking backward on one side of the door you see the past record of sin, slavery to unrighteousness, and habituation in the ways of wickedness. As you pass through it, you see before you the potential for an entirely new life of righteousness: slavery to goodness and joy in doing it. Conversion is passing from one reality to another very different one. The radical nature of this transformation must never be minimized in counseling. Some counselors are willing to settle for too little; and because they hold out so little that's exactly what they get. In the chapter before us, Paul holds out for nothing less than **newness of life** (lifestyle).

Because Christ has passed through the experience of death triumphantly (being raised from it), He will never again experience death. It is entirely behind Him (v. 9). And that means death no longer has any power or authority (**lordship**) over Him. Likewise, counselees who are in Christ should **count themselves dead to sin but alive to God** (v. 11). After all, that is the course of affairs for Christ Himself (v. 10), the same course that, positionally, the believer is *reckoned* to have followed.

Having explained these matters, Paul turns to exhortation, the very exhortation that counselees often need. He writes, **Therefore, don't let sin reign in your mortal body with the result that you obey its desires**. This body of the Christian, about which Paul began to write in verse 6, now becomes the subject of Paul's greater concern. Once it was enslaved by sin. Now it has been freed from that slavery. So this **mortal body**—the one that is dying because of sin, not the new body to be received at the resurrection—must no longer be subject to sin. Sin must no longer **reign** in and over it. If you allow it to do so, you will **obey its desires**. The desires of sin, habituated in the body by years of service to sin, will be to do unrighteousness. So sin must no longer be obeyed. Its **desires** (that

Christian Counselor's Commentary

> 13 and don't present your bodily members to sin as instruments of unrighteousness, but rather, present yourselves to God as persons who have been raised from the dead and are living, and your members to God as instruments of righteousness.
> 14 Sin must not be your lord and master; you aren't under law but under grace.
> **15** What then? Should we sin then because we aren't under law but under grace? Of course not!

---

over time have become habitual desires of the body) will tend in the wrong direction. Your body (which includes the brain, programmed by your sinful nature) will desire to do sinful things that you know you must not do. So you both desire and do not desire to do them. That is the struggle in which your counselee is engaged if he truly is a believer.

How may you obey God and not the desires of sin that also have become the desires of a habituated body long trained in sin's service? By conscious efforts to **present your bodily members to God** rather than to sin. As you once willingly used the body for the purposes of sin, now a conscious, prayerful effort to regularly (note the present tense) **present your body to God for His use** is required. Previously, your bodily members were used as **weapons (or instruments) of unrighteousness**; they now must be trained to become **weapons (instruments) of righteousness**. There is a process of learning to use the body (including the brain) for God instead of for sin. The counselee has a new Master. That is what counseling is all about: enabling the counselee to understand and live according to these facts concerning himself.

Again, Paul reiterates that sin is **no longer your master**; therefore **you are not under its authority** (v. 13). You are free! Act, live like free men and women. Grace—all that God's goodness and mercy has done for you—now rules your life. Out of gratitude for grace, serve God!

Paul raises another objection in verse 15. He had heard it many times before: **Should we sin because we aren't under law but under grace?** The answer is as before. How did his imagined inquirer reason? He asked, "If you are not saved by keeping the law, but by the mercy and grace of God, why not sin? After all, it is the power of God that saved me. If I am not to sin, then let this same grace keep me from sinning as well!" But God does not work in sanctification as He did in regeneration and justification. In the latter instances He acted on His own, instantaneously. But, in sanctifying there are two differences: 1) He has determined that believers will play a part, and 2) sanctification takes time. God does not sanctify

Romans 6

16 Don't you know that you are slaves of the one to whom you present yourselves for obedience? You are slaves of the one to whom you give obedience, whether it is sin leading to death, or obedience leading to righteousness.

---

instantaneously. Your counselee is involved. There are certain forms of counseling purporting to be biblical that teach he does not have a part. They teach that if change in the believer is to take place, God, apart from human obedience, will bring it about. That is false. It is true that God enables one to do His will (cf. Philippians 2:13), but *he* must do it. God could have chosen to change everything immediately, as He will remove the remnant of the lifestyle that must be changed at death or at the coming of Christ, but for His own purposes He has chosen not to do so in this life. Otherwise the exhortations found in verses 12 and 13 would be pointless.

Explaining his earlier exhortations, Paul says you are **the slave** of the one to whom you give obedience by presenting the members of your body for his service. Sin's service leads to death; God's to righteousness (v. 16). He wants you to **know** that fact. Evidently there were those for whom this was vague. He wanted the Romans to be clear about the matter. It is plain that, regardless of what one *says*, it is the one whom he *obeys* that is his master. Obedience to sin leads to death; obedience to God leads to righteousness. There is a vast difference. How then can Christians choose to obey sin? That is the inconsistency that Paul is probing.

There is then, throughout this section, both explanation and exhortation. The latter is based on the former. It is ever Paul's concern to make clear why he calls God's people to the paths of duty and action that he sets forth in any given place. Counselors should follow his example. Here, in the course of exposition, he provides the clearest explanation of why God wishes a change of life in His children. He has brought them out of the past by His mighty act on the cross and by the resurrection from the dead. These divine acts provide both justification and power for sanctification. To continue to live as one did in the past is to deny the gracious work of God. In effect, because it is inconsistent with His death and resurrection (which was not for His sake but for the sake of those for whom He died), the failure to grasp the importance of newness of life is fatal to counseling. Counseling is for God's glory in Christ. It is one's effort to help others to honor Him, out of gratitude. To live as if the death of Christ meant nothing to one's lifestyle, had no effect upon his thinking, belief or actions, is to live in a manner inconsistent with the cross.

Christian Counselor's Commentary

> 17 But thank God that you, who were once slaves of sin, now have obeyed from the heart the pattern of teaching to which you were handed over,

In addition, Paul is careful to explain not only *why* one's life must be different after the cross, but *how* that may occur. It takes place as one **obeys the pattern of teaching to which** he was **handed over**. That obedience began with the hearing of the gospel in faith; it continues with the heeding of the commandments of God. And it is to those commands, found in a divinely-deposited pattern of teaching (now recorded in the Scriptures) that each believer has been handed over by God. That is to say, he was delivered (handed over) to it—to do it—instead of those things he did in the past (cf. Mt. 28:18-20). Because in redemption the former slave of sin has been handed over to a new master, Jesus Christ, he is handed over to His will (v. 17).

In this verse there are several noteworthy items that should not be missed. One ought to be eternally grateful that he is no longer a slave of sin. This gratitude should lead to **thanking** God. How much gratitude do you discover in the counselee before you? That is an important matter. If he is filled with anger, despair or some similar emotion, rather than gratitude, do you think he will be motivated to **obey from the heart**? Perhaps before you can progress further in counseling you must remind him of what he has in Christ. Remind him of the old days of slavery to sin and of the new potential for righteousness that is now his. Remind him of the fact that God Himself has become his new master and that He will not allow anything to happen to His servant that He does not countenance (we will soon come to Romans 8:28!). In short, explain once again the main thrust of this passage.

But, notice also, Paul speaks of obedience **from the heart.** There is a great difference between obedience of an outward sort and obedience that stems from the heart of the counselee. The heart is the inner person that no one but God and he, himself, knows. God the Heart-Knower, however, is concerned about whether one's obedience is forced, outward and insincere or whether it stems from an inner desire to please Him. He wants no Pharisaical obedience, obedience that conforms outwardly but has no corresponding reality within. He wants His servants to be like cups washed inside and out, not on the outside only. One may not wish to obey God's will because it is hard, embarrassing, etc., but he must want to obey because of gratitude in his heart for the cross and all the many benefits

18 and having been freed from the authority of sin you became slaves of righteousness.
19 (I am using human illustrations because of the weakness of your flesh.) In the same way that you presented your members as slaves to uncleanness and lawlessness to bring about more lawlessness, now you must present your members as slaves of righteousness to bring about sanctification.

---

that flow from it. In other words, one obeys God not because the task to which he is called is pleasant, but because he wants to please God. That is obedience from the heart. And it is precisely the sort of obedience about which many counselees need to learn.

Finally, this obedience is not to some present-day revelation (there is none) or to supposed "promptings and checks in the spirit" (there are none), or "feelings" and "impressions," "leadings" and "feelings" (these may come from anything, but not from God) but to a recognized, formulated body **(pattern) of teaching** to which one is **handed over** when he is saved. That means you do not have to determine what sort of conduct you should pursue during the new life you are leading; God, your new Master, has outlined it for you in His Word. The Christian is committed (**handed over**) to a standard lifestyle that is set forth in the Bible. That is because his new Master wants him to use his life to bring about righteousness wherever he goes (v. 18). He is under a new authority—the authority of God exercised through the deposit of truth found in the Bible. Never allow counselees to appeal to anything other than the Scriptures as the basis for obedience. Too many depend on what others say, what they themselves have reasoned out, or what some church or church leader has told them.

The entire metaphor of sin and God as slave-masters, Paul explains, is to help his reader to understand (v. 19). There is a **weakness** of human **flesh** (that is, of unaided, sinful human ability) to comprehend. Because of the patterns of living in the past, one is habituated to think improperly. So Paul must go to lengths to explain. Vivid imagery helps. There is a lesson here for counselors. Use examples, use imagery. It helps clarify matters, it helps make points memorable, etc. Counselees (especially new converts) need all the help they can get in understanding and applying God's truth. They are still filled with the ideas of the world. Indeed, many older converts also have been strongly influenced by contemporary non-Christian thought. It takes all you can do, at times, to make something clear to such persons. If Paul, who was writing inerrant, inspired material was willing to work at making his points clear, so should you.

Christian Counselor's Commentary

20 When you were slaves of sin, you were free from the authority of righteousness.
21 What fruit did you have at that time from those things about which you are now ashamed? The end of those things is death!
22 But now, having been freed from sin, and having become God's slaves, you have the fruit of sanctification for yourselves, and its result is eternal life.

He continues to squeeze all he can out of the slave/master analogy. Just as when you were a faithful slave, willingly **presenting the members of your body** to your master for his service, so now **present them** to God. Previously, you worked (consciously or not) **to bring about lawlessness** in sin's service; now use those bodily members for producing the righteousness of **sanctification** (growing out of sin and into righteousness). It is a matter of who is the master and what are that master's requirements. Ask the counselee, "If you were faithful in the past in doing lawless deeds, how much more so ought you to be in doing those things that lead to your sanctification?" This presenting of your body (you'll read more of this in the twelfth chapter) is the process of rehabituation.

And one more argument is added. Under sin's slavery, what was the result? It was death; that was the **fruit** of your labors. What now, in contrast, will be the result of labor for Christ? **Sanctification and eternal life** (vv. 20-22). What a contrast! The **wages that sins pays his servants is death** (physical, spiritual, eternal), but **the gift** (you don't earn it) **of God is eternal life**. Even the new slavery for God is a gift. You deserved to remain in the service of sin, but by grace God freed you from sin's **authority** and graciously brought you into His own service, thus removing you from the realm of **death** to the realm of **eternal life**.

Paul's words are calculated to motivate. They are designed to melt hard hearts, to move slothful ones, to energize despairing persons. Use them for the purposes for which they were given and you will find that they will bring the results you desire. A counselee says, "I don't know what to do?" You reply, "God has graciously given you a body of teaching that He wants you to obey." Another complains, "I seem always to be falling back into sin." You respond, "There is no need to; you have been freed from sin's authority." Still another despairingly says, "Oh, what's the use; what does one get out of it anyway?" Your answer? "Well, God says sanctification and eternal life. And both of these are calculated to lead to His honor and glory. That's what!" On and on it could go; but you get the point, I hope. All in all, this is a most instructive chapter for the Christian

Romans 6

23 The wages that sin pays is death, but God's gift is eternal life by Christ Jesus our Lord.

---

counselor. There so much by way of explanation, hope and application. Give it all the time you can in your personal study.

Chapter 7

> 1 Don't you know, brothers—after all, I am speaking to those who know the law—that the law has authority over a person as long as he lives?
> 2 A married woman is bound by law to her husband while he is alive; but if her husband dies she is released from the law referring to her husband.
> 3 That means, then, that she will be called an adulteress if she marries a different man while her husband is living. But if her husband dies, she is free from the law, and if she marries a different man she isn't an adulteress.

Paul is still addressing the problem of sanctification (becoming more like Christ) in this chapter. The law cannot bring it about. He poses several problems. He writes not as a detached theologian but as a practitioner of Christianity, both as an individual struggling with his lifestyle and as an instructor of others. If one had to be perfect in order to help others then even Paul would have given up. But it is not whether one is perfect or not that is at issue, it is whether or not he is doing the right things about his imperfections. That is the key issue.

Paul, in accord with what he said about the weakness of human understanding (6:19), opens this next discussion with an illustration (vv. 1-4). Take the situation of a husband and a wife, he says. Those who know the O.T. law know that God's law about marriage and remarriage holds so long as one lives. Incidentally, he says nothing about exceptions because that would confuse the illustration and lead away from its point. Those who try to prove doctrines about marriage, divorce and remarriage from the passage, therefore, make a mistake. What is the provision to which he refers? He explains: **a married woman is bound by law to her husband while he is alive; but if her husband dies she is released from the law about her husband. That means she will be called an adulteress if she marries a different man while her husband is living. But if her husband dies, she is free from the law, and if she marries a different man, she isn't an adulteress.** That much is clear. But now, in an unexpected twist, he says, **So, my brothers, you died to the law through Christ's body, so that you might become the wife of a different man, the One Who was raised from the dead so that we may bear fruit for God.** Here, instead of the expected "He died," we read **you died**. But the twist is necessary because of the previous discussion in chapter 6 about the believer having died in Christ. Either way, **death**—and that is the point—

Romans 7

> 4 So, my brothers, you also died to the law through Christ's body, so that you might become the wife of a different man, the One Who was raised from the dead so that we may bear fruit for God.
> 5 When we were in the flesh, the sinful passions through the law were at work in our members, bearing fruit for death.
> 6 But now we are released from the law, dead to what firmly held us in its grip, so that we might serve in the newness of the Spirit and not in the oldness of the letter.

---

makes the way clear to the pursuit of a future marriage. Here, that marriage is the marriage of the believer to Jesus Christ. It is **death** that has made this possible.

And from this marriage there should be **fruit**. Here the double entendre is at work. He spoke of fruit as the result of two lifestyles in the O.T. Here, once again, he continues to speak of fruit as a result of a way of life, but also calls those two lifestyles marriages, from which there are children (fruit). The goal is **to bear fruit for God** as one bears fruit in a marriage.

The thrust of this illustration is simple. As in the last chapter, Paul once more reiterates that the death of the Christian through the crucified **body of Christ** demands newness of life. In all that is to come in the chapter we are now examining, that fact must not be lost. It is the background and the presupposition upon which all else rests.

In verse 5, Paul refers to the pre-regenerate state of the Christian. At that time, he says, he was **in the flesh**. That is to say, he was unregenerate. He was not justified in God's sight and was incapable of doing good (cf. Romans 8:8, **Those who are in the flesh can't please God**). Rather, the **sinful desires (passions)** that **the law** forbids **were at work in the members** of his body, which had been habituated to sinful ways and, therefore, passionately wanted (desires) to do them. But as these desires motivated him to do their work, that led only to **death** as its **fruit**.

But now, says Paul, we are **released from the law** (a divorce from a marriage that meant we were trying to be saved by keeping the law). We are free from the sinful passions that **held us** in their **grip**. Now, having been justified and regenerated in Christ, we can serve God in the **newness** that the indwelling of **the Spirit** makes possible instead of trying to be saved by the old, unsuccessful way of attempting to keep the law. **The letter** means the law.

Well, if we are married to another, instead of the law by which we attempted to be saved, Paul asks, **Is the law sin?** The answer to this question, like those before, is **Of course not** (literally, "Let it not be so"). The

Christian Counselor's Commentary

> 7 What shall we say then, that the law is sin? Of course not. On the contrary, I wouldn't have known what was sin except by law. For example, I wouldn't have known about covetousness if the law hadn't said, **You must not covet.**
> 8 But sin, taking advantage of the opportunity that was provided by the commandment, produced in me every sort of covetousness. Without law, sin is dead.
> 9 At one time, I was alive apart from law, but when the commandment came sin came to life again
> 10 and I died. And I discovered that the very commandment that was to lead to life led to death.
> 11 Sin, taking advantage of the opportunity that was provided by the commandment, deceived me, and by it killed me.

law has its place. Paul shows its proper function from his own experience: If there had been no law, he says, then **I wouldn't know what was sin**. Sin is the breaking of God's law. **I wouldn't have known about covetousness**, for instance, **if the law hadn't said, "You must not covet."** So the law has an important part to play: it shows one his need for salvation. It exposes his sin to him, so as to drive him to Christ. However, sin **took advantage of the situation.** It stirred up **the sinful passions** when one saw **the commandment,** which resulted in **all sorts of covetousness.** Sinners, seeing a wet paint sign, have a desire to touch it. There may be many who have played around the edges of what they knew was displeasing to God who never thought that they would fall over the edge, but did. That happens to saved sinners too. You must recognize the pull of sin for what it is. If there had been no law, sin wouldn't have come alive to him with such fury; it would have seemed inert, as if **dead**.

Once, before the law was applied to me, Paul says, he considered himself **alive** (i.e., everything seemed OK so far as he was concerned; in his own sight he was alive; he was at peace). But then **came the commandment,** he recognized his sin, and **it came alive** to him once more. The law, with its commandment forbidding covetousness, brought the fact of his sin to mind—things were not OK. He was in trouble with a holy God Who would have no truck with sin. **When sin came alive, I who seemed to be alive, died** (v. 10^a). The **commandment** that (if kept) would **lead to life,** instead (because it was not kept) led to death. Sin **deceived** him and killed him. The law and the commandment are both **holy, just, good.** The problem is not with the law, it is with the sinner—the one who was misusing the law.

Romans 7

12 So then, the law is holy and the commandment is holy and just and good.

13 Did that which is good become death to me then? Of course not! On the contrary, it was sin—so that it might appear to be sin—that produced death in me by that which is good, in order that by the commandment sin might become as excessively sinful as it is.

14 We know that the law is spiritual; but I am fleshly, sold as a slave to sin.

15 I don't understand what I am producing: What I want to do I don't practice, but instead what I hate is exactly what I do.

16 But if it is what I don't want to do that I do, I agree that the law is fine.

17 The fact is that it is no longer I who produce it, but the sin that is dwelling in me.

The law is spiritual (that is, something given and used by the Spirit for His purposes), but though he is not **in the flesh,** the converted sinner is still bound up in **fleshly** ways; largely, he is **still sold out to sin** as a master whose ways he finds it difficult to reject (v. 14). That is the problem with most of your counselees. They are living as if the emancipation, the divorce, their death, had never taken place. What can be done for them? That is Paul's concern. But first he wants to describe the condition. This is most helpful, because if Paul had struggles with a *war within* (see my book with this title), it is not unique to your counselee. He should be told so.

What is this struggle like? There is *confusion*: **I don't understand what I am doing,** Paul says (v. 15). Confused counselees should be alerted to the common nature of this problem. They are not alone in it. Around what does this confusion revolve? One finds contradictory forces at work, battling one another. With his regenerate nature he finds that he **wants to do** things that will please God, but nevertheless fails to **practice** them. On the other hand, what he has come to **hate** as a Christian, he discovers himself doing. Clearly, says Paul, if I do things I don't want to do, I thereby testify that **the law is good** (v. 16). The problem's in me, not in the law. It is no longer **I** (the new regenerate I) who produces sin, but the sinful practices of brain and body habituated in my members. The struggle is with the past carried over into the present by a habituated body.

Nothing good from the past **dwells** in this body, that is **in his flesh** (another term he uses for this habituated body). He is aware of his desire to do good, but also of the actual products of his life which so often are evil. The summary statement of this is found in verse 19.

> 18 I know that nothing good dwells in me, that is, in my flesh. I am aware that I want to do good, but I am not producing fine things.
> 19 I don't do the good that I want to do, but rather what I practice is the evil that I don't want to do.
> 20 So if it is what I don't want to do that I do, it is no longer I who produce it, but the sin that is dwelling in me.
> **21** So then, I discover that it is a law that whenever I want to do a fine thing, I am aware of evil.
> 22 I delight in God's law in my inner person,
> 23 but I see a different law in my bodily members fighting against the law of my mind and holding me captive to sin's law that is in my members.

So, he repeats, it is not the new me that **produces** sin; it is the sin that dwells in me (in his bodily members: cf. v. 23). His sinful nature, with which he was born, programmed the parts (**members**) **of his body** to respond to various situations in life sinfully. So, in sanctification, the problem is to reprogram them in righteous ways, **presenting** the same members of the body to God for righteousness. Paul finds it to be **a law** (a habitual occurrence; something that happens regularly) that **whenever he wants to do a fine thing,** he is aware of the **evil** tendencies with which he must struggle. To do good is rarely easy. Your counselee struggles too. You must realize that change for him is not easy.

The believer finds himself **agreeing with God's law**, now written on the heart in regeneration. **Within**, in his heart of hearts, there is little problem (v. 22). But this other **law** (habituation of the body to sin) **fights against the law of his mind** (by which he wills to do God's will) and **holds him captive**. It is not enough to cognitively think straight. Nor is it enough to will the right thing. One must overcome **the law of sin in the members**. Failure to help counselees overcome the problem of a habituated body that produces sinful responses is, perhaps, the greatest cause of failure in counseling that attempts to be biblical. People's members must become rehabituated. The **captivity** of which Paul writes is the strong captivity of **habit**. For more on this, see my book *Winning The War Within*.

This struggle, especially in those instances where the law of sin wins the battle, makes one **miserable**. Paul, taking the place of one who is captive to his own sinful habits, cries out, **Who will rescue me from this body of death?** (v. 24) Every struggling, failing counselee can vibrate to that sentence. But one must not leave him there. The answer comes ringing back: **Thank God, it is Jesus Christ our Lord Who will!** Without a

24 What a miserable person I am! Who will rescue me from this body of death?
25 Thank God, it is Jesus Christ our Lord Who will! So then, on the one hand, I, myself, am serving God's law as a slave with my mind, but, on the other hand, with my flesh I am serving sin's law.

---

doubt, this is the most welcome sentence in the entire chapter. And in the chapter that follows you will see how God has, in Christ, provided the help needed to overcome the habits of the body. In the latter part of the last verse of chapter 7, Paul sums up: **So then, on the one hand, I, myself, am serving God's law as a slave with my mind, but, on the other hand, with my flesh I am serving sin's law**. That says it all.

Counselor, despairing Christians need to hear those reassuring words about Christ and, with Paul, **thank God** that there is a way to win the war within.

CHAPTER 8

1 Therefore there is now no condemnation of those who are in Christ Jesus,
2 since the law of the Spirit of life in Christ Jesus has freed you from sin's law and death.
3 What was impossible for the law to do because our flesh weakened it God accomplished by sending His own Son in the likeness of sinful flesh (and concerning sin), and He condemned sin in the flesh,

---

The eighth chapter refers back to what Christ has done for the believer. He has paid the price for his sin and, therefore, **there is no condemnation of those who are in Christ Jesus**. The word **no** is quite emphatic: there is not even a single kind of condemnation that can be brought against the Christian successfully. This is so because they are **in Christ Jesus**. By virtue of being united to Him in Spirit baptism (cf. ch. 6, vv. 1-4), they are counted to have lived the perfectly righteous life He lived. How could there be condemnation of one who is perfect? Those who fear loss of salvation can be comforted by explaining this verse with its strong denial of any sort of condemnation to the regenerate believer.

And how does one know that he is **in Christ Jesus**? The sort of person of which Paul is speaking is described in verse 2: he is one who is now living under **the Spirit's law of life**, not **sin's law of death**. That is, he has been freed from the power of sin as a slave master. It does not mean that he is not struggling (chapter 7 makes that clear). But the very presence of the struggle shows that he is now under the law of the Spirit. The Spirit and the flesh are at war. He regularly wants to do those things that the Spirit has commanded in His Word and that He increasingly—but not without the Christian's frequent failures— is enabling him to realize in his daily life.

Already the **Spirit** has been mentioned in this chapter. While He is virtually absent from the previous two chapters, you will find His presence dominating the present chapter. Why is that? Because it is through the Spirit working by His Word that God sanctifies His children. It is not by their unaided struggle to keep the law. It is the Spirit Who opposes the habituated flesh (cf. Galatians 5:16-18) and enables us to win battles and gain ground. **What the law couldn't do, God accomplished by sending Christ in the likeness of sinful flesh** (not in sinful flesh: Christ's body, though flesh, was not wrongly habituated to sin because He did not have a

Romans 8

4 so that the law's requirements might be fulfilled by us who don't walk according to the flesh but according to the Spirit.

5 Those who walk according to the flesh set their minds on fleshly things, but those who walk according to the Spirit set their minds on spiritual things.

6 Now to have a fleshly mind is death, but to have a spiritual mind is life and peace,

7 because the fleshly mind leads to hostility toward God, since it doesn't subject itself to God's law; nor can it.

---

sinful nature to so habituate it). In His body, offered as a sacrifice on the cross, **He condemned sin**. And it was by His substitutionary life and death that the law's requirements (both positively and negatively) were fulfilled by us (v. 4). And now, as we **walk according to the Spirit** (that is, according to His Word and power) rather than by the desires of the wrongly-habituated body, we (at last) are able to do those things that the law commands.

In the rehabituation process, the focus of one's thinking must change. In verse 5, Paul explains that **those who walk according to the flesh** focus (**set their minds**) on **fleshly things** (things that satisfy the desires of the flesh). On the other hand, those who **walk according to the Spirit focus on spiritual things**. About what does the counselee speak most frequently? Is it about pleasing the Lord or about pleasing himself or others? What does he say are his objectives in counseling? In life? Are they worldly or spiritual? According to what principles does he operate? What does he say fills his mind from day to day? Ask these questions, and if you receive an honest reply you will know whether he is failing because his mind is focused wrongly. But as important as the mind is, it is not changing the mind alone that makes the difference. **Setting the mind on spiritual things** must lead to the actual pursuit and attainment of those things. The counselee must go beyond good intentions, correct goals; he must be taught how to **walk by the Spirit**. Paul further explains: **to have a fleshly mind is death** (v. 6). The word for **mind** used here means the **resultant thought** of the mind. That is, what one determines to do. To have a mind that determines to do wrong, that cares nothing about pleasing God, means that one is not saved—he is headed toward eternal **death**. A mind focused on reaching spiritual attainments to God's glory, on the other hand, means that one has **life** eternal and in this life will know true **peace**.

Not only does the fleshly mind not care about God or spiritual things,

Christian Counselor's Commentary

> 8   Those who are in the flesh can't please God.
>
> **9** Now you aren't in the flesh, but in the Spirit, if indeed God's Spirit dwells in you. But if anybody doesn't have Christ's Spirit, he isn't His.

it is **hostile to** God. How does Paul define this hostility? Not by saying that one consciously fights against God but, rather, by observing that his mind **refuses to subject itself to God and His law, nor can it**. Rebellious, self-sufficient thinking that will not submit to God's Word is the basic **hostility** that he mentions. This works out eventually into rebellious living. It is the mind that thinks its own thoughts, rather than thinking God's thoughts after Him, that is in view here. That basic hostility to the Word of God began with Satan in the garden when he attacked God's Word. Instead of the counsel of God, man turned to and accepted the counsel of Satan. Ever since, that has been the problem with human beings; they have turned to the way that seems right, but its end is death.

Moreover, Paul acknowledges that the unregenerate mind is unable to think otherwise: **nor can it** (v. 7^b). On the subject of human inability, see chapter 2 of my commentary on I Corinthians. This point is carried to its logical conclusion: if one cannot think thoughts that are anything but hostile to God and that lead to a walk in the flesh, then those with such minds (who are **in the flesh**) **cannot please God.** This is a pivotal verse on human inability. It is one that you should memorize and use frequently. When your counselee protests about the behavior of another who is unsaved ("I can't understand why she always does those things") tell him "I can," and explain this verse. Rather than complain, he should pray for that person's salvation and live a life calculated to demonstrate what God can do for the walk of a believer. Cats don't bark and dogs don't meow. Unregenerate people will think and act like they are unregenerate. They cannot do otherwise. It is hard enough to get regenerate persons to act like they have been regenerated!

In verse 9 Paul observes, **Now you aren't in the flesh, but in the Spirit, if indeed God's Spirit dwells in you. But if anyone doesn't have Christ's Spirit, he is not His**. The notion that one is regenerated, justified and saved but at some later time must receive the Spirit is totally false. If anyone has the Spirit (by definition) he belongs to Christ. But if he doesn't have the Spirit, he does not belong to Christ. All Christians are spiritual; that is, they are indwelt by the Spirit Who is at work sanctifying them. Some counselees will plead that they are not spiritual, that they have not yet attained to the point where they can obey certain commands

Romans 8

10 If Christ is in you, although your bodies are dead because of sin, nevertheless your spirits are alive because of righteousness.

11 Moreover, if the Spirit of the One Who raised Jesus from the dead dwells in you, this One Who raised Christ Jesus from the dead will give life to your mortal bodies through His Spirit Who dwells within you.

12 So then, brothers, we are debtors; but not to the flesh to live according to the flesh.

13 If you live according to the flesh, you are going to die. But if by the Spirit you put to death your bodily practices, you will live.

---

of the Bible. Don't listen to such excuses. If anyone has the Spirit of the Lord, he is 1) able to know God's will from God's Word and 2) able to do it in the wisdom and power of the Spirit. If he goes on insisting that he can't, perhaps he should be faced with the possibility that he is not a Christian after all, but one bereft of the truth.

You have been greatly enlightened in your inner person (**spirit;** cf. v. 10) even though you begin the Christian life with a body that is still **dead** to righteousness because it is programmed to sin. The spirit wants to do good but is confronted with a body that wants to do evil. The body hasn't yet been raised to newness of life as the soul has (the soul, of course, still has much to learn and relearn). **But, if the Spirit Who raised Jesus from the dead dwells within, He will also give life to the mortal body**. In that fact lies the Christian's hope. Here the life imparted to the body by the Spirit is not the life it will receive at the coming of Christ. That will be its consummation. But the **life** envisioned in verse 11 is the ongoing work of the Spirit as He fights against the flesh (cf. Galatians 5:16-18). In other words, the Spirit will continue to enable the body to be habituated to the righteous ways of God. Even in this life He is in the process of reprogramming the members of this body that will die. **We are debtors (to God); not to the flesh** to live according to its desires. We don't owe anything to the past. We are future-oriented. We are freed from the hold of sin and we have a positive Force at work within enabling us to live for God.

The plea of Paul to your counselee, then, is to start living as if this were true. Believe that you have the resources and avail yourself of them. Too often preaching (and counseling) fails to make clear how many strong resources exist. Hold out for nothing less than obedience from the heart as you direct counselees by the Scriptures to walk in newness of life.

If you live according to the flesh, there is but one end—**death** (v. 13). But **if you live according to the Spirit, you are putting to death your [sinful] bodily practices,** and—you will **live**! Clearly, the sanctify-

Christian Counselor's Commentary

> 14 As many as are led by God's Spirit are God's sons.
> 15 Indeed, you didn't receive a Spirit who once again enslaves you to fear, but rather, you received a Spirit Who adopts you, by Whom we call out, "Abba" (that is, Father).

ing work of the Spirit extends to the practices (habits) acquired by the body. If you are thus **led** into paths of righteousness by the Spirit through His Word, you will live because that is evidence that you belong to Christ. To be **led** is not some subjective experience; it is the Spirit opening your heart to understand and reprogramming your body to perform those things that God has ordered you to do—in the Bible. The Spirit is the Author behind the human authors of the Bible. Of all the Persons of the Trinity, the Bible is most closely associated with Him. He produced the Bible over thousands of years by moving holy men of old to write it. Now, is He going to turn around and "lead" people through some other means that make the Bible irrelevant? Certainly not!

Guidance does not come from circumstances, as many think. Perhaps that is the most serious error in which counselees entangle themselves when seeking God's will. Circumstances may be interpreted in any number of ways. A young man's car breaks down on his way to ask a young lady to marry him. How should he interpret the circumstance? Some would say, "Well, since I can't get there tonight, I guess the Lord doesn't want me to marry her." But another says, "I'm going to get there if I have to hitchhike; the Lord is testing me to see if I really mean business." A third says, "Well, I guess this will teach me to take better care of my automobile!" The circumstance does not come with its interpretation built in; you must add it. And you have no biblical warrant to think that one such interpretation or another is truly the Lord's. It isn't; it is yours.

Paul continues to describe what the Spirit's coming into the Christian's life means (v. 15). In a tender passage he says that the Spirit frees from **enslaving fear and adopts you** as a son of God who has the privileges of intimately addressing Him, the Creator of the universe, as **Abba** ("Daddy"). How comforting this should be to the fearful. Few things are as difficult to handle as problems associated with fear. Yet here is a magnificent solution to them all. When afraid, like a little child cuddling up to his father, the Christian comes close to God and cries "Abba" for help. To know that the fear of death is gone, that nothing can happen that is not for his good and that he can take all his fears and troubles to a heavenly Father Who has adopted him as His own son or daughter is the epitome of

Romans 8

16 The Spirit Himself testifies together with our spirit that we are God's children;
17 and if children, then we also are heirs, not only God's heirs but heirs together with Christ—if, indeed, we suffer with Him so that we may be glorified with Him.
18 For this reason, I don't count the sufferings of this present time worthy of comparison with the glory that is going to be revealed to us.

---

comfort. Don't fail to point this out to your counselees whenever appropriate.

Because two witnesses are needed, **the Spirit** (in His Word) **testifies together with** one's own spirit that he is saved (v. 16). Notice, it is not that the Spirit testifies *to* the Christian's spirit, but *along with* his spirit. His testimony is objective, the believer's is subjective. The idea is the same as in 9:1 where the two witnesses that testify *together* are Paul and his conscience. Doubting Christians have not only to look within, but also to the pages of the Bible which clearly tell us all who believe the gospel are saved.

Now, in a transitional verse (v. 17), Paul declares that adopted **children**, in accordance with the laws of adoption, are **heirs**. It is not enough to have the privilege of turning to God in fear and difficulty as a child does to his daddy; no, God has also provided a limitless inheritance for all who love Him. It is an inheritance that one shares with Christ. Where is the faith of the one who complains like the Psalmist in Psalm 73? Why should one be concerned if here he must **suffer with** Christ? That only proves that he is **heir** to a fortune that will never fade away. Again, counseling should be done in the atmosphere of eternity. Because many wrongs and inequities are never righted in this world, it is important to keep the counselee's eyes fixed on the heavenly rectitude that will take place.

Because of what lies ahead for God's children in this inheritance, Paul says, **I don't count the sufferings of this present time worthy of comparison with the glory that is going to be revealed in (or, possibly *to*) us** (v. 18). We are to be **glorified** (v. 17) along with Christ. That is, we will share in the same glory that He, now, as a glorified man, knows in heaven. Nothing on earth compares with this. A body may now suffer agonizing pain, but to be freed from the pain of hell forever makes it pale into insignificance. To know that one will receive a body which will never again suffer pain, illness, crying etc., but will be perfect is simply incomparable. The glory that is coming is so great that we don't yet have the

> 19 The creation anxiously waits, eagerly anticipating the revelation of God's sons.
> 20 The entire creation was subjected to futility, not because it wanted to be, but because of the One who subjected it with the hope
> 21 that the creation itself will be set free from its slavery to corruption and realize the glorious freedom of God's children.
> 22 We know that the entire creation groans together in labor pains until now.
> 23 And not only the creation, but we ourselves who have the Spirit as a first fruit also groan inwardly as we eagerly anticipate our adoption, that is, our bodily redemption.
> 24 After all, we were saved with this hope. But when you see what you hope for, that isn't hope. Who hopes for what he sees?

---

ability to comprehend it; so it has yet **to be revealed to us**.

The entire creation was affected by the fall and God's consequent curse. It too **awaits the revelation of God's children**. When the curse is lifted and there is a new heavens and a new earth formed out of the purified elements, that too will be remarkable. Does your counselee have *this* sort of perspective with which to look at his situation?

The creation became **subject to corruption and futility** (see Ecclesiastes) not of its will, but because God subjected it to such **slavery**. Yet He did so with **the hope** of future redemption (vv. 20, 21). Indeed, the creation **groans in labor pains** (that is, anticipating that God will bring forth the new creation) along with us (vv. 22, 23). All the misery of the present world in which we live, among persons and animals alike, should not lead to despair, but because of the promise of God to redeem it all it ought to lead to hope. And the Spirit Who lives within the believer is the first-fruit (promise) of the full redemption that awaits us (v. 23).

When one was **saved**, it was not merely for the forgiveness of sins, but **with the hope** of eternal life, eternal inheritance and ultimate freedom from sin and misery. But we must have patience. It is not yet realized. We don't anticipate that which we already have, do we (v. 24)? So then, you must teach your counselees to **eagerly anticipate it with patience**. That is the crux of the matter.

But we are **weak**; we have a hard time obeying, learning patience, waiting, believing. The Holy Spirit, Who is the first-fruit of our heavenly redemption, **helps us** in our weaknesses. We don't even know **how to pray or what to pray for.** But, because we can't frame our words properly, He reads the heart and with **sighs** sends off our innermost prayers to

25 But if we hope for what we don't see, we eagerly anticipate it with patience.

26 In the same way the Spirit helps us in our weakness. We don't know what to pray for or how we ought to pray, but the Spirit Himself intercedes for us with groanings that can't be put into words;

27 and the One Who searches our hearts knows what the Spirit has in mind because the way that He intercedes for the saints is in keeping with God.

28 We know that God makes everything work together for the good of those who love Him, for those who are called according to His purpose,

29 because those whom He foreknew, He also foreordained to be conformed to His Son's image so that He might be the First-born among many brothers.

God. Even our prayers are assisted! Think of that. One does not have to become eloquent in prayer; even his stumbling prayers are heard and shaped and made **acceptable** to God. All that is necessary is their genuineness (v. 26). And God Who (alone) knows the heart of the one praying understands **what the Spirit has in mind because He intercedes for the saints in a manner that is acceptable to God**.

Now comes the verse that is so important to every counselor, Romans 8:28. Many Christian counselors have it framed and hanging on the wall. Doubtless, whether on the wall or not, it ought to be heard by the counselee often enough that he comes to think about it all during the week. We don't know how God will **work all things together for good to those who love Him and are the called according to His purpose**, but we must believe it. Notice the restrictive clause. This precious promise is for **those who love Him**, who have been **called t**o serve His purposes. The promise was made only to believers. But, for them, there could be no more reassuring one. It is possible that a counselee will express doubt about the application of the promise to his circumstances: "How could *this* possibly work together for good?" In such cases, you should make it clear that the verse doesn't say "some things" work together or even "most things" do, but, rather, ***all*** *things work together for good.*

This promise follows hard on the heels of the words about the prayers of Christians and should be read in the light of those who, through the Spirit, ask Him for the help they need. These verses refer especially to those who are suffering bodily afflictions of one sort or another. The day will come, as it did for Joseph, when even the wrongs done by others can be said to be meant for good by God and to bless His people (see Genesis 50).

30 And those whom He foreordained He also called, and those whom He called He also justified, and those whom He justified He also glorified.

31 What then should be our response to these facts? If God is for us, who can be against us?

32 If He didn't spare His own Son, but delivered Him up for all of us, won't He also with Him freely give us everything?

How is it that this is so certain? God has made it so by His involvement in every aspect of salvation, from start to finish (v. 29). He effectually **called** the believer to salvation (v. 28). And the one He called was **already foreknown** by Him. That is to say, He knew that He would do so from all eternity. God's foreknowledge is foreknowledge of what *He* will do. He does not have to look into the future for information. Long before time began He **foreordained** (or predestinated) him to be conformed to Christ's image (v. 29). No wonder Christ could know that He was only **the Firstborn** (preeminent One) **among many brothers** who would be redeemed by His death! It was all planned out by God before His death. Moreover, in verse 30, Paul observes that God **called, justified and glorified** those He foreordained. He did not only plan what He would do, He also executed the plan, working it out at every step so that nothing could go wrong with your salvation. These words are intended to bring comfort and assurance. Use them for that purpose. Even though we have not yet been glorified, with God it is as certain as if it had happened; His promise is that good.

Paul asks, **What then should be our response to these facts** (v. 31)? Exactly the question to ask fearful, doubting, discouraged counselees. The answer should be to ask the question with which Paul concludes the verse: **If God be for us who can be against us?** Why, of course, that's it! If God has proven Himself for us so as to do all this, who, what could ever stand in the way of our eternal salvation and of His continued fatherly care right now? Get your counselee to see this. Until he does, he will probably be inadequately motivated.

Paul presses the point—**If God didn't spare His own Son, but delivered Him up for us, won't He also with Him freely give us everything** [we need]? That is the ultimate reason for assurance, comfort and hope. It is what makes prayer and Christian living worthwhile. Nothing else can. This is not only a great passage for the theologians, but it is preeminently for those who are defeated, despairing and dispirited. And it is for those who are beginning to doubt. It is practical. Don't shy away from

Romans 8

33 Who can bring a charge against God's chosen ones? God is the One Who justifies.
34 Who can condemn? Christ Jesus is the One Who died—or rather Who was raised—and sits at God's right hand and also intercedes for us.
35 Who can separate us from Christ's love? Can affliction, or distress, or persecution, or famine, or nakedness, or danger or sword?
36 As it is written, **For your sake we are put to death all day long; we are considered sheep to be slaughtered.**
37 No! In all of these things we are more than conquerors through the One Who loved us.
38 I am convinced that neither death nor life, nor angels, nor rulers, nor things present, nor things to come, nor powers,
39 nor height nor depth, nor anything else in creation can separate us from God's love in Christ Jesus our Lord.

---

it because of the theological concepts inherent in the terms used. Learn what they mean and then use this passage *as it was meant to be used* —to help weak Christians.

All that follows in verses 33 through 39 builds on what has been said already. It is a beautiful, reassuring heaping of truth upon truth for counselors to use. The devil himself cannot **bring a charge against God's elect. God has justified** them (they are counted sinless and perfectly righteous because of what Christ has done). No one can throw out a condemning word that will stick (v. 34). Christ **died and was raised and now sits at God's right hand to intercede for us**. We have a lawyer in heaven Who sits at God's right hand to plead our case. He pleads His own work on the cross, which is more than sufficient for all His own. He **loves us** with an everlasting love. **Who, what can separate us** from that love? Certainly not the things about which counselees complain if those greater things mentioned in verse 35 cannot. Read the verse and ask, "If these things could not separate Paul from Christ, do you think the lesser troubles that you are experiencing can?" Paul backs up his remarkable statement with Scripture in verse 36.

Then he answers the question about separation. **No**, he says, **these things** cannot separate us from Christ's love (v. 37). Indeed, not only can these things not separate us from Him, He enables us to **conqueror** them. And, in conclusion, he finds one final way to say that NOTHING can interfere with Christ's love for His own (vv. 38, 39). In these two verses Paul is virtually saying, "It doesn't matter what you suggest, height, depth, rulers, powers (present or future)—you name it—nothing in cre-

Christian Counselor's Commentary

ation can separate us from His great love!" What a marvelous statement of Christian security. How can anyone think that his salvation is uncertain after reading and understanding these verses? It is impossible.

CHAPTER 9

1 I am speaking the truth in Christ. I am not lying. My conscience testifies together with me by the Holy Spirit
2 that I have great pain and continual anguish in my heart.
3 I could wish that I myself were cursed, as one who is separated from Christ, for the sake of my brothers, my kinsmen according to the flesh.

The book now takes a new turn. In the theologically-charged atmosphere of chapter 8, Paul thinks of the theological problem of God's election of a people and the individuals who make up the people of God. In short, he discusses *election*.

Many people wouldn't touch election "with a ten foot pole." But Paul is not among them. Rather than think of election (God's **choosing** or, literally, "picking out" some from among others) as something mysterious, and therefore a subject to be avoided whenever possible, he brings it up. That is the Bible's way. From time to time counselees will want to discuss the matter. They may be confused about it, full of questions as to how election relates to their particular problems, etc. You must be prepared to answer—biblically. You may be able to avoid the issue in preaching, but it cannot be avoided in counseling. It is important then for you to understand what God says about election so that you can respond to the many earnest and troubled questions about it that will be raised in the course of biblical counseling.

Paul eases his way into the matter with a discussion of the plight of Israel. He begins by assuring them of his great love for his **kinsmen according to the flesh** (v. 3^b). In order to bolster what he is about to say in this verse, he opens the discussion with the words, **I am speaking the truth in Christ. I am not lying. My conscience testifies with me by the Holy Spirit** (v. 1). Those are strong protestations against any possible charge that might be made to the contrary. Obviously, since Paul seemed to think so, there are times when it is not only appropriate, but also necessary, to reassure the counselee that what you are about to affirm is the exact truth. Usually, that is when you are going to make a statement that is hard to believe. What is it that occasioned such an introductory word from the great apostle? Simply this—that he was so deeply **pained** and so **continually in anguish within** (v. 2) for his people who for the most part had rejected the gospel that he could wish to be damned to hell for all eternity in their place were it possible for that to gain eternal life for them. Of

Christian Counselor's Commentary

4 They are Israelites, who have had the adoption, and the glory, and the covenants, and the giving of the law, and the worship, and the promises.
5 From them have come the patriarchs and, according to the flesh, Christ, the God Who is over all and blessed forever. Amen.

---

course it could not. Nothing of the sort was possible. If they rejected the sacrificial death of Jesus Christ, in which He bore hell for His own, there could be no other remedy.

But notice what the statement says about the heart of the apostle; that is the important thing about verses 1 through 3. He so greatly loved his people that he was willing to go to hell, if possible, to save them. I cannot bring myself to the point where, contemplating that thought, I truly can say that I would be willing to go to hell for anyone else. Can you? I have not yet attained to that kind of self-abnegation and love for my neighbor. Yet Paul says it and means it. He tells us, "I want you to know that I have examined **my conscience** and can tell you honestly before **the Holy Spirit** Who dwells within me that this is true of me" (v. 1). If it were necessary to have such love in order to counsel, then none of us would. But that we should long to so care for the eternal welfare of our counselees is certainly an ideal to which each of us must aspire. Counselor, how much love do you have for counselees? Well, you can check it out by asking how much it **pains** you when they do wrong, how much **anguish** you feel when they go astray. Even if you cannot truly say you **could wish that you were cursed, separated from Christ for their sake**, do you recognize pain and anguish within when it is warranted?

Paul describes his kinsmen as those who have had all the benefits of God's grace showered upon them (vv. 4, 5). They were adopted, saw God's glory in the cloud, entered into covenants with Him, received the law, were the progenitors of the patriarchs and—preeminently—the Messiah! How much love God set upon them! Yet, on the whole, they have rejected the Savior. He came to His own [creation] but His own [people] did not receive Him (John 1:11). That is why Paul had so much anguish. Does it especially pain you when you discover that a potential counselee turns out not to be a believer after all but merely one who came to get something for himself? He cares not one whit for pleasing God, living according to the truth, or loving his neighbor. He goes away soon after you have discussed agenda matters with him, saying, "If you think that I came to talk religion, you've got another think coming! You can stuff all that Christianity so far as I am concerned." Well you should have great

Romans 9

6 Now it isn't as though God's Word failed; you see, not all of those who are descendants of Israel are Israel.

---

anguish and pain for him. The more you do, the more like Paul (who was like Christ; cf. Matthew 23:37, 38) you will become.

On mentioning Christ and thinking of all that He did for him, Paul cannot help but burst into a doxological utterance in which he calls Christ **the God Who is over all and blessed forever** (v. 5). Here is a clear affirmation of the deity of Jesus Christ. The **Amen** at the conclusion of the doxology is a ringing second affirmation of the truth that he has just uttered. "What I have just stated," Paul is saying thereby, "I say all over again—it is true!" In verses 1 and 5, Paul writes emotionally. There are exclamation marks all around. He is caught up in the comments that he is dictating to his amanuensis. It is not wrong in counseling to express strong emotion from time to time whenever it is appropriate to do so. Recently, a couple, their preacher and I all teared up in a session. It was spontaneous, uncontrived and natural in the circumstance to do so. The moment called it forth. Not to have allowed emotions to be expressed would have been artificial, unnatural. Don't buy into the nonemotional, white-coated approach of many of the self-styled "professionals." Rather, take your cue from the writings of the New Testament.

Paul has intimated that the vast majority of his kinsmen are lost. He is concerned for them, as we saw. But he also wants the members of the Roman church to understand why this has occurred. It is not as though something about God's providential workings in history has gone awry. No, exactly not that. **God's Word** (in which you will find His many promises to Israel) didn't fail. What failed was **Israel** (v. 6). How is that? Because, as both Testaments teach, **not all of those who are descendants of Israel are Israel**. What does he mean by that? Simply this: some who are a part of the outward community are not a part of the inner body. Not all who profess allegiance to God do so genuinely. There is an outer circumcision of the flesh and an inner circumcision of the heart. True Israel consists of those who belong not only to that which is outer, but to that which is inner. The outer membership is but symbolic of the inner reality—just as baptism is. He will explain this point in detail before he is finished.

But for now, before entering into this explanation, let us notice how carefully Paul endeavors to make every matter clear. Perhaps you have noticed already that he repeats, in different words, the same point over

Christian Counselor's Commentary

> 7 Nor, because they are Abraham's descendants are they all his children. But **those who are in Isaac's line will be called your descendants.**
> 8 That means that it isn't those who are children by flesh who are God's children, but rather that those who are children by promise are counted as descendants.
> 9 This is the way that the promise was stated: **At this time I shall come and Sarah will have a son.**

---

and over again. Here, as usual, he will do so, coming at it from various angles. Why so much repetition? Well, remember, most people did not have their own copies of the Bible. They had to get God's message *as it was read to them.* That meant that they needed to take time to digest it—particularly if some points were difficult to understand or to accept. So repetition did two things: it took time so that there was adequate opportunity for the message to be contemplated, and it hammered it home to the listener so that he could carry it away. Now, your counselee has a Bible (or can easily get one). Should you use repetition? Certainly. Though people have Bibles they often do not use them, or use them incorrectly. They have difficulty in interpreting them. So, for the very reasons that Paul repeated himself, you too should repeat yourself in counseling. Make sure that no counselee goes away confused; be sure that whether he likes what he hears or not he understands it. There is no place for obscurity in counseling. Indeed, there is an additional reason for repetition. When people come for counseling, often they are emotionally excited, troubled, full of the problems that they want to detail. They may listen only halfway, or in a less-than-optimal manner. Repetition, especially when it approaches a matter from various angles, is needed to assure understanding.

In verse 7 Paul explains that not **all** who are genetically **descended from Abraham** are **his children**. It is only those who are **in Isaac's line** who are. Does that mean that one line is genetically his and others are not? No, precisely not that. To be a child of Abraham is not a genetic thing at all. It is the children of promise (such as Isaac was) who are God's children (v. 8). All those who have trusted in the promise of the Messiah is what he has in mind. Racially, they may be Hebrews or Gentiles. It makes no difference. They are *counted* as descendants if they are **heirs according to the promise**. He has explained all this in an earlier place. Now, repeating it, he also applies it to a very important fact—the rejection of Israel after the flesh. And of the greatest importance: while true believers are **Abraham's children,** they are also **reckoned** to be **God's children** (v. 8).

Romans 9

10 And not only that, but also when Rebecca had conceived children from one man, our forefather Isaac,
11 even though they were not yet born or practicing anything good or bad, so that God's purpose might continue to be by His choice
12 (not by works, but by the One Who calls), she was told, **The older will serve the younger.**
13 As it is written: **I loved Jacob, but I hated Esau.**
14 What shall we say then? Is God unjust? Of course not.
15 He says to Moses, **I will have mercy on whom I will have mercy, and I will have pity on whom I will have pity.**

The promise was given to Sarah that she would have a son (v. 9). That son was a son of promise, as God said. He was a miracle son; not one born according to the normal course of human sexuality. The circumstances were all against Abraham and Sarah having a child at their advanced age. But God fulfilled His promise, even when the faith of others failed. And from that miracle child were born two other children: Jacob and Esau. It is about these two that he is going to speak (vv. 9, 10).

The same principle of selection is seen in the choice of one of these two sons, both born in the same birth. It was determined before they were born (they having done nothing to influence the choice: v. 11) that, contrary to usual practice, **the older will serve the younger** (v. 12). Why was this? **So that God's purpose might continue to be by His choice** (v. 11). God freely determines whatever He wishes. He does not look down the corridors of time in order to determine what people will do in order to choose or reject them. No, the choice is His from start to finish. It is independent of what human beings do; He does not govern the universe by reaction. Out of His good pleasure God effectually **calls** some and not others. As the Old Testament said about the two brothers: "**I loved Jacob, but I hated Esau.**"

Now Paul takes up the natural objection that follows. As he does so, you recognize that he has heard it all before. Counselors soon do. If God determines the future state of each according to His will and not according to their works (v. 12), **is God unjust**? From time to time in counseling you will be confronted with the same question. Take heed then to his reply. He cites the case of **Pharaoh** where God told **Moses** that He **will show mercy and pity** to those to whom He determined to do so (v. 15). Obviously, Paul's answer to the question is: the Bible teaches that this is how God operates. No one deserves anything from God but eternal punishment. So it is out of sheer **mercy and pity** that anyone at all escapes

Christian Counselor's Commentary

16 So then, it isn't a question of somebody willing or running but rather of God having mercy.

17 The Scripture says to Pharaoh,

For this very reason I raised you up, so that I could demonstrate My power by you, and so that My Name would be proclaimed throughout the whole earth.

18 So then, He shows mercy to whom He wishes, and He hardens whom He wishes.

---

hell. And if God for His own self-sufficient reasons determines to save them, then who is there to complain of injustice? Mere justice, apart from mercy and pity, would have consigned every man, woman and child to hell. Why, then, is it unjust for God to show mercy to some?

In verse 16, Paul makes it clear that it is not a matter of **human willing** or trying to win some race (**running**) that saves, but it is strictly a matter of mercy from God. Continuing with the example of Pharaoh, Paul points out that the Old Testament says God **raised up Pharaoh in order to demonstrate His power by him and thereby receive honor throughout the whole earth (or land)** as His mighty deeds against Pharaoh are **proclaimed** (v. 17). That statement itself will occasion another objection, but for now notice what Paul is saying. God determines who will do what *for His own purposes*. The hardness of Pharaoh's heart led to the mighty works of God in Egypt that spread His Name far and wide. Pharaoh, in God's providence, served the purpose of making this possible.

Concluding, Paul says, **So then, He shows mercy to whom He wishes, and He hardens whom He wishes**. In this verse (v. 18) Paul moves one step farther. It is not only mercy shown to some that is the effect of God's willing, but also the hardening of others. Again, Paul raises the objection that naturally flows from the statement that he just made: **You will say to me then, "Why does He still blame people; who can resist His will?"** That Paul was teaching the absolute predetermination of some to heaven and some to hell in the words that precede verse 19 is certain. Otherwise, no one would ask the question he says will be asked. Only such teaching elicits that question. The interpretation of others who want to soften Paul's teaching fails since, in one way or another, it takes the edge off the teaching so that no one asks the question any longer. An astute counselor, faced with this question, will make the point that I have just tried to make. He will say, "My friend, you may have problems with this doctrine, but you must admit that it is what Paul was teaching since you—as he said you would—have asked the question that always proceeds from it."

Romans 9

19 You will say to me then, "Why does He still blame people; who can resist His will?"
20 But who are you, my friend, to talk back to God? The thing that is formed won't say to the one who formed it, "Why did you make me like this?" will it?
21 Or doesn't the potter have the right to make out of the same lump of clay one jar as a decorative item and another jar for everyday use?
22 What if God, wishing to demonstrate His wrath and to make known His power, endured with great patience the vases of wrath fitted for destruction,
23 in order to make known the riches of His glory toward the vases of mercy, that He designed beforehand for glory,

---

Now we turn to Paul's response. He gently, but firmly, puts the objector in his place: **But who are you, my friend, to talk back to God?** "If this is what God has said, then accept it; stop objecting. Man is born a sinner. As such, from the beginning he pictures himself as more than he really is and (consequently) pictures God as less than He is." This is one of those corrective passages that not only puts man in his place as a creature, but also puts God in His as the Creator and Sustainer of the universe. We all need, from time to time, to read and reread this passage so as to bring us down to the place where we belong. Perhaps some counselees, riding their high horses, could use a good dose of selected verses from Romans 9!

Turning to another figure, Paul pictures the **potter and the clay**. The pot won't tell the pot maker that he doesn't like the sort of pot he has been made. After all, **the potter has a right to make from the same lump of clay pots both for decorative use and for menial use, doesn't he?** asks Paul. God, in creation, determined to make two sorts of persons; that is what Paul is getting at. He made those who would become Jacobs and those who would become Esaus; those who would become Moseses and those who would become Pharoahes (v. 21).

Now, in verses 22 and 23, Paul deals definitively with the problem that has been raised and, incidentally, with the so-called problem of evil. God **wanted to demonstrate** the various sides of His nature. So He **fitted** some pots (jars) **for destruction**, so that in them He could **make His power and wrath known**. It took **endurance** to do so, but He endured their sin and stupidity and thereby demonstrated to all sentient creatures in the universe how powerful He is. Unless there were sinners who justly deserved His wrath, He could not have done so. So He determined that, in

24 even us whom He called, not only from among the Jews but also from among the Gentiles.
25 As He also says in Hosea:
I will call "My people" those who are not My people; and the one who wasn't loved I will call "My loved one."
26 And in the place where it was said to them, "You are not My people," they will be called "sons of the living God."
27 And Isaiah calls out concerning Israel:
Though the number of the sons of Israel be as the sand of the sea, only a remnant will be saved;
28 the Lord will fully execute His sentence upon the earth and He will do it very shortly.

---

harmony with their free and uncoerced decisions, He would fit some for destruction. On the other hand, He **designed beforehand** other pots **to receive mercy** upon whom He poured out the **riches** of His mercy and glory. These deserved nothing but wrath but, in pity and grace, He provided salvation for them. Unless there had been sinners, He could never have shown the other, gracious side of His nature. Sin, therefore, serves God's purpose of demonstrating what He is like. For a more detailed discussion of these verses, see my book *The Grand Demonstration* that deals with these and related matters.

Now Paul returns to the subject with which he began the chapter—the plight of the unbelieving Jews. He identifies himself as a pot designed for mercy (v. 24) along with the believers—both Jew and Gentile—in the church at Rome. Note well, Paul has no difficulty in identifying himself as a child of God, a vessel of mercy, who will spend all eternity in glory. Counselees uncertain of their final destiny need to come to the same place if they are believers. It is abnormal for Christians not to know who their Father is, where their home is and who their brothers and sisters are. This needs to be insisted on. People who spend all their time trying to determine whether or not they are saved usually spend far too little time telling others about Christ and serving Him. It is a deceitful self-centeredness that keeps questioning one's salvation while wallowing in a morass of subjectivism.

The quotations from **Hosea** (vv. 25-26) and from **Isaiah** (vv. 27-29) indicate two things: Israel has not fallen so as to have no **remnants** and a new Israel composed of believing **Jews and Gentiles** will take the place of the old. Accordingly, argues Paul, Gentiles who were not out **running after (pursuing) righteousness** were the ones who **caught it through**

Romans 9

29 And as Isaiah predicted,

> **Unless the Lord of Armies had left us descendants, we would have become like Sodom and would have looked like Gomorrah.**

30 What shall we say then? That the Gentiles who didn't pursue righteousness caught it, a righteousness that is by faith;

31 but Israel by pursuing a law that would make them righteous failed to catch up with the demands of the law.

32 Why? Because they didn't pursue it by faith but as though they could do so by works; they tripped over the "stumbling stone."

33 As it is written:

> **See I am placing a stone in Zion that people will trip over and a rock that will make them fall, but whoever depends on Him will not be put to shame.**

---

faith, and Israel, by attempting **to catch up with the demands of the law,** failed to do so (vv. 30, 31). Again Paul is teaching justification **by faith, not by works** (v. 32). Thus, they **tripped over the stumbling stone**—the Cross of Christ. They thought they could earn salvation rather than have someone earn it for them. So whoever **depends on** Christ and not on himself **will not be put to shame** at the last Day.

This chapter deals with the ways of God and man. It shows God supreme, the Master of His creation and creatures. It shows man dependent upon Him at all points. Due to lack of space, I have not dealt here with the supposed inequities and unfairness of the sovereignty of God in depth; my full remarks on these issues may be found in *The Grand Demonstration*, mentioned above. Here, the important thing for the Christian counselor is to show that God does not act arbitrarily, but for His own purposes, purposes that in the end always glorify Him.

CHAPTER 10

1 Brothers, my heart's desire and request to God for them is for their salvation.
2 I can testify about them that they have enthusiasm for God but it isn't based on correct knowledge.
3 Out of ignorance of God's righteousness, and by trying to contrive their own, they didn't submit to God's righteousness.
4 Christ is the end of law as a way of obtaining righteousness for everybody who believes.

Again, as this chapter opens, we find Paul expressing his **heart's desire**—the **salvation** of his people (v. 1ff.). They have **an enthusiasm for God based on** faulty premises: **ignorant of the righteousness that God gives through faith, they attempt to contrive their own**. Obviously, according to Paul, sincerity and effort are not going to cut it. For all those who think that so long as one is sincere he is all right with God, this passage stands as a strong corrective. One cannot come to God his own way; he must come *God's* way (cf. Acts 4:12). There is no other way to eternal life. God's righteousness is presented as a gift to those who trust in His Son. There is no righteousness apart from the work of Christ on the cross with which God is satisfied. His is the perfect righteousness. All other humanly-contrived righteousnesses are imperfect. Indeed, they are **as filthy rags**. To offer such righteousness to a holy God and expect Him to receive it is an insult—especially when He Himself has provided a perfect righteousness through the substitutionary death of Christ. No one, therefore, can be saved by his own good works.

And, if you will note closely, **ignorance** is no excuse. Ignorance is the result of man's sin and thus provides no sufficient reason for rejecting the offer of salvation that is proclaimed by preachers from God. **Christ**, as Paul continues to say (v. 4), **is the end of the law as a way of obtaining righteousness for everybody who believes**. There is no need to go on trying to keep the law as a way of salvation. It does not work. That is because men are sinners who cannot keep it. How wonderful it is to know that the futile attempt to keep the law has been superseded by a perfectly satisfactory way of obtaining righteousness: it is reckoned to all those who **believe**. If, as Moses wrote, one could keep the law perfectly, he would receive **life** (v. 5). No one can.

But, in contrast, about the righteousness that comes through faith, by

Romans 10

> 5 Moses writes this about the righteousness that is by law: "The person who does it will live by it."
> 6 But of the righteousness that is by faith he says: **Don't say in your heart, "Who will ascend into heaven?"** (that is, to bring Christ down),
> 7 or **"Who will descend into the abyss?"** (that is, to bring Christ up from the dead)."
> 8 But what does it say? **The word is near you, in your mouth and in your heart** (that is, the word of faith that we are preaching);

which one is accounted righteous in God's sight for Christ sake, Moses does not say that it is impossible to attain (as if you had to go to heaven **to bring Christ down** or to **descend into the abyss to bring Him up from the dead** to save you; cf. Deuteronomy 30:14). No, unlike trying to keep the law, the attainment of God's righteousness is not some impossible task for you to perform. Christ has already done the seemingly impossible: He has **come down** from heaven, died and **risen**. The work is complete. So don't tell yourself in your heart that salvation is yet to be accomplished by your efforts. The message that you must believe is **near**; all you must do is believe and profess faith and **you will be saved** (v. 9). Indeed, it is as near as your own **heart and mouth**! We preach **the message (word)**, says Paul, and all you must do is to declare the belief of your heart (vv. 6-8).

People are always trying to add their own efforts to what God has done. Some want to make salvation a *far off* thing. They insist that one "prepare" himself for regeneration by Herculean labors to become "sensible" of all his sin. They say he must forsake all known sins (as if that were possible for an unregenerate person), etc., etc. Then, in time (often after a long time), he may be ready to hear the gospel. This sort of thing was taught by a number of New England Puritans as well as some in England. It was devastating to people, and a false way of salvation. It placed salvation far off, something to be attained by works rather than something to be received by faith in a message that one hears preached. The gospel is not good works to perform but good news to be believed. Just so, you must help confused counselees who may have been taught and are struggling with this doctrine, since it has been recently revived. This teaching leaves people uncertain about their salvation, wondering if and when the Holy Spirit might find them ready to be regenerated. Back in those days Puritans constantly found it necessary to deal with "cases of conscience" as they were called. These were counseling problems created unnecessarily by the proclamation of this false view of salvation. The preachers brought people into a quandary about their faith, then counseled them (wrongly)

9 because if you confess with your mouth, "Jesus is Lord," and believe in your heart that God raised Him from the dead you will be saved.
10 It is with the heart that a person must believe in order to be justified and with the mouth that he must confess in order to be saved.
11 As the Scripture says, **Whoever depends on Him won't be put to shame.**
12 There isn't any difference between a Jew and a Greek; the same Person is Lord of all and is rich to all who call on Him,

---

about it. That is why Puritan counseling had to do almost exclusively with assurance of salvation. When you discover persons who are troubled with assurance, make sure that, in one way or another, they are not trying to help the Spirit of God to bring about their regeneration. If you do not find full-fledged Puritan preparationist teaching, you will almost always discover that the counselee believes that in some way he must assist the Holy Spirit. The preparation doctrine is not found in the whole of Scripture. And this passage, in particular, militates against it.

Verses 9 and 10 make it clear that this salvation is as close as your heart and mouth. If you will **confess with your mouth** that you believe **Jesus is "Lord"** you will be saved. But that confession is not some magic word that is uttered like "open sesame." No, it must be the expression of a true belief of the **heart**. The gospel that Christ died for our sins and was raised from the dead to become Lord of the universe as the God-man (He always was as God) must be believed for justification and salvation. There is no separation between believing on Jesus for salvation and then, at some later time, making Him Lord of your life. Paul considers belief in and acceptance of the Lordship of Jesus Christ part of the original message that he preached (cf. Acts 2:36). If you run into counselees confused about this matter, this passage together with the one cited from the book of Acts should be sufficient to clarify the issue.

In verse 11, Paul sums it up with a Scripture quotation (Isaiah 28:16). Faith is dependence on God's Word. It is relying wholly on what He promises in the gospel. The one who casts his lot with Christ will, when it all turns out in the end, find that he is on the winning side with nothing about which to be **ashamed**. Indeed, everything about the Lord on whom he believes will swell his heart with satisfaction and pride.

This way of salvation is precisely the same for **both Jew and Greek** (v. 12). Christ is Lord of both, and richly deals with all who **call on** Him by faith as Joel 2:32 indicates (v. 13). Note how close the preaching of Paul is to that of Peter in the citation of Joel in Acts 2:21. Here, the

Romans 10

13 since whoever calls on the Lord's Name will be saved.

14 But then, how can they call on somebody in whom they haven't believed? How can they believe somebody whom they haven't heard? And how can they hear without a preacher?

15 How can they preach unless they are sent? As it is written: **How beautiful are the feet of those who announce the good news about good things.**

16 But everybody hasn't obeyed the good news. Isaiah says, **Lord, who has believed what he heard from us?**

17 So, faith comes by hearing and hearing through the Word of Christ.

---

important word is *all*. This inclusive term comprises both Jew and Greek, as he says. There are not two ways of salvation, one for the Jew and another for the Gentile, as some have taught. Nothing could be farther from the truth. And that such a viewpoint is false is exactly what Paul wants to say. Jews do not come to Christ through ceremonies and works while Gentiles come through faith in the gospel that the apostles preached. No, both come in the latter manner, or they do not come at all.

In verses 14 and 15, Paul runs backwards from faith in the gospel to its source. One **calls on** Christ in faith to be saved only when he **hears** about the death and resurrection of Jesus for sinners. But he hears about this Christ and **believes** on Him only if someone **preaches** the message of salvation to him. And preachers preach the message only because they have been called, ordained and **sent out** to do so under the authority of God. God has sent them with the message of redemption and life, a beautiful word to those in death and darkness occasioned by sin!

Actually, in verse 14, it is said that one believes Christ. That means He preaches when the preacher preaches a message true to the gospel. It is not merely preachers who preach, but they are mouthpieces for Christ Who, Himself, calls on men to be saved. When they reject the message, it is the Savior Whom they reject, not merely a preacher.

As in Isaiah's day, however, not everyone who hears believes. As then, so today many refuse to **obey** the command to repent of sin and believe the gospel. To speak of "obeying" the gospel is not a way of calling for works on the part of the one who obeys. It is obedient faith that is in view: faith that when one hears the call to believe does so (i.e., obeys the preacher's call to depend on Christ for salvation) (v. 16). See John 6:29. **Faith comes through hearing the message (word) about Christ.** There is no other way.

Paul wants to make it clear that the Jews had heard (v. 18). It was not

Christian Counselor's Commentary

18 But I ask, didn't they hear? Yes indeed—**Their sound went out into the whole earth, and their words to the very ends of the inhabited world.**

19 Again I ask, "Didn't Israel know?" First Moses says, **I will make you jealous over those who aren't a nation; I will make you angry over a senseless nation.**

20 Then Isaiah quite boldly says, **I have been found by those who didn't seek Me; I have appeared to those who didn't ask for Me.**

---

that they didn't know. The message went out to all the earth (or land). But, as the next quotations indicate, all but a remnant refused to believe the gospel (vv. 19-21), just as he said at the end of the previous chapter (9:27-29). And the judgment mentioned there that would **shortly** come upon them did in 70 A.D. with the destruction of the temple, the city and Judaism as it was then practiced. And, as Isaiah says (in the same spirit as Hosea, cf. 9:25, 26), a new people of God ("**My people**") would receive all the promises made to Israel of old. The kingdom would be taken from them and given to a people who would believe—the church. Here he says that He was **found by those who didn't seek Him,** a clear allusion to the same thing. But of Israel he says, I tried to woo them, but they were a **disobedient and antagonistic people** (v. 21). Here, the sad note of One who does all that could be expected—and more—and yet is rejected, is sounded.

In counseling too there comes a time when nothing more can be done, at least for the moment. A pastor recently brought a couple to my office for help. The wife wrote on her PDI (Personal Data Inventory) that she wants a divorce. He wanted to continue the marriage. She was seeing another man and engaging in an adulterous relationship. Told that she must repent, give up the other man and return to her husband, she refused. Informed that she had no biblical reason for a divorce, she said, "I know, but I'm going to get it anyway."

With no commitment on her part to resolve problems and to work toward reconciliation with her husband, there was no use in beginning counseling. All I could do was plead, warn and explain that to proceed as she planned was a clear violation of God's requirements and of her marriage vows. I urged her to repent of this plan to go on sinning and let me help them not merely repair their torn marriage but to point them to ways in which God can turn it into "a marriage that sings!"

When she said that she understood all that I was saying, and that she appreciated the offer, but that she intended to go on with her plans, all I

21 But about Israel He says, **All day long I have stretched out My hands to a disobedient and antagonistic people.**

---

could do was to encourage her pastor to continue in the steps of Church discipline that had been begun at his church. Such situations break a pastor's heart. Like Isaiah, he finds himself **reaching out his hand** to help people who are bent on disobeying and will not take hold of it to receive help. It is my prayer as I write that if she is put out of the church for persisting, like the man in Corinth, she will at length repent and return (see II Corinthians 2). But, by then, she may have done such damage to herself and her marriage that it will be irreparable.

This chapter is not the most fruitful for mining counseling principles. Yet, there is something here for counselors. Note how Paul treats his subject. *He is writing out of pain and agony over the faithlessness of Israel, but that does not keep him from declaring the hard facts.* That is an important point for the counselor to recognize. On the one hand, the caring note allows him to say loving things. But on the other, caring does not mean withholding truths that condemn, warn, etc. Too many counselors err on the one side or on the other. They see the plight of the counselee and soften the message or they proclaim the hard truths without compassion. Neither is correct. One must teach hard truths compassionately. But he teaches them simply *because* he recognizes why the counselee is in his plight and that there is no way out of it apart from a proper recognition of sin and the appropriate action that follows therefrom. Think hard about how Paul approaches Israel here, in the previous chapter and in the one to come.

CHAPTER 11

1 I ask then, "Did God push His people aside?" Of course not! I, indeed, am an Israelite, a descendant of Abraham from Benjamin's tribe.
2 God didn't push aside His people whom He foreknew. Don't you know what the Scripture says about Elijah, how he pleads with God against Israel:
3 **Lord, they killed Your prophets, they tore down Your altars; I** alone am left and they seek my life?
4 But what is the divine response to him? **I have reserved seven thousand men for Myself, who haven't bowed the knee to Baal.**
5 So, in the same way at the present time there is a remnant chosen by grace!

This chapter concludes Paul's discussion of the plight of Israel and his explanation of God's ways in regard to her and the promises made to her. He begins by asking another question: **Did God push His people aside?** The answer? **Of course not!** Well, how is it that He has rejected them and instead created a new, international nation for his people? In two ways. First, there is a remnant, as Isaiah had predicted. Paul, a genuine, card-carrying Hebrew if there ever was one, was a Christian (v. 1). No more was it true that all Jews had rejected Christ than it was that all had turned from Jehovah in **Elijah's** day (v. 2). There is always a remnant. Elijah thought that he alone survived (v. 3), but God showed him that He had reserved 7,000 men for himself who had not bowed the knee to Baal. In **grace** God **chose a remnant** for Himself from among the Jews (v. 5). Many counselees may feel alone in their willingness to follow Christ. Family, friends and others may turn aside. Whole congregations may desert them. But if they are really true to God they are never really alone. God will faithfully bring others into their lives who have not bowed the knee. However, in many cases where the counselee is crying that he alone stands against the world, it is of his own doing. He is not a part of a remnant; he has departed from the biblical mainstream. The counselor must be careful to distinguish the two so that he may not encourage a counselee in deviant behavior. On the other hand, if he is truly a part of a divine remnant in his community, genuine encouragement must be offered. It is safe to say that there is rarely a time when one stands entirely alone. If he does, he is probably wrong.

Paul makes it clear that if it is the result of God's grace that a rem-

6   But if it is by grace, then it isn't any longer by works; otherwise grace wouldn't be grace any longer.

7   What then? What Israel enthusiastically sought, he didn't find; but the chosen ones found it, and the rest were hardened.

8   As it is written:
>   **God gave them a stuporous spirit—eyes that couldn't see and ears that couldn't hear—a condition that continues until this very day.**

9   David says:
>   **Let their table become a trap and a net, a stumbling block and a retribution to them;**

10 **let their eyes be darkened so that they can't see, and let their backs be bent forever.**

---

nant is left, then that remnant is not composed of that mass of people who have rejected Christ for works. No, people are part of the remnant purely by the grace of God—not because they were any better than the others who turned aside. That is always a point to make. It is possible to develop a remnant mentality that leads those few who huddle together against the world and the rest of the church to make special claims for the holiness and faithfulness of their little group. It is easy for a counselee to become proud and spiteful toward others who do not belong to his little coterie. A counselor must guard against feeding that mentality. Rather, he should challenge it as Paul does here, declaring that anything good about a faithful group is the result of grace and not anything in the members of the group themselves (v. 6).

What the Israelites as a whole sought by good works and self-righteousness, but didn't find, the chosen ones did. The rest, like Pharaoh, were hardened against God. The quotations from the Old Testament that follow say it clearly. God gave them up because they gave Him up. We are back to chapter 1 again, only this time in reference to Jews. And, as Paul comments, the condition has not changed in his day; it continues (as in ours). "If they **won't** see or hear, then let them **not be able** to do either", is what God says in those verses. They are terrible words. But from time to time you will find yourself turning to them when you consider the total unwillingness and hatred evidenced by the family and friends of some of your counselees. Their utter hatred for God is most likely due to this double hardening. In such instances, it is important for you to assure your counselee that it is not unusual for people to become hardened against God and His gospel; after all, that is precisely what these quotations say is true of the Israelites.

Christian Counselor's Commentary

> **11** I ask then, did they trip in order to fall? Of course not! Rather, because of their trespass salvation has come to the Gentiles to provoke them to jealousy.
> 12 Now if their trespass results in riches for the world, and if their failure results in riches for the Gentiles, how much more will their fullness result in?
> **13** Now I shall speak to you Gentiles. Inasmuch then as I am an apostle to the Gentiles, I take pride in my service to them,

---

In verse 11 Paul asks another question: did their **fall**, in **tripping** over the Stone, constitute the only providential end or purpose that God had in view? The answer: **Of course not**. There was also a positive purpose: through **their trespass, salvation came to the Gentiles**. And a second, ancillary purpose was also in view: **to provoke them to jealousy** (i.e., to motivate them to desire the salvation of Christ also). Now **the trespass results in riches for the world and the Gentiles.** But if that is so, **how much more so** will it be when **the times of the Gentiles** are fulfilled and Hebrews also respond to the gospel in large numbers (**fullness**) rather than merely as a remnant? Paul sees here not only the redemption of some from every tribe and tongue and nation, but also the eventual salvation of numbers of Hebrews as well. As we saw in the last chapter (cf. v. 12), they will come to Christ in the same way as the Gentiles. They will bow the knee in faith, having the work of Christ **counted** to them. When that time comes, they will be saved by grace, through faith, discarding every pretense of self-righteousness. So people hardened in one or more generations, in spite of that fact, may propagate a line throughout history that in the long run, by God's providence, will turn to Him in repentance and faith. Hardness today does not mean rejection for all generations.

Having set up the situation—there is now a remnant of Jews who believe, the Gentiles have received the good news and the times of the Gentiles have begun, there is coming a time when Hebrews also will in larger numbers than a remnant believe—Paul turns to the Gentiles at Rome (and throughout the ages) to discuss their situation in relationship to unbelieving Hebrews (v. 13).

God called Paul to be **an apostle to the Gentiles** (see Galatians 2:8). He was **proud** of the fact that he had a message to the world that would change it. He was therefore happy to **serve** in this capacity (v. 13). And, along the way, he was appealing to the remnant of Jews who might be **provoked to jealousy** and believe (v. 14). After all, he did take the message to the Jew first and after that to the Gentile. If the **rejection** of Israel

14 trying somehow to provoke some of my own flesh to jealousy and save some of them.
15 If their rejection means the world's reconciliation, what would their reception mean but life from the dead?
16 Now if the first piece of dough is holy, so is the lump; and if the root is holy so are the branches.
17 But if some of the branches were broken off, and you—a wild olive shoot—were grafted in among the rest and now share the sap of the root of the olive tree,
18 don't brag to the branches. If you must brag remember that you don't support the root; the root supports you.

---

had such a wonderful result—the **redemption** of people from all over the world—how wonderful would their **reception** back into fellowship with God and His church be! Why, it would be like a resurrection, he says (v. 15). This threefold note of rejection, redemption and reception (in one way or another) permeates the discussion of this chapter. To see that is to understand Paul. If **the first-fruit of dough** is consecrated to God (**holy**) so will be **the entire lump**; if the **root,** then also **the branches**. How is that? The part that is basic to the whole lends its qualities to the whole. The patriarchs (firstfruits; root) were **holy** (set aside), consecrated to God; so too are those who proceed from them who, like them, are men of faith (v. 16).

They were the **branches** on the patriarchal tree (the people of God; the church). But, because of unbelief, they were **broken off**. And Gentiles, like **a wild olive branch, were grafted in**. These **now share the sap of the root** (the blessings of the covenants and promises made to the fathers). But just because you Gentiles are in and the Jews for the most part are out, Paul says, be careful not to **brag** about it. There is nothing to brag about; all is of grace. If you've got to brag, don't brag about your place in the tree but, rather, brag about the goodness of God to the Patriarchs (the **root**—cf. vv. 17, 18).

Paul continues, raising an objection: **But the branches were broken off so that I could be grafted in**. He speaks as a questioner who thinks of himself as better than those that were broken off. **Fine**, what you say is true, Paul replies. But remember, **they were broken off because of unbelief**, not because you were better than they (all you have is of grace). The only reason you **remain in place** is because you believe (and that belief, as you know, is the gracious gift of God). So, **stop that haughty thinking**; instead, **be concerned**. After all, if God broke off natural branches

Christian Counselor's Commentary

19 You will reply, "The branches were broken off so that I could be grafted in."
20 Fine. But they were broken off because of unbelief, and you remain in place by faith. Stop your haughty thinking; instead be concerned.
21 If God didn't spare the natural branches, He won't spare you either.
22 See then God's kindness and strictness; on the one hand, strictness toward those who have fallen, but on the other hand, God's kindness to you, provided you continue in His kindness (otherwise you will be cut off).
23 Those also, if they don't continue in unbelief, will be grafted in; God can graft them in again.
24 If you—an olive tree that was wild by nature—were cut off, and contrary to nature were grafted into a cultivated olive tree, how much more easily will these natural branches be grafted into their own olive tree?

25 I don't want you to be ignorant of this secret, brothers (or you might become conceited), that hardness has come upon a part of Israel until the full number of the Gentiles has come in.

---

when necessary, He won't hesitate to break off the wild ones as well (vv. 20, 21).

Proud counselees take heed! All you are or have is of grace. At best, most of your counselees are but wild olive branches that have been grafted into Christ's church. They are there because of grace. They must not become haughty of their place and position as the Jews did. Rather, they should walk in utter humility and gratitude for the goodness that God has showered down on them. They *deserve* nothing from God but His keenest displeasure. The attitude Paul is inculcating in the gentile believer is precisely the one that needs to be adopted by every counselee. As you know, counselor, it is not every counselee who thinks that way. It is your task to help him do so. Otherwise, God is likely not to bless your efforts to extricate him from his problems.

In utter balance (as the ways of God always are) Paul calls on the reader to recognize the **kindness and strictness of God**. The latter to the fallen Jew, the former to the Gentile grafted into the kingdom of God. But at the end of verse 22 comes the warning: either appreciate His kindness or experience His strictness—you too can be **cut off**! And Jews who come to faith can also be **grafted in**; God can accomplish that (v. 23). If that which was wild can be grafted in, how much more that which is **natural** (v. 24)? Be clear about one thing: Israel has been **hardened in part** (the remnant excluded) only till all the elect Gentiles **have come in**to the body of Christ (v. 25). In this way, the tree is composed some of the natural

26 In this way, all Israel will be saved: As it is written,
>   **The Deliverer will come from Zion,**
>   **He will turn away ungodliness from Jacob.**
27 **And this is the covenant they will receive from Me when I take away their sins.**

28 As far as the good news is concerned, they are enemies for your sake, but as far as the choice is concerned, they are loved for their fathers' sakes.

29 God's gifts and calling are not recalled.

30 Just as you disobeyed God at one time, but now have received mercy as the result of their disobedience,

31 in the same way these now have disobeyed so that by the mercy you received they also may receive mercy.

---

branches constituting the remnant, some Gentiles, and in the future some additional Jews (after the full number of the Gentiles has come in). At the end of the thousand years (the millennium) when Satan is unchained to go out to deceive the Gentiles once more, there will be a turning of Jews to the Lord (see Revelation 20; for more information, consult my book *The Time is at Hand*). In substantiation of this, Paul quotes the Old Testament (vv. 26, 27). The expression **all Israel** includes both believing Jews and Gentiles. In relation to the gospel the Jews are **enemies** for the sake of the Gentiles, but as far as the choice is concerned they (the Jews) are not forgotten **for the fathers' sakes**. God remembers Jews because He set aside their patriarchal fathers to Himself. For the sake of the fathers, therefore, in time He will bring into the church a larger number of believing Jews. There were **gifts and callings** granted to the fathers; that is why He will remember them. God cannot **recall** these. He is no "Indian giver."

"You Gentiles were disobedient to God as the Jews are, but **have now received mercy as the result of their disobedience**. Their breaking off has opened a place for you to be grafted in. But **the mercy you received is the means by which they will receive mercy**" (vv. 30, 31). Ultimately, the Gentiles' reception will provoke Jews to the jealous faith of which Paul wrote earlier. And he may indicate as well that the gospel will be preached by Gentiles to Jews who, when the time has come, will believe in larger numbers than a mere remnant. Summing up, Paul marvels at **the depth of God's riches, wisdom and knowledge** in bringing about salvation through mercy to people living in the entire world (vv. 32, 33). And He has done so through human **disobedience**! No one can advise God. No one could have dreamed up a plan like His. His ways are

> 32 God has delivered all mankind into disobedience so that He may show mercy to all.
> 33 O the depth of God's riches, and wisdom and knowledge! How inscrutable His judgments are, and how untraceable His ways!
> 34 Who has known the Lord's mind or who has been His counselor?
> 35 Or **who has previously given something to Him that He is indebted to return to him?**
> 36 Indeed everything is from Him, and through Him and for Him. To Him be glory forever! Amen.

untraceable. He is unique. That is the purport of the remaining words in verses 33 through 35. We all (Jew and Greek) are indebted to God; not the reverse. All that happens is related in every way to Him for His glory.

Well, there you have another chapter not directly addressing counseling issues, but one in which pride and bragging *are* addressed, in which the sovereignty of God is asserted—a chapter in which we see the ways of God worked out even through the sin of man. He truly makes the wrath of man to praise Him. That, of course, is the message for the counselee. The trials and tribulations in which he may find himself are all part of a divine program for God and for God's glory. There is nothing we deserve but wrath, yet He has provided mercy and grace. All that is happening will, in ways we could never have dreamed (let alone counseled God to follow), turn out for good to His people and glorify Him. That is what a counselee must turn to, remember, and hold on to throughout every trial.

Chapter 12

1 I urge you then, brothers, because of these mercies from God, to present your bodies as living, holy, pleasing sacrifices to God, which is the reasonable way to serve Him in worship.

In this and the chapters that follow, we have a veritable goldmine of counseling principles and practices. These chapters (especially 12-14) are usually thought of as the practical chapters in which the truths taught in previous ones are now applied concretely to life. While that is not exactly true there is something to it. At any rate, you will turn to these chapters again and again if you are wise and care to do genuinely biblical counseling.

Paul has made it clear that all Jew or Gentile alike have that is worthwhile is the result of the many **mercies** of God's grace. They did not earn them. Paul now appeals to those mercies from God's hand as the motivating power that should drive a Christian's life (v. 1): **I urge you then, brothers, because of these mercies from God, to present your bodies as living, holy, pleasing sacrifices to God**. In other words, godly living ought to be the natural expression of gratitude to God for His many gifts and kindnesses. Few counselees come with this in mind. If they are interested in obeying God at all, thoughts of **presenting their bodies as sacrifices to God** too often mingle with motives of receiving something in return. But we ought to do so, whether something good returns to us or not. It is very important to cultivate a grateful spirit in the counselee so that he will serve God in any and all circumstances regardless of what those circumstances hold for him.

To **present your bodies** is a return to the discussion of chapter 6 (see v. 13 in particular). God wants us to become servants who are willing to live for Him Who died for us. This is **the reasonable way to serve Him in worship** (worship being not only the meeting that takes place twice on Sunday, but the attitude of thankful sacrificial service that is rendered to God throughout the rest of the week as well). Again, Paul calls for the Christian to turn over his body to the Spirit in order to serve God by it. Please be clear about the fact that it is the body, as understood in chapter 6, and not something else (as some want to read it), about which Paul is writing here. The body with all its members must be presented to God the new Master for habituated service.

Christian Counselor's Commentary

> 2 Don't be conformed to the way of our modern age, but be transformed by the renewal of your mind, so that you may be able to determine what God's good and pleasing and perfect will is.

Obviously, this is not some mindless submission to God. One does not simply "yield" himself or "let go and let God." It is a thoughtful, purposeful turning over the use of your **body** to the Lord's work that he is cultivating in Christians: service is said to be **reasonable**. And it is a **pleasing sacrifice** of yourself to **living** service that is in view. This is to be done in a way in which you are **to determine what God's good and pleasing and perfect will is**. The **mind** must be **renewed** (made over anew; see Ephesians 4 for more about this). Paul writes, therefore, of an intelligent, intellectually competent process. One must be so **renewed** in his understanding of God's thoughts and ways from his study of the Scriptures that he is able to **determine** in various life situations what His new Master would have him do (vv. 1, 2). This is no magic make-over—some sort of second blessing; no, it involves study, work, prayer and all those activities that enable one to grow in his knowledge of the Lord's **will**. And, in it all, there will be a **transformation** of the individual that estranges him from the ways and thinking of the world. Less and less he will find that the **modern age** holds interest for him. It is not that he becomes cynical about it, but that he sees it as perishable, sinfully-oriented, displeasing to his Lord. More and more he becomes acclimated to his Savior and His ways, seeing in Him the only thing in life that is permanent and worthwhile (cf. I Corinthians 15:58).

As he presents the members of his body to the Lord in His new service, he discovers meaning and purpose in life. Counselees failing to do so may become cynical, defeated and disheartened with life, as do others who remain in the service of sin. The thing to do, then, with a counselee who gives evidence of having given up is to remind him of what Paul says here, help him to discover how he is failing to present the members of his body for the Lord's service and set him on the proper course. In it all, he must be constantly renewing his mind by the study and application of Scripture to his life. Otherwise he will not learn to do those things that are **good and pleasing** to God because he will remain ignorant of His **perfect will**.

Incidentally, there is no such thing as God's perfect will and some lesser will of God. God wills nothing that is not perfect. Speaking of His perfect will here, Paul is not distinguishing it from some lesser, not-so-

Romans 12

3 Now, by the grace given to me, I tell every one of you: Don't think more highly of yourself than you ought to, but think soberly according to the measure of faith that God distributed to each of you.

---

perfect will. What he is doing is making clear that the slave who does the will of his new Master does that which is according to a perfect plan. God's will is perfect *as over against* the will of sin, the Christian's previous master. He is now able to please his Master (cf. 8:8 in contrast). He is now in the service of God, fulfilling His perfect will. Be sure that your counselee doesn't become entangled in the ideas of some who think that if you miss the perfect will of God, He will allocate you to a lesser position where you must now settle for something less. God doesn't; neither should He. There is only one expressed will of God that can be determined and approved of: the revealed will of God found in the Bible. And it, in its entirety, is nothing less than perfect.

Paul now begins to discuss matters that are pertinent to doing God's will in the right frame of mind. Your counselee must look to the gifts that God has given him and not to **think more highly of himself than he ought to.** This counsel runs counter to the views of those who are in the self-esteem, self-worth camp. Man's problem is not lack of self-esteem but the opposite. Nowhere in the Bible are we told to raise our self-esteem or that of others. Everywhere, as here, we are brought down from the too lofty heights to which we already have raised ourselves.

Counselees who are concerned about the way others talk about them, complaining that these people have destroyed their self-esteem, have it all backwards. If they really lacked a sense of self-worth they would not complain; instead, you'd hear them saying "Tell me again; I deserve it!" Their protest indicates that they think they are worthy of better treatment. You may have to debate this with those who have been so deeply-dyed in the self-love teaching that, at first, they will have difficulty seeing it. These people have been taught to view reality upside down.

God, in accordance with His sovereign purposes, **distributed to each** Christian **a measure of faith** (i.e., a portion fitting to his faith as a gift of the Spirit). He must discover what his gifts are and be satisfied with them. That is not to say that he will not develop them to the full; he should. But he should not complain when he is not chosen as a member of the choir because of his gravel-Gertie voice. If he thinks **soberly** (sensibly, according to reason) about his gifts, he will be the first to decline an invitation to sing in the choir. Instead, he will know what abilities God

Christian Counselor's Commentary

> 4 Just as we have many members in one body, and the members don't all have the same function,
> 5 in the same way, we who are many are one body in Christ and individually members of one another.
> 6 We have differing gifts by the grace given to us: if prophecy, it is to be used in proportion to our faith;
> 7 if service, in serving; if one is gifted as a teacher, in teaching;
> 8 if he is a counselor, in counseling; if he is a contributor, in liberality; if he is a manager, in diligence; if he is one who is gifted to show mercy, in cheerfulness.

---

gifted him with and find his *rightful* place and function within the congregation. Recognizing that others too have varying **gifts** and degrees of the same gifts, he will not condemn them for doing what they have not been gifted to accomplish (cf. vv. 4-6). Hands, feet, eyes, Paul says, all have different functions; but all are necessary for the health and accomplishments of a physical body. The same is true of the body of Christ (v. 4, 5). What are some of those gifts? Paul now begins to enumerate a few of them (the list is hardly exhaustive but, as with his other lists, merely suggestive).

In verse 6, he speaks of **differing gifts**. But note the important fact that these are given in **grace**. God the Spirit distributes them *as He wills*. We complain about the distribution only at the risk of complaining about God! Complainers think they are wiser than He. Surely their self-esteem needs lowering. Many counselees need instruction about these points. You, of course, must have a firm grasp on them yourself so that you may not only think to turn to this passage, but be able to apply it carefully to the specific complaints of your counselees or to other situations in their lives that you may uncover.

Paul lists gifts, some of which are extraordinary and temporary ones, others ordinary and permanent. **Prophecy** was a gift given in the apostolic age to serve while the New Testament was being composed. When it was complete, prophecy vanished (cf. I Cor. 13:8). But those who possessed the gift should exercise it according to the measure that the gift was granted to them—not less or more. Again, we see the Spirit as sovereign both in dispensing gifts and in the degree to which they are dispensed to each.

In verses 7 through 8 the point is that one is to use his gift for the purpose for which it was given. Gifts are not for show, for selfish use, etc., but each is for the benefit of the entire body. Here is an area into which

Romans 12

9 Love must be without hypocrisy; loathe what is evil, adhere to what is good.

---

one might wish to wander with his counselee. If he has ordinary gifts and abilities you might inquire as to whether they are being used. And if the answer is yes, you might want to continue to ask, "for what purposes?" And if the answer seems to be that they are being used for the purpose for which they are given, then you might ask, "Are they are being used for the benefit of the whole body?" One may have the gift of management, may use it diligently in managing a motel, business, etc., but it may not be used in managing any aspect of the Lord's work in the congregation. The likelihood is that, in inquiring about the use of gifts, you will find a disproportionate number of counselees who either fail to exercise their gifts for the purposes for which they were granted and an even larger share who use them exclusively for their own private interests rather than in the interest of the congregations to which they belong. Checking a counselee out on this matter can be decisive to his future welfare and that of his congregation. Moreover, many counselees who complain of a variety of ills have as a major problem the failure to utilize time well. They waste much of it, using little or no time in the service of Christ and His church. If they were to get off their duffs, they would find life more interesting, the church of Christ more exciting, and many of their ills would disappear. Check out the counselee, I say, as to the development and use of his gifts. Many, if they use them at all (you will find), use them only in their own selfish interests. No wonder they are miserable! Counter this with the passage at hand.

In a triad of exhortations, Paul urges **Let love be without hypocrisy, loathe what is evil, adhere to what is good** (v. 9). This is a marvelous exhortation—one of those verses worth memorizing for frequent quotation off the top of your head when counseling. It fits so many situations. The three go together. One who *genuinely* **loves** (over against he who only *pretends* to love) finds doing **evil** to others **loathsome** (a strong term in the original). It revolts him; he attempts to steer a wide course around anything that has even the semblance of evil in it. On the other hand, one who shows the love of God to others **adheres** (the word is the word for gluing two things tightly together) to what is **good** for the other person. He will not let go of it, but sticks to it like glue to paper. No one can detach him from a good work. Test out a counselee on how much he loathes evildoing to others. You may, indeed, find that evildoing is pre-

Christian Counselor's Commentary

10 Have warm affection for one another with brotherly affection; prefer one another when showing honor;

---

cisely what he is intent on. Later in the chapter such a vengeful spirit will be dealt with. But if there is no strong abhorrence of evil that is done to others, the chances are that there is little good done. In our day, when the headlines and the TV nightly news broadcasts feature evildoing in society, it is easy to become immune to the heinousness involved in it. We tend to become dulled in our perception of how God, with His pure eyes, looks on those who plan to do evil. A fresh sense of God's perspective can be gleaned from the verse before us. When necessary, you will find that using this verse can make all the difference.

Verse 9 ranges the territory of all men; verse 10 pertains to relations between believers, members of the same family of God. **Have warm affection for one another.** It is easy for one's relationship to his brother to grow cold. Many counselees have broken off any significant fellowship with other believers. They may attend church, but they hurry to the door at the conclusion of the service to get out before someone can speak with them. They have no contact with other believers during the week. That sort of lifestyle does not engender **warm affection**. It is only when believers are intimately a part of each other's lives that such affection grows. Again, this is a point at which to check out your counselee. Ask, "Who are you close to at church? Who is the person you'd turn to if you had a need?" and questions of that sort. You will soon discover, in all-too-many cases, there is no one really close to him. You must encourage (and often to instruct) the counselee how to make the effort to grow close to other Christians. He cannot get along otherwise. And he does so by doing **good** to others, taking initiative and becoming warm in his approach to them.

The phrase **with brotherly affection** qualifies the command in an important way. One must always be careful not to develop sexually-immoral relations when trying to relate to another with warm affection. And, in addition, one does not develop such relationships for his own advantage—to borrow from another, ask for privileges from him, or in some other manner trade on the relationship. The best way to develop proper relationships is to labor together in the work of Christ's church.

And, in doing so, one should be careful **to prefer one another when showing honor,** in every legitimate context. If another can play the piano better than you, put him forward; let him receive the thanks for doing so rather than hanging on to the piano bench yourself. If another has done

11 don't slacken in diligence, be aglow in spirit, serving the Lord.
12 Rejoice in hope, endure affliction, persevere in prayer,

---

something worth mentioning to the body, or to individuals in it, then don't fail to do so. And when you do it, don't hog the spotlight with him. Many people like to toot their own horns; the Bible is opposed to this. But honestly tooting the horn of another is right, so long as it is not flattery or manipulation of any sort.

The series of staccato exhortations begun in verse 9 continues, and will do so for a few verses thereafter. **Don't slacken in diligence**, Paul writes. There are so many things to discourage, if one only allows them to do so. It might be instructive for you to keep a growing list of the reasons counselees present for giving up. You will discover if you do that the list is a long, ever-increasing one. But this verse makes it clear that none of these reasons is more than an excuse for slackening. Indeed, if one sees that there is difficulty in the way, that things are not going as he would have wished, that is just the time to jack up his effort, not to slacken. Tell your dispirited counselee so: "Well, you certainly have painted a discouraging picture. I guess there is only one thing to do about it—double your efforts for Christ!"

Paul continues, **be aglow in spirit**. Ah! There it is. It is not enough to double one's efforts, but he must do so with hope, with good cheer and with boundless enthusiasm. He must glow in the effort. After all, whatever the outcome—and not all outcomes will be what we want in this world of sin—to work with glowing heart for the Lord is itself an achievement. And it certainly makes life easier for you and all around you. Counselor, part of your job is to become a cheerleader. You must help Christians become excited about serving Christ. But if you are dour and sour, others will never catch the **glow** from you!

In verse 12 Paul urges your counselee **to rejoice in hope**. After all, what a hope he has: eternal life in perfection with God sharing in the inheritance in light that is His. There may not be much else to rejoice in from time to time, but there is always the future expectation that God has held out before His people. When nothing else brings joy, even in the midst of suffering, that hope can prevail. And it will enable him **to endure affliction** too. In this world, the Christian has been promised tribulation. Counselors must be utterly realistic about this. None of this talk about "Trust Jesus" and the world will suddenly become "a bowl of cherries." That's unbiblical. The hope is for endurance here in the midst of trial and

13 share in meeting the saints' needs, pursue hospitality.

---

suffering, and peace and pleasure at God's right hand forevermore—at death! One is not to give up on praying. To **persevere in prayer** is to pray about something until the final results are in. It means not to give up if the first few times one prays for something he does not receive it. It may be that in God's estimation the person who prays is not yet ready for it. It may be that God has other plans. It may be that God wants to see if you will persevere. It may be that... (for whatever other reason He has providentially determined that you have not received what you wanted when you asked for it).

And Christians are specifically to show warm affection by **meeting each other's needs** when they become apparent. The type of needs in view are not mentioned. There is no qualification. You are to meet his needs so far as you are able to do so by sharing whatever you have that he needs. Another checkpoint for your counselee: is he totally wrapped up in himself, or does he reach out to others?

And specifically, says Paul, **pursue hospitality**. This was important in the early church because Christians had lost friends and relatives through ostracism. They needed the fellowship of the saints. Traveling from place to place, missionaries needed to receive hospitality (cf. III John). Today, in the cold, impersonal world in which Christians live, hospitality is every bit as important as it was then. We no longer have neighborhoods, we drive our heated and air-conditioned cars in a bubble in which we live apart from others. The same is true of our homes with their windows slammed shut. We need one another. Many counselees suffer from their failure to realize this and to do something about it.

I have written a small book based on an exposition of verses 14 through 21 entitled *How to Overcome Evil*. For that reason, I shall not develop these verses as fully as I might otherwise. Yet, although I do not give as much time to them as I might have had I not written the book, I do not want you to get the idea that they are not all that important to counseling. I cannot emphasize strongly enough the utter necessity of using these verses with those who bear grudges and harbor resentments against others. They deal with the problem of vengeance (which also will be dealt with in the next chapter of Romans) and they set forth the great alternatives to the sinful responses of those who do not know Christ, who retaliate when injured by others.

14 Bless those who persecute you; bless and don't curse.
15 Rejoice with those who rejoice and weep with those who weep.

Bless those who persecute you: bless and don't curse. Those words go contrary to unregenerate nature. But to bless is precisely what God wants His regenerate children to do. When others **persecute** (in this instance, Paul probably is thinking about verbal abuse) you must say good things to and about them (**bless him**). Surely, that is the first in a series of instructions God gives you and your counselee in which He expects you to replace the natural response with which you were born (to retaliate in kind) with its biblical alternative. Here, clearly, is a biblical put-on that is calculated to replace the unchristian response. It is what you must tell those O-so-many counselees who come with fire in their eyes ready to do someone in. It is the advice that you give to those who go about spreading rumors about another, to those who would run down offenders behind their backs to you as well as to others. You have here a direct, clear-cut command to read to them. And you should do so. Many counselors, whose counseling is not solidly based on biblical exegesis, will encourage counselees to pour out venom against someone else—for whatever reason they may have. But that is utterly contrary to the spirit of these verses and verse 14 in particular. You win the battles of the Lord by blessing enemies, not by cursing them. Hard? Nobody in the Scriptures said Christianity was easy!

Your counselee may have a hard time finding anything good that he can say about the one who persecutes him. He may be so filled with bile that it runs out of the sides of his mouth. So, in many cases, you may have to help him. Explore the things the other person has done in other areas. Think of his good qualities as a husband, as a father or as a worker. Help your counselee to develop options of thinking other than those he has been considering.

In order to respond correctly to those who would persecute and say nasty things about you, take a look at what it is that your enemy grieves and rejoices over. If he has recently lost a loved one, send him a sympathy card—with a kindly personal word written on it. If he has lost his job, commiserate with him (in a good way, of course). If he has just been able to purchase a brand new car—the car of his dreams—rather than stand jealously apart, drooling for such a car for yourself, move in, share his delight, enjoy his enjoyment at having it. In short, **rejoice with those who rejoice and weep with those who weep** (v. 15). Sometimes it is easier to

> 16 Think in harmony with one another, not being haughty but associating with the lowly. Don't become conceited.
> 17 Don't return evil for evil to anybody; plan ahead to do what is fine in the eyes of every one.

weep with another than to rejoice at his good fortune. Especially when he is an enemy. Counselees will need help in doing what God requires in this case; but they can. The very fact that God commands something should engender hope. God never commands His children to do what they cannot, if they do it His way by His grace. In every command, then, lies a possibility for change and for growth in Christ.

Among believers, there is to be no squabbling. They are **to think in harmony with one another**. That does not mean that they will always agree on everything, but agreement and harmony are more likely to occur under conditions where believers make it a point not to be disagreeable. The harmony in view is, especially, between people who differ because of differing economic, intellectual and social status: **not being haughty, but associating with the lowly. Don't become conceited**. There are many manifestations of the attitude that Paul is denouncing. It appears sometimes between people and preacher. He has knowledge they do not and may think of them as uneducated, unspiritual peons. It is his task to lovingly instruct so as to impart knowledge and wisdom; not to look down on those who do not possess it. Members of the congregation sometimes flock together with those birds who have the same feathers. That is particularly sinful. Those who have wealth and education should be cultivating the members who do not, lending help to them in every way that is proper. And those who are lowly in the sight of the world should not be considered such in the sight of any member of the church. No one should become conceited about his attainments—regardless of what they are. Obviously, counselees often express opinions of others that indicate they need a good dose of Romans 12:16.

Again, verse 17 goes against the grain. As persons born with sinful natures, the pattern that nature develops is a retaliatory one. "He did it to me and I'm going to give it back to him with spades!" That is the way many think; even if they do not say so. When speaking to a counselee whom another has wronged ask, "Don't you want to get even?" If he is honest, most likely with some vigor he will say "Absolutely!" That is when you quote **Don't return evil for evil to anybody; plan ahead to do what is fine in the eyes of every one** (v. 17). He will have a hard time

18 If possible, so far as it depends on you, be at peace with everybody.

---

accepting this. But read it again, and again. Get God's instruction across to him in such a way that he cannot wiggle out of it.

He will be hard put in many cases to come up with something **fine** to do for the one who does evil. The word used is more than "good"; it means something that is well done (so much so that anyone looking at it would have to say, "Well now, that was really nice"). How will he go about thinking of something fine to do in return for evil done to him? Remember what Jesus said. He told us to give something to eat to an enemy that is hungry, something to drink to a enemy that is thirsty. Therein lies the answer. He should research the one who has done evil to him *to discover some need of his that he is able to fill*. In some instances he will know right off what to do but in many others research will be necessary. Give that research as a homework assignment. Perhaps he could inquire of those who know him, talk to a member of his family, etc.

And, to do something **fine**, one must **plan ahead**. A fine dinner is not thrown together at the last minute. It takes planning. Similarly, all that we do in representing our Savior through our response to another must be done with prior planning so that it will be done well. It must be done in such a way that He is not disgraced but, rather, honored.

Verse 18 is especially important in a whole variety of situations. It deals not with the believer's relationship to other Christians so much as with his relationship to unbelievers. Note the careful qualifications: **If possible** (it may not always be, because of the attitude of the unsaved person with whom you are dealing), **so far as it depends on you** (you cannot answer for what another does; but you must answer to God for what you do), **be at peace with everybody**. This is a powerful directive to be memorized, rehearsed and ready at your fingertips always. What it says is that if there is animosity between you and someone else, then it should never be you who is the source of it. In the cases of believers, there is always the process of church discipline, if another will not be reconciled (cf. Matthew 18:15ff.). But in the case of unbelievers you do not have recourse to that. So, there may be disharmony between you and unbelievers that cannot be dissolved; but if so, that must always be because of him and not because of you.

In verse 19 Paul mentions one way in which Christians sometimes try to rob God (of course it is impossible to do so). They take **vengeance**

Christian Counselor's Commentary

19 Don't avenge yourselves, dear friends, but rather make room for wrath, since it is written:
   Vengeance is Mine, I will repay,
says the Lord.
20   But if your enemy is hungry, feed him; if he is thirsty, give him a drink, since by doing this you will heap burning coals on his head.

---

on another when God has said, **vengeance is Mine; I will repay**. We have not been given the right to do this as private citizens. God alone knows how to avenge rightly. Neither you nor your counselee knows the heart of the one who has done the wrong. "You may take more severe vengeance on him than God, Who knows his heart, would. On the other hand, God may have come down harder on him than you. Vengeance is God's business; not yours," you must tell your counselee. God also says **Make room for wrath**. What does that mean? If you park in the boss' parking space, look out! He will let you know in no uncertain terms that you have transgressed his territory. He, and he only parks there! God, and God alone takes proper vengeance; it is His place to do so. If you are standing in His place, attempting to administer vengeance, get out of the way; that's God's place—He may park through you! There is a strong warning here for the believer who becomes a vigilante and, without warrant from God (indeed, against His explicit prohibition of it), takes vengeance into His own hands. If you fail to issue this warning, you place your counselee in jeopardy. Don't.

The next verse is one that many have a hard time understanding. It is given in the context of warfare (cf. terms used in v. 21). By **feeding** or **giving drink** (meeting his needs) an **enemy** is subdued. And **that is like heaping burning coals** (literally of charcoal) on his head. How is that?

Picture the enemy advancing through a narrow pass. Unknown to him, your troops hold the heights. Above him on both sides, undetected, are soldiers with bellows heating to white heat the coals of your smokeless fuel. On command, they shovel the coals on the heads of the enemy. What is the result? He is done for. He is no longer a threat. He is conquered by this very effective means. When you do good to those who do evil to you, you subdue your enemy. Do enough long enough and it will be like heaping charcoal on his head—he will no longer be a formidable foe. Don't just quote the verse; explain it to your counselee. Let him see how effective God is saying that this method of putting an enemy out of the business of being an enemy is.

21 Don't be conquered by evil but conquer evil by means of good.

Finally, as a summary to the entire section (14-21) Paul writes, **Don't be conquered by evil but conquer evil by means of good.** That says it all. God expects you to win the battles you fight. Don't allow your counselee to take a defeated, hangdog attitude. He is to be the victor in his battles with evil. However, he will lose if he uses his own weapons and follows his own strategy. Rather, he must strictly adhere to the principles of spiritual warfare outlined in these verses at the close of chapter 12.

CHAPTER 13

> 1 Every individual must subject himself to the governing authorities, since there is no authority except from God; and those that exist have been ordered by God.
> 2 So then, whoever opposes the authority opposes what God has ordered; and whoever does so will receive judgment.

In chapter 12 we considered the personal ethics of an individual Christian as they relate to God and his fellow man. In this chapter, we shall see him in relationship to the state, and to the world opposed to Christ. What he was not permitted to do as an individual (take vengeance), he would be authorized and commanded by God to do as an officer of the state (cf. v. 4, **he is God's servant, and** *avenger*). In that official capacity he may bear the sword; but not as an individual. Sometimes counselees are confused by seemingly contradictory statements that they simply do not understand. What one does in his official capacity he has no right to do as a private individual. To understand this distinction is crucial for the interpretation of this chapter in the light of the previous one. Your counselee must be apprised of the distinction, if you would have him understand his relationship to others who have wronged him.

But the chapter does not speak of the Christian in the position of a magistrate (though all that is said of that authoritative position would apply to him *par excellence* were he an official of the state). It deals with his relation to the civil authorities. The thrust is clear: he is to **submit** to them (v. 1) and **pay taxes** to support them (v. 6ff.). He is not to **resist or oppose** them in any way, but must recognize that if he does so he opposes not them but, in the final analysis, opposes God Himself (v. 2). How is that? God ordained them. They exist because of His providential working in history (**God has ordered** them). This is of importance to some who may express subversive ideas in counseling. More and more you are likely to hear such things, but revolution and anarchy do not please God. He wants your counselee to **subject himself to the governing authorities** (v. 1). Opposition to the state, Paul warns, leads to God's **judgment** (v. 2). You must likewise warn whenever necessary.

The ruler is God's ordained servant to bring about **good** and to put down **evil** (v. 3). In a world of sin this does not always happen as fully as one would like. Nevertheless, to the extent that there is law and order in the land, the Christian should be grateful. After all, it is God who has

Romans 13

3 Rulers aren't a cause for fear to those who do good but to those who do evil. Do you want to have no fear of the one in authority? Then do good, and you will have his approval

4 He is God's servant to you for good. But if you do evil, fear, since he doesn't bear the sword in vain; he is God's servant, an avenger who brings his wrath on those who practice evil.

5 Therefore, it is necessary to be subject, not only because of wrath but also because of conscience.

6 This is the same reason why you pay taxes, since the authorities are God's agents who must attend to this very matter.

---

brought about those conditions. There should be no **fear** of the authorities if the Christian is law abiding. Rather, he should receive the **approval** of the ruler (v. 3). But Christians who transgress the law have reason to **fear** (v. 4); God has given the **sword** to the ruling authority to *use*. He does not carry it **in vain**. God has made him, in his official capacity, one means of exercising the **vengeance** that He said was His (12: 19).

But a Christian should obey the law for the highest reason—not to escape punishment only, but out of **conscience** (v. 5). That is, knowing the commands of God to subject himself to rulers and their laws, he does so not because he thinks the laws are reasonable, nor because the ruler is such a fine person, or even to escape his **wrath**, but he does so in order to please God. Again, the high motive—gratitude for what Christ has done (cf. 12: 1)—should prevail in the life of the Christian. At all points, he must endeavor to make this the driving force of his life. Counselees will be heading toward solutions to their problems only when they become aware of this and determine, above all else, to please God.

The only exception to what has been said is when the government requires a Christian to sin. If it requires him to worship a false God (as it did later in the Roman world) or to stop preaching the gospel (as the authorities in Jerusalem did; cf. Acts 4:19; 5:29), then the Christian must respectfully decline. God never gave the government or any of its officials the right to require anyone to sin. Notice, the apostles indicated that the authorities were acting on human authority and not divine when they required them to cease preaching: **we must obey God rather than** *men*.

It is also out of conscience (not the fear of the IRS) that your counselee should pay his taxes (cf. **this is the same reason why you pay taxes**...v. 6). The authorities (once again) are viewed as **God's agents** for collecting them. All sorts of taxes are to be paid and every kind of **honor and respect** is to be given to those who bear authority from God. The

Christian Counselor's Commentary

7 Pay all of them what is due; tax to whom tax is due, revenue to whom revenue is due, respect to whom respect is due and honor to whom honor is due.

8 Don't owe anybody anything except to love one another; whoever loves the other person has fulfilled the law.

9 **Don't commit adultery, Don't kill, Don't steal, Don't covet,** and whatever other commandment there may be, is summed up in this statement: Love your neighbor as yourself.

10 Love doesn't do anything to harm a neighbor; therefore love is the fulfillment of the law.

11 Besides this, you know the sort of times in which we live, that the hour has come for you to rise up from your sleep; our salvation is now nearer than when we believed.

---

honor is due them not because of their actions, their personalities or their lifestyles, but because of the God-ordained positions that they occupy.

These principles must be made clear to those who have failed to pay taxes (a significant number of persons come to counseling over guilt about the matter). Often you will be led by their disparaging remarks about governing authorities who levy taxes to ask them whether they have been cheating the government. This is an important clue that you should not miss in counseling. "You haven't been engaging in income tax evasion by any chance, have you?" you will find yourself saying more often in the future, whenever you hear an overemphasis on the evils of taxes and those who pass tax plans.

From the idea of paying taxes, Paul moves on to the duty of the Christian to **owe nothing to anyone** (no longer does he focus on the government). The only debt that one can never pay is the debt of **love** that he owes to all others (v. 8) that he must go on paying, installment after installment, so long as he lives. After all, says Paul, love **fulfills every requirement of the law** toward others (these are listed in v. 9). Put negatively, Paul points out love will do nothing to **harm a neighbor** (v. 10). Love impels one to do every good toward him that he would do toward himself, and with the same zeal (the meaning of the appendage **as yourself**). Obviously, there is too much zeal for one's self and far too little for others among counselees. Self-esteem is not the problem, but the opposite.

Now Paul picks up the theme of the **sort of times** in which they are all living (v. 11). The days are dark. If a Christian is to have a witness in this world he must get up early, since the hour has come to awaken from

12 The night is well along and it is nearly day. So then, let us put off the works of darkness and put on the weapons of light.
13 Let us walk decently in a manner that is appropriate to the daytime; not in carousing and in drunken bouts, not in sexual orgies and debauchery, not in strife and jealousy.
14 But rather, put on the Lord Jesus Christ and don't make plans to satisfy the desires of the flesh.

---

sleep (any indolence or lethargy that may have set in). He has battles to win for the Lord (vv. 11, 12). **Salvation is nearer** than when one first came to **believe**. The **night** of prevailing sin has just about run its course; it is **nearly day**. Put off any sinful patterns of life and, instead, take up **the weapons of light**. Jerusalem will soon fall; Rome will follow. The persecutions that are beginning will accelerate, then run their course. Get into the fray by walking **decently in a manner that is appropriate to daytime** (a lifestyle that can stand up under the light of day). This is a life opposed to that of the unbeliever, which is characterized by those sinful activities mentioned in verse 13. Instead, he must become more and more like Christ, being careful not to **make any plans that would stir the desires of the flesh** (v. 14).

All great material for your counselee! Wake up. Put on God's armor and prepare for battle. Shake off the lethargy of sinful sleep when you ought to be up and about in the service of Christ. Walk not in the darkness of sinful ways, but in those patterns of life that can withstand the scrutiny of daylight. And be careful not to deceive yourself or others, so that while you seem to be doing so well, you are actually planning to indulge your sinful desires.

How often has that last item on Paul's list popped up in your counseling? I find that it is all-too-frequent. People promise all sorts of things in counseling that, at the very same time, they contradict in secret. A man tells you he wants to be reconciled to his wife, but all the while he is seeing another woman and planning to get a divorce. Proper homework, which, by the nature of things, always is inconsistent with such intents and actions, will in short order ferret out the truth. Warn counselees that they should not think they can get away with such plans. Even if you fail to uncover their hypocrisy, God knows all about it. Nothing can be kept hidden from Him. And, in time, "the truth will out."

CHAPTER 14

> 1 Welcome the person who is weak in the faith; don't criticize his views.
> 2 One person believes that he may eat anything; but the weaker one eats only vegetables.

Perhaps the only problem in the Roman church of which Paul had knowledge was the problem of things indifferent (or as they are sometimes called the *aideophora*). There seem to have been people who had difficulty with eating meat—a kind of vegetarianism of that day (cf. v. 2)—and there were some who had problems eating meat that had been declared unclean (cf. vv. 14ff.). Presumably these were converted Jews. Who the first group were we simply do not know. These Christian Hebrews also wanted to impose the keeping of the Jewish Sabbath on others in the church. These issues were causing (or in time would cause) problems for the congregations at Rome. As a converted Jew himself, Paul was well-qualified to address these matters.

Plainly, Paul stands with those who will eat meat, will eat any kind of meat, considering it clean, and those who consider every day holy to God rather than singling out one from among the rest as particularly so. Himself and those he sides with in their interpretation of these matters he calls the **strong** brothers; those on the other side of the issue he views as **weak**. It is important to recognize this since the thinking of those in many churches today flip-flops this assessment. The counselor must understand this very important point or he will only add to the confusion of many counselees.

But it is the *attitudes* of each group with which Paul is most concerned—not the correctness of their views. Either group can cause trouble in the church by maintaining its adherents are right, the other's wrong, and that those who are opposed should be either ousted from the church or in some way restricted. Both attitudes are wrong. The strong are those who have no scruples on these matters, and should ultimately help the weak to gain better views. Yet as he begins, addressing the former, Paul says, **Welcome the person who is weak in the faith; don't criticize his views**. That is a magnanimous statement which is to be followed wherever this sort of situation develops in a church. There are to be no second class citizens in the church because of matters of difference. The word **welcome** indicates that **weak** brothers and sisters—those who have a con-

3 The one who eats must not look with contempt on the one who doesn't eat, and the one who doesn't eat must not judge the one who eats, since God has received him.

---

science about matters of the sort mentioned in the passage—are not to be excluded or looked down upon by the strong. It is so easy for Christians to do this. But Paul envisions both existing side-by-side in Christ's church (v. 2). The difference in views is not to separate them or to cause rifts in the congregation. There will always be weak brothers in the church. And why not? According to verse 3 God Himself has received them. Those God receives no one has the right to exclude. The strong are to recognize this and make a place for them. They must tolerate their erroneous views for a time and hope, at length, to lead them into a stronger position. But they may not ostracize them either by refusing to welcome them into membership or by looking down on them when they become members.

Nor are they to be everlastingly **criticizing** them for their errors. Many "enlightened" Christians think that it is their duty to pounce on them, trying to convert them to sounder beliefs. That is exactly what Paul forbids. Through the preaching of the Word and through proper discussions at appropriate times doubtless most weak Christians eventually will come around. After all, the Holy Spirit is at work in them. We ought not to erect barriers to church fellowship that God does not countenance. And the sort of thing that Paul is treating here is of exactly that sort. While you may side with the views of one or another person in counseling, you may find yourself having to reprimand the one who holds your own beliefs because of his *attitude* toward a weaker brother or sister. Sometimes this is difficult for counselors to understand: "After all, Tom is right. What he says is biblical. And what John says is clearly not so." Ah, yes! But, now check out their attitudes about the difference. Tom may be all wrong in the way in which he views John and John's attitude toward Tom may be right. Often, however, as Paul seems to indicate here, the attitudes of both may be wrong. At least, Paul shows how people on either side of these issues can be wrong.

It is possible to **look with contempt** on a weaker brother. It is that which God forbids in verses 3 and 10. That characterizes the attitude that God finds so reprehensible. But, as the rest of verse 3 indicates, the weaker brother can also sin by **judging** the stronger. In some ways this latter tendency seems more prevalent in some Christian circles than the former. Because they do not partake of the food or because they strictly

> 4 Who are you to judge somebody else's household servant? To his own lord he stands or falls. And he will stand because the Lord is able to make him stand.

observe the day, weaker Christians actually think of themselves as stronger than their brothers who see matters differently. They are likely to try to get them to see things their way and, when they do not, to judge them. "You are not as spiritual as we are," they think if they do not say it. There is the danger of laxity among the strong but the danger of pharisaism among the weak. And there must be no tyranny by the weak in the church.

Paul says that we are all the **Lord's servants**. Who, then, but their **Master** has the right to judge? (v. 4). The **Lord makes both to stand** in the day of judgment; thus, no one now has the right to condemn or try to knock others down. That last phrase, **the Lord is able to make him stand**, is a powerful assurance for believers that has aphoristic quality. It has a life of its own and is capable of being applied correctly to any situation in which one is attacked—either from without or (as here) from within the church. One stands here and now, and ultimately as he appears before His Lord, only because of the strength he receives from God. God may enable one to stand against any and all opposition.

But there is something more in the statement. If one or the other of the persons mentioned in the chapter complains to you that he "can't take it anymore," that someone in the church is persecuting him beyond his ability to withstand, there is not only I Corinthians 10:13 to turn to, but also this verse. And what is said here goes beyond what Paul says in I Corinthians. In addition to all the hope that the wonderful verse in I Corinthians gives, Paul in this verse implies that if one falls *it is his own fault*. God is able to make him **stand**. If he doesn't stand in the face of criticism, etc., it is because he has failed to access what God has provided for him to be able to do so. He has no complaint that he can rightly level against the Church or against God.

Paul now mentions another problem: the keeping of days. Not recognizing that God has declared all days holy, each day a Sabbath, and that He has substituted a day on which His church is to meet that is not the Jewish Sabbath, the weak brothers look on Saturday as more holy than other days of the week. Here, Paul makes it clear that this is not so. But, if one wishes to do so, he may observe the day much as he did before becoming a Christian, and no one is to criticize him for it. On the other hand, the one who views every day as holy to God, and the first day as the

5 One person regards one day above another day; another regards every day the same. Each person must become fully convinced in his own mind.
6 The one who observes the day, observes it for the Lord, and the one who eats, eats for the Lord since he gives thanks to God. The one who doesn't eat, does so and gives thanks to God.
7 None of us lives for himself, and none of us dies for himself.
8 If we live, we must live for the Lord; if we die, we must die for the Lord. So then, whether we live or die we are the Lord's.

---

day designated for God's people to meet, is not to be criticized either. The weaker is to meet with the people of God on the first day; but he may also observe the seventh if he wishes, in his home.

In verse 5 we are given the additional exhortation to **let each become convinced in his own mind.** There is, therefore, the need to discuss, persuade and preach about such matters, but there is no place for either group to judge or criticize. The key thing is that both are to do what they do about eating or observing days **for the Lord** (v. 6). Convinced as they are of their view, within the parameters of their views they must do all they do (or refuse to do) to honor God. They are both to **thank** God. Paul doesn't say for what, but clearly for all that He has done, including whatever truth they recognize from their viewpoint.

Verses 7 through 9 are important not only to the discussion at hand, but to many other matters as well. They are global in application, not restricted to the discussion of food and days. None of us is **to live or die for himself** (v. 7). The self-love people need to spend time understanding and applying this verse to themselves. It is their idea, at least as it is expressed by some of them, that people should live to meet their own "needs" (often expressed as needs for security and significance). Such Adlerian views are championed by Larry Crabb and others. And, as Maslow puts it in his hierarchy of needs, even those things done by those in the top category (self-actualization) are involved in need-fulfilling activities. But this verse puts the matter straight: one is to live and die for Christ, not **self**. Even suicide is forbidden by the verse, it being a selfish act that, in the eyes of the self-murderer, is done to fulfill some "need" of his own. Most so-called needs are not needs at all, but desires. The suicide thinks so highly of himself that, disregarding what effect his act may have on others, he dies in order to avoid some thing or things that he thinks he is too good to have to bear. And, worst of all, he totally disregards the command of God not to murder. In life or death whatever we do, there-

Christian Counselor's Commentary

9 Now it was for this purpose that Christ died and lives again, that He might be Lord of both the dead and the living.

10 Why do you judge your brother? Or why do you look on your brother with contempt? We shall all stand before God's judgment seat,

11 since it is written:

> **As I live, the Lord says, every knee will bend before Me, and every tongue will confess to God.**

12 So then, each of us will give an account of himself to God.

13 Therefore, we must stop judging one another. Rather, make this judgment—not to put a hindrance or a stumbling block in a brother's way.

14 I know, and am convinced by the Lord Jesus, that nothing is unclean in itself, but it is unclean for anybody who counts it unclean.

---

fore, it is to be done for the Lord and not for us (v. 8). That is how both the weaker and the stronger brother should regard their activities.

Christ died so **that He might be Lord of both the dead and the living**. Whatever may be the state of His people, He—no one else—is their Lord. That is the point to make to counselees who want to lord their views over others.

Now, Paul makes it plain that no one has a right to judge his brother (v. 10); God is the Judge. To attempt to take over God's task is a sin. It is to attempt to unseat Him and put one's self on His judgment throne. That is the point of verses 10 and 11. Moreover, in making this point, Paul nails down the fact that each brother who fails to hear what the Scriptures say on the matter will Himself be **judged** for that. Not only will his brother **stand before God** to answer for his beliefs and actions, but he himself will be forced to do so, too. The implication is clear: be sure you do nothing to a brother that will need to be condemned on that day.

In verse 13 Paul takes his argument a step farther. If one fails to listen to these exhortations about judging, he will likely put a **stumbling-block in his brother's path**. This stumbling-block is something that makes it hard for another to please Christ. It is a temptation over which he may trip and fall. The **hindrance** is a difficulty that makes another's way hard; the **stumbling-block** is an occasion for sinning. The hindrance makes it hard to do right; the stumbling-block makes it easy to do wrong. Both are to be avoided.

Dealing with meats that some thought continued to be **unclean** (or common), Paul asserts the strong view that none are (v. 14). And he has this on the direct authority of Christ (perhaps given in a revelation to him or as he understood the words of Christ to Peter in Acts 10:14, or from

Romans 14

15 Now if you are hurting your brother because of food, you are no longer walking by love. Don't let your food ruin a person for whom Christ died.
16 So then, don't let what is good be blasphemed;
17 after all, God's empire isn't eating and drinking, but righteousness and peace and joy by the Holy Spirit.
18 Whoever serves Christ in this is pleasing to God and is approved by people.

---

what He said in Mark 7:19). Yet, even so, as long as he causes no trouble for others, one may eat only those meats he thinks are "clean." If a strong brother hurts a weaker one **because of his food** (presumably by persuading him to eat against his conscience) his whole approach is wrong. It is not an act of **love**. Perhaps it is an act of pride—wanting to show the weaker brother how strong he is, or whatever. But love must rule in the matter. One, in order to preserve his own rights, may never ruin a brother for whom Christ died (v. 15^b). If he fails to heed this advice, he will blaspheme what is good. That is to say, he will give others (outsiders as well as those within the church) an occasion to speak ill of what is actually the right (strong) position on the matter. Rubbing another's nose in one's view is what Paul has in mind. So, counselor, watch out for the one who is in the right, that he does not always insist on his rights. To do so can be devastating to others, and to churches as well.

After all, Paul observes (v. 17), **God's empire isn't about food** (or its lack) but about really important matters like **righteousness, peace and joy** which **the Holy Spirit** brings about. Make these things the issues you contend for. And do so, as the Holy Spirit directs you in the Bible. What you are doing when you make these things paramount is to **please God**, so that rather than **blaspheme** by speaking evil against God's church, people will **approve** of what His church members are doing. This emphasis is even more ultimate than caring for your brother's welfare—as important as that may be. God's Name is at stake. Jesus told us to do **good** and thus bring others to glorify His Name (Matthew 5:16).

Note also that peace, joy and righteousness are not dependent on circumstances or other persons ("I'd be happy if only she would..."). They all come from the Holy Spirit. Since this is true, neither do you have to whomp them up. They are the by-products that the Spirit provides when one follows His Word. Don't let counselees make these elements dependent on people, things or situations.

So then, we must pursue peaceful ways and whatever builds up

Christian Counselor's Commentary

19 So then, we must pursue peaceful ways and whatever builds up one another.
20 We must not undo God's work for the sake of food! Everything indeed is clean, but it's wrong for a person to eat anything that is a stumbling block.
21 It isn't good to eat meat or to drink wine or to do anything that affords an occasion for your brother to stumble.
22 The belief that you have, keep between yourself and God. The one who doesn't have to judge himself about what he approves is happy.

---

one another. What a wonderful verse for counselors! How often you will find a good use for it. This is God's way for Christians to live with one another. To **pursue** is the word for hunting something, tracking it down until you find it. It is a forceful term. Building up others is the business of preachers and of the entire church. Here, then, in this summary statement are the divine criteria for your actions and attitudes toward your brother or sister. Do my words and actions bring peace between us? Do they build up the other person? There is a way to persuade that does; there is a way to persuade that doesn't.

What **food** one eats is so unimportant when compared with God's work in lives. Don't make it so important that you **undo the work of God** s (v. 20). Here is an important matter to bring up in almost any counseling discussion. Even though all food is clean—the old distinctions are gone—**don't eat anything that leads a brother into sin by your example**. That too is of significance in the discussion (cf. v. 21; note the addition of drinking wine added in this verse).

Don't go pressing your beliefs about such matters on others; **keep** (observe) **them before yourself and God** (v. 22). You will **be happy** if you go on acting in a manner consistent with those beliefs and do not have to **judge yourself** for violating them. In other words, you must not violate your conscience. The important principle that grows out of that statement is the concluding verse of the chapter. I call it the *holding principle*. If you **doubt** and *do* the doubtful thing, you sin; whatever you do not do **in faith** (i.e., believing it is right before God) **is sin**. If it's doubtful, it's dirty. Even if something is right in itself, but you think it might be wrong, you sin if you do it. Why? Because you did what you thought was (or might be) a sin against God. Thinking that way, you did it anyway; therefore, your *attitude* was sinful. You were willing to go ahead and do something that you thought might be rebellion against Him. That is a rebellious attitude. That is sin.

23 But whoever doubts is condemned if he eats, because he doesn't eat in faith; and whatever isn't done in faith is sin.

Now this principle is essential to understand rightly. Many times a course of action may be doubtful. The counselee is perplexed about what to do. How will you advise him? You say, "If there is the slightest question in your mind about whether what you are proposing might be sinful, you must abandon that course of action or put it on hold until you can be certain that it is not." The valuable principle given here is: don't take action unless you think that action is right before God.

Take an example. A man is faced with a choice between remaining in the job he presently has or taking a new one which (he thinks) might reduce significantly the amount of time that he will be able to spend with his wife and children. Because of the number of days he will possibly be on the road for the new company, he may also miss church services at least once a month. Yet much of that is mere supposition. Should he take it? Obviously, the answer should be no. Unless and until he can resolve these matters by information that shows these deleterious factors actually *do not* characterize the new job, he should remain where he is. To do otherwise would be sin. You do not recommend that he move forward to change the status quo except by faith—faith that a contemplated action is pleasing to God.

The fourteenth chapter is not difficult to understand; and it is brief. Yet this holding principle, together with the attitude that God wishes your counselees to develop toward their brothers in Christ, makes it one of the most important. Learn to turn to it frequently. Possibly no other chapter, containing no other principle, offers the counselor (and his counselee) as much direction in questionable matters. You will find yourself using the holding principle every week. When people say, "The Bible doesn't have an answer for my problem," frequently the answer that it gives (and you must assure them that it is an answer) is **whatever isn't done in faith is sin**. So, the Bible tells you don't do it so long as you aren't sure it is right before God.

CHAPTER 15

> **1** We who are strong ought to bear the weaknesses of those who aren't strong rather than please ourselves.
> **2** Each of us must please his neighbor for his good, to build him up.
> **3** Even Christ didn't please Himself, but as it is written, **The insults of those who insulted you have fallen on Me.**

The first few verses of this chapter continue the theme of the previous one: how to treat a weak brother. Paul makes his point: **We who are strong ought to bear the weaknesses of those who aren't strong rather than please ourselves**. And, in so many counseling cases, that's exactly what it comes down to! Often, the counselor must call on an irritated (or even irate) counselee to take it on the chin for the sake of another who is not so well-informed as he. Counselees rarely want to hear this, I've found. They "want something to be done about so-and-so," or they "want justice." Such cries are self-oriented. They should stand out for the alert counselor. When listening to that sort of thing, he will clearly discern that the counselee has little or no concern for the weak brother, but only for himself. While that is not an easy thing to tell him it is precisely what the counselee needs to hear. Perhaps the best way to introduce him to his own self-centeredness is to read this verse and ask, "Who do you want **to please**?" That puts it the way Paul does. It should bring conviction to those who reluctantly look anywhere but to themselves.

Then you can read verse 2: **Each of us must please his neighbor for his good, to build him up**. The proper biblical concern should be for the weak one; that is one practical way of loving one's **neighbor** as one loves himself. Having to put up with the (often) nonsensical ideas and actions of weak Christians provides a concrete opportunity for putting the second great commandment into practice. Doing so frequently means **bearing** (v. 1) their weaknesses. Sometimes this is more difficult than putting up with others who do not know Christ. It is easy to reason, "Why is he/she so thickheaded? By now there is every reason for him/her to be straight on this matter. After all, haven't I explained matters a hundred times?" Weak brothers or sisters can be very aggravating at times. But, love is manifested in patience (**bearing** with them).

As motivation, Paul refers to Jesus, **Who didn't please Himself**. Instead, as the Scripture puts it, He took the insults that should have been borne by elect sinners upon Himself (v. 3). It is interesting to note the way

Romans 15

4 Whatever was written before was written for our instruction, that by the endurance and the encouragement that the Scriptures give us we may have hope.

---

that Paul describes it. Insults to believers are really, in the final analysis, insults leveled toward Him. That should take the edge off of all such insulting remarks by weaker brothers as well as by others. Ultimately they are borne by the Savior Himself. If He is willing to do so, why shouldn't we be?

Having referred to the Scriptures, Paul now mentions their purpose: **Whatever was written before was written for our instruction, that by the endurance and the encouragement that the Scriptures give us we may have hope**. The Bible is not some record of past events recorded for curiosity's sake; it is the living Word of God to His church in all generations. And it is given in order to provide **hope** in times of difficulty for His people. It does so by **instructing** us in God's will, by strengthening us to **endure** suffering and hardship and by giving us the **encouragement** we need to carry on in hard times. In other words, all that Paul has been urging, and has yet to urge, it is possible to achieve because God has provided all that is necessary to do so in His holy Word. When a counselee protests, "I can't" (a favorite word of counselees), he should be told, "Yes, you can. If at the moment you can't that is because you have not been empowered by **Scripture**. Let's look at the problem in the light of Scripture. It is there, and there alone, that you will find the resources that you need."

God wants every believer to have **an abundance of hope** (cf. v. 13). This hope is provided **by the power of the Holy Spirit**. But just how does the Spirit empower His people with hope? Not through any mystical means, not through promptings or checks in the spirit, not through direct revelation. Well then, how? Through the Scriptures. In the Bible, the Holy Spirit is always shown to be intimately related to the Bible. He moved men to write it (II Peter 1:21), He turned it into the very breathed-out word of God (II Timothy 3:16), He illumines believers to understand it (I Corinthians 2) and He is said to speak by means of it (Hebrews 10:15). So, when you place verse 13 and verse 4 side-by-side, it becomes clear that not only joy and peace, but also endurance and encouragement, come from the Bible as the Holy Spirit empowers believers by means of it. Quell all ideas to the contrary. Never allow counselees to seek the Holy Spirit's power apart from the strength that the Scriptures give. Don't let

Christian Counselor's Commentary

5 May the God from Whom endurance and encouragement come give you unity of thought among yourselves by Christ Jesus
6 so that unanimously, with one mouth, you may glorify the God and Father of the Lord Jesus Christ.
7 Therefore, welcome one another just as Christ also welcomed us to God's glory.
8 I tell you that Christ became a servant to the circumcised on behalf of God's truth to confirm the promises made to the fathers,

---

them wander hopelessly seeking help in other places, trying to call on the Spirit to work directly; He doesn't. He produced the Scriptures, and He works through them. They are peculiarly His Books.

The **endurance and encouragement** that **God** gives, by the Spirit applying His Word, fosters **unity** in a church. It is possible that there may have been the beginning of signs of disunity between the weak and the stronger brothers at Rome. If so, Paul has effectively pointed them all to the solution of the problem. This unity must begin by developing **a unity of thought**. The agreement to put up with one another, to be more concerned with the other person than one's self, and the agreement to refrain from judging and despising others would, in time, also lead to unity of thought regarding food and the keeping of days. But, as always, it begins with the Scriptures. The Bible tells us how to relate to one another so that we may eventually properly discuss its teachings. No matter how clear a point may be, it will be hard for another to accept it from his brother if he is on bad terms with him. So the Bible, as Paul indicated, will straighten out relationships so that, in time, doctrinal agreement may also be reached. In counseling, counselees often want to discuss the points of disagreement before they deal with the relationships. When bad relationships get in the way of unity in thought those relationships must be dealt with first. Priorities in counseling must be observed carefully. Then, having worked out differences of relationship and doctrine, the whole church may **glorify God unanimously, with one mouth** (v. 6). That is the goal.

The conclusion to the whole matter is found in verse 7: **Therefore, welcome one another just as Christ also welcomed us to God's glory.** Throughout this section, since 14:1, Paul has been dealing with the problem of welcoming and assimilating the weak. It is an instructive section. But don't fail to see and utilize the many principles pertaining to interpersonal relationships that appear in it. These are aphoristic and may be used in any number of situations. Why not list those that you have gleaned in the discussion, then apply each to at least three different counseling cases

Romans 15

9   and to give the Gentiles cause to glorify God for His mercy. As it is written

Because of this I will confess You among the Gentiles, and sing praise to Your Name.

10 Again it says:

Be glad, Gentiles, with His people.

11 Again:

Praise the Lord, all you Gentiles,
and let all the peoples sing His praises.

12 And again Isaiah says:

There will be a Root of Jesse
and One Who rises to rule the Gentiles;
on Him the Gentiles will place their hope.

---

you have had? Such an exercise will not only sharpen your thinking but will prepare you for the future.

Paul, moving naturally out of the topic by showing how **Christ became a servant** to others, goes on the summarize much of what he said earlier about the salvation of elect Hebrews and Gentiles alike. In verses 8 through 10, he demonstrates that this was God's plan and purpose. Quoting various verses that mention the salvation of the Gentiles, he shows that what has happened is not some afterthought but that the Gentiles always were in God's mind. He had prophesied in various places that they would come into the faith. In the last verse, he quotes the words **There will be a root of Jesse and One Who rises to rule the Gentiles**. Then he continues, **on Him the Gentiles will place their hope.** That naturally leads then to the discussion of hope that we mentioned previously (under verse 4).

Next, Paul says, **I am convinced about you, my brothers, that you yourselves are full of goodness, filled with all knowledge, and competent to counsel one another.** This, of course, is a pivotal verse for Christian counselors. The word for counsel used in this verse is *noutheteo*, the term from which I gleaned the adjective Nouthetic. Because it is so full, and has no exact English counterpart, I simply brought the word over into English. It means to bring about *correction* by verbal *confrontation* out of deep *concern* for the counselee. If you remember those three words beginning in "c" you will have it.

Paul believes that the average Christian in Rome has the capability for giving counsel of this sort. He does not restrict it to those officially ordained to the work. Unofficially, every believer ought to be able to offer

Christian Counselor's Commentary

> 13 Now may the God of hope fill you with every sort of joy and peace in believing, so that you may have an abundance of hope by the power of the Holy Spirit.
>
> **14** I myself am convinced about you, my brothers, that you yourselves are full of goodness, filled with all knowledge, and competent to counsel one another.
>
> 15 I have written to you rather boldly about some things, by way of reminding you, by the grace God gave me

---

biblical counsel to his fellow believers. Note what he says it takes to do so: goodness and knowledge. The need is for **competent (full) knowledge** of God's will and a **competent (full)** desire to help others (**goodness** means good-heartedness toward them that grows out of one's own goodness of life). If one does not possess **full knowledge** of the Scriptures, his counseling will be deficient. Unlike a preacher who knows what he is going to say from the pulpit, and whose attention is fixed on one topic and passage, the counselor has little idea what may arise in a given counseling session and what passages may be pertinent. He must be prepared for most anything. Therefore his knowledge of the Bible must be **full**. And if his attitude toward counselees is not beneficent, he will soon give up on many of them, finding them (at least initially) intransigent. It is a good-hearted attitude alone that puts up with much of the bitterness, nastiness, discouragement and resistance found in counselees. Verse 14 maps these things out. So, of what sort should training in counseling be? It should focus on the attitudes and life of the counselor-to-be and his knowledge of and ability to use the Scriptures.

Paul now looks back over the letter (or thinks back about what he has written) and concludes: **I have written to you rather boldly about some things**. That was his way—he was straightforward. You never had to guess about where Paul stood. Counselors should take a leaf from his book. It is not astute or scholarly or professional for a counselor to be obscure. He is obligated to set forth God's Word in clarity and to apply it with vigor.

And some things he realizes are only **reminder**s (v. 15). It is interesting, as you go through the New Testament, to see how often the biblical writers think it is necessary to give reminders to their readers (see especially Peter's letters which are little else). Why is that? Because people tend to forget. I cannot tell you how many times I have told a counselee something that, as he was hearing it, rang bells. It was not new material, but it had been forgotten—or it had been dismissed as irrelevant to the

Romans 15

16 that I should be a servant of Christ Jesus to the Gentiles, serving as a priest of the good news, in order that the offering up of the Gentiles may be acceptable, sanctified by the Holy Spirit.

17 So then, I have reason in Christ Jesus to take pride in my work for God.

18 I won't dare to speak anything but what Christ has accomplished through me to bring about the obedience of the Gentiles, by my word and work,

19 by the power of signs and wonders, by the power of the Holy Spirit, so that from Jerusalem and all around as far as Illyricum, I have fully preached the good news about Christ.

---

problem at hand. Often, it is because the person fails to recognize the relevance of a biblical teaching that he forgets it. Reminding, and applying, make the difference. So don't hesitate to remind counselees of things they have been taught before but have never "learned" in the sense of having seen their application to particular situations.

God's **grace** in enabling Paul to understand and remember as well as to see such relevance was the power behind his own counsel. It is apparent that God apportions His grace (help we don't deserve, but upon which we are dependent) in various ways. But counselors will be given grace as they prayerfully study His Word and seek ways of applying it in counseling. I can remember how few really difficult cases appeared in the early days. That was grace! Yet, as I have grown in ability to counsel, cases have become more difficult. God is good to give grace *when it is needed*. Depend on Him.

This grace, he says, enabled him to **serve Christ by serving the Gentiles**. Note the double nature of service. People often see a conflict between the two: "Do I serve the church or Christ?" But the conflict is only apparent. One serves Christ *by* serving His church. There is no conflict. Like **a priest**, he is offering **the gospel** to men and women who need to hear about Christ. And as **Gentiles** believe, he **offers them up** to God. He wants his work to be **acceptable** to God, **set aside** from all other service **by the Holy Spirit**.

So because of what **Christ** has done through him, Paul is **proud** of his ministry. Notice his pride was not in himself but in Jesus (v. 17). Pride must always be focused on Him; never on self. It is clearly **Christ** who **has accomplished the obedience of Gentiles** through Paul (v. 18). Through the divinely-provided **signs and wonders** given to him as an apostle, Paul **fully preached** Christ from one part of the Mediterranean

Christian Counselor's Commentary

20 So I have made it a point of honor to announce the good news only where Christ hasn't been named already, so that I wouldn't build on another person's foundation.

21 Indeed, it has been written:
>   Those who weren't told about Him will see,
>   those who haven't heard will understand.

22 This is the reason I have so often been kept from coming to you.

23 But now that I no longer have any such place in these regions, and since for a number of years I have had a desire to come to you,

24 I hope to see you as I travel through your community on my journey to Spain, and have you provide what I need from there, after first enjoying your company for a while.

25 But now I am going to Jerusalem to serve the saints,

26 because Macedonia and Achaia have been pleased to make a contribution to the poor saints in Jerusalem.

27 They were pleased to do so, and they are debtors to them. If the Gentiles have shared their spiritual things, they ought to be of service to them in material things.

---

world to the next. He could be proud of what Christ did through him. And he has **made it a point of honor to preach only where Christ has not yet been named**. It was not his job **to build on another's foundation**; he laid foundations, but then went on from there. He followed the Bible's teaching about **those who weren't told about Him** so that they too would **see and understand** (v. 21). Because he was engaged in this work, and because Rome had already received the gospel, Paul had **been kept from coming** to Rome (v. 22). But now at last it looks as if it were possible since he had finished the work in the regions where he had labored in the past. He would be able to realize his long-standing goal of seeing them. He was planning to go to **Spain**, and hoped to visit Rome on the way. He wanted to spend some time with them and then, provided with the necessary funds and supplies to make the trip to Spain, he would depart. This letter, in part, allowed them to know something of him so that they would be prepared when he arrived. Yet, first, he was going **to Jerusalem to serve the saints** there by delivering the gentile offering to them (vv. 23-26).

Paul fully disclosed his plans so that no one could claim that he was fickle, or that he vacillated. There could be any number of hindrances, but this was what he expected to happen. And, indeed, his plans did not turn out precisely as he had anticipated.

Now, in verse 27, he says that the generous gifts by the churches of

Romans 15

28 So when I have finished this, and have sealed this fruit for them, I shall leave for Spain, going by way of you,

29 and I know that I shall come with the fullness of Christ's blessing.

30 I urge you, brothers, by our Lord Jesus Christ and by the Spirit's love, to struggle with me in your prayers to God for me,

---

Macedonia and Achaia were, in effect, the payment of a debt. Since the Jews (through the remnant) were the source from which the gospel **went forth to the isles**, there is a sense in which they are indebted to the Jews. It is not farfetched then to say that there would be at least a fair exchange if the Gentiles gave **material** help to the Jews from whom they received **spiritual** help.

It is interesting to see how Paul reasoned by implication. Counselors afraid to reason from the implications of biblical facts to conclusions that direct counselees in proper directions will often find that they have a lack of advice to give. While one can reason in a faulty or careless manner in drawing implications and inferences, he may also draw valid ones. Danger ought not to scare you off from doing such reasoning; it only should make you especially careful. Much counseling requires the ability to reason by implication (if such and such is true then so and so must also be true). Good and necessary consequences should not be avoided. One must, however, be sure that the inference or the application growing out of the implication is true. That requires examination, thought and care. But those are some of the elements involved in Christian counseling; biblical counseling is not a question of focusing on emotion but on facts. True counseling draws conclusions regarding truth and its implications for life. When these are properly applied to behavior and give rise to a new, biblical lifestyle, appropriate feeling will follow as a consequence.

All this to explain about his proposed trip to Rome on his way to Spain. He believes that he will see them and, in coming, Christ will favor his trip with His own **blessing** (through revelation: see Acts 23:11). The unspoken implication here is that if Christ's blessing will be upon it so should theirs be also (vv. 28, 29). But Paul recognized that the road ahead would not be smooth. So (v. 30) he asks for the **prayers** of the Roman Christians. If the **Spirit** has really put **His love** within them (cf. 5:5), then he urges them to manifest that love by praying for him as they together struggle against great difficulties in the work of evangelization. He knew that those who had refused to **obey** (i.e., rejected God's command to believe the gospel) would oppose him in Judea. He knew the temper of the

Christian Counselor's Commentary

> 31 that I may be rescued from disobedient persons in Judea, and that my service for Jerusalem may be acceptable to the saints.
> 32 Then by God's will I shall come to you with gladness and be refreshed together with you.
> 33 The God of peace be with all of you. Amen.

Sanhedrin for which he Himself once had worked. He was walking into trouble. But the promise of the Lord was that he would witness for Him at Rome (how little Paul knew about how he would get there or in what way or to whom he would bear this witness!).

Now, notice this. He *knew* that he was going to Rome. That, Jesus had made clear. Yet he urged prayer for deliverance from those who would oppose. How was that? He knew already that he would be delivered; otherwise Christ's promise would fail—and that was an impossibility. Yet he urged prayer for deliverance. Counselees sometimes ask about such matters. You must be prepared to explain. God's sovereignty is unlike the fatalism of Islam. The Muslim says, "I shall die on such and such a day at such and such an hour *regardless* of what I do." Biblical Christianity says, "I shall die on such and such a day at such and such an hour *because* of what I do." Christianity also affirms the means, not merely the end. So Paul can speak of **God's will** being certain (v. 32) so that there was no doubt he would **come** to Rome, yet because of the contemplated opposition in Palestine, he **urges prayer** for the deliverance that would make it possible for him to come. And he looked forward to that visit as a time of great **refreshment and gladness.** All counselees should be encouraged to look at the fellowship of the saints in like manner. Rather than view church attendance as a chore, they should strain at the bit to attend. And, indeed, every participant in the gatherings of the saints should not only seek refreshment and gladness there but also endeavor to provide those things for others. The letter proper closes with verse 33 in which Paul leaves a cheerful benediction with them. Chapter 16 is a word of greeting, exhortation and good will toward those with whom he was familiar.

CHAPTER 16

1 Now I want to introduce to you Phoebe, our sister, who is a deaconess from the church of Cenchrea,
2 so that you may receive her in the Lord in a way that is fitting for saints, and help her in any matter in which she may need your assistance, since she, indeed, has been a benefactor of many, including me.

The last twenty-seven verses of the book of Romans focus on people. Paul was no impersonal practitioner. He worked everywhere with teams and used the services of fellow-workers (or co-laborers, as he called them) to the full. In no way was he a lone ranger, a solitary figure roaming the Roman world. He enjoyed and in every way possible furthered the fellowship of the saints. Indeed, this chapter is an example of one way in which he did so. Many counselees fail in their Christian walk because they refuse to cultivate fellowship with fellow-believers. One important counseling task is to encourage and (at times, when necessary) to assign homework that will promote fellowship. Shyness is one form of pride. People are shy because they are afraid they will make a *faux pas*. Because doing so would embarrass them, they develop a "shy" lifestyle. They are too proud to face the consequences of their fallibility.

First, Paul introduces the Roman church to **Phoebe, a sister and a deaconess of the church at Cenchrea**. Presumably, she was the one who faithfully carried this precious epistle to Rome. How impoverished we would be had she lost it! There is no problem with women becoming deaconesses. Some conservative Christians rail against "womens' ordination." But ordination is simply the "setting apart" of someone to a particular task; it is merely an appointment. The key to the issue is the task itself. Deacons were set apart to assist the elders, to take over the temporal work that elders should not get bogged down in as they are pursuing the ministry of the word and prayer (see Acts 6). It would be possible to ordain a sexton to his task of keeping the church buildings clean. To ordain women to tasks that the elders give them along with male deacons is certainly not unthinkable, and has nothing to do with liberalism. Deaconesses were ordained from Reformation times on. The title and the task it signifies gives no authority; it only obligates to work. Of course, it is possible to translate the word in its non-official sense as "female servant." But, since she is already designated **a sister**, it is likely that this second appellation signified the role to which the church had appointed her.

Christian Counselor's Commentary

3 Greet Priscilla and Aquila, my co-workers in Christ Jesus,
4 who risked their necks for my life, to whom not only I but also all of the Gentile churches give thanks;
5 and greet the church at their house. Greet Epaenetus, my dear friend, who is the first fruit from Asia for Christ.
6 Greet Mary, who expended much labor for you.
7 Greet Andronicus and Junius, my kinsmen and my fellow prisoners, who are well known by the apostles, who (as a matter of fact) were in Christ before me.
8 Greet Ampliatus, my dear friend in the Lord.
9 Greet Urbanas, our co-worker in Christ, and Stachys, my dear friend.
10 Greet Apelles who has been tested and approved by Christ. Greet the members of Aristobulus' family.
11 Greet Herodion my kinsman. Greet the members of Narcissus' family who are in the Lord.
12 Greet Tryphena and Tryphosa, who labor in the Lord. Greet Persis, my dear friend, who has expended much labor in the Lord.
13 Greet Rufus, chosen by the Lord, and his mother and mine.

She is to be welcomed (**received**) and not rejected. She is to be dealt with in a manner that is **fitting for a saint**. She is to be given all the **help** necessary to carry out any additional tasks that Paul had assigned to her. And this is fitting in her case in particular since she has done so much for others (v. 2).

Two **co-workers** (nonofficial workers) who **risked their lives** to save Paul from some (to us) unknown danger, who opened their home for **the church** to meet and to whom **all the gentile churches** owe **thanks** are **Priscilla and Aquila**. And the Roman congregation that met there was also to be **greeted**. **Epaenetus** was Paul's **first** convert in the province of **Asia** (now called Asia Minor). He too is to be greeted. And **Mary, who expended much labor**, is also the recipient of greetings. Andronicus and Junius (fellow-Hebrews with Paul who had spent time in **prison** with him) are noted. All **the apostles knew them well**. They were Christians from before Paul's conversion. **Ampliatus** is called **a dear friend in the Lord** along with **Stachys**. And **Urbans** is designated a **co-worker**. **Apelle**s has undergone some **testing** (probably through persecution) which Paul will not forget; the man did so faithfully, and was **approved by Christ**. **Herodian** is also a Hebrew. Two **families** are noted: that of **Aristobulus** and that of **Narcissus**. As **laborers** and **friends, Tryphena, Tryphosa and Persis** are mentioned. **Rufus** and his mother (who acted as if she were Paul's own mother) come to Paul's mind. And, in verses 14

Romans 16

14 Greet Asyncritus, Phlegon, Hermes, Patrobas, Hermas and the brothers who are with them.
15 Greet Philologus and Julia, Nereus and his sister, and Olympas and all the saints who are with them.
16 Greet one another with a holy kiss. All of Christ's churches greet you.

17 Now I urge you, brothers, to watch out for those who, by disregarding the teaching that you have learned, cause divisions and give occasion for stumbling. Keep away from them.
18 Such people don't serve our Lord Christ as His slaves, but are slaves of their own appetites; and by fine talk and flattery they deceive the hearts of the unsuspecting.

19 Although word of your obedience has come to everybody, and makes me happy about you, I want you to be wise about what is good and innocent about what is evil,

---

and 15, a bevy of additional names appears. All these are to **greet one another with a holy kiss** (a sign of chaste love in the church).

In verse 17, Paul begins to take up a few additional matters. First, there is a warning against those who, **by disregarding correct teaching, would cause divisions and give some an occasion for falling**. It is clear that Paul thought poor teaching leads to the destruction of churches and individuals. Never let your emphasis as a counselor become less crisp in this regard than Paul's. People are always setting life over against **learning**. The antithesis is false. What one learns affects how he lives. Never forget that.

Those who teach false doctrine are **not Christ's servants**; they live for themselves—to satisfy their own desires—and they **deceive unsuspecting persons by fine talk and flattery**. Any flatterer needs watching. In counseling, counselees may seek to flatter you in order to receive favorable treatment. But counselors must be impartial. There is no doubt that you are a fine church, says Paul; **everyone** tells me so. I am **happy to hear** such things. But let me give you a parting word of advice in aphoristic form: **be wise about what is good and innocent about what is evil**. What a marvelous statement to memorize and hold ready to bring to bear upon many problems. Soon the devil's work among you will be **crushed by you** as Christ crushed the head of the serpent on the cross. You will put his activity to an end. Satan cannot be handled by compromising with him; only by crushing him. He is to be defeated at every turn. Christians who are defeated come to counseling for help and need to be given the assurance that they can defeat the enemy instead.

Christian Counselor's Commentary

20 and the God of peace will soon crush Satan under your feet.
May help from our Lord Jesus be with you.
21 Timothy, my co-worker, greets you along with Lucius and Jason and Sosipater, my kinsmen.
22 I, Tertius, who recorded this letter, greet you in the Lord.
23 Gaius, my host (and host of the whole church), greets you. Erastus, the city treasurer, and Quartus our brother greet you.
24 May help from our Lord Jesus Christ be with you all. Amen.
25 Now to the One Who is able to strengthen you by my gospel even the proclamation about Jesus Christ, according to the revelation of the secret that was kept quiet for ages,
26 but now has been disclosed by order of the eternal God, and through the prophetic Scriptures has been made known to all the Gentiles to bring about obedience by faith,
27 to the only wise God be glory forever and ever. Amen.

They need God's grace for achieving this (v. 20). He wishes it for them.

Those with Paul also send greetings (vv. 21-23). At least one of the recipients (**Erastus**) is a well-known political official. Very few such are mentioned among the early believers. **Tertius,** who was Paul's amanuensis (secretary), also sent his greetings. Now comes a closing benediction (vv. 25-27) that befits such a magnificent letter. It is one of the great small bits of literature in existence. God **is able to strengthen** the Roman Christians—and your counselees. Don't let them forget it. Again, as Paul indicated in chapter 15, that strength comes though the **revelation** of the **gospel** and Christian truth that comes from the **prophets and apostles** and was recorded in the **Scriptures**. The letter ends on the note that the God Who gave the Bible is **alone wise**. And so, to Him there is to be **glory forever and forever**.

CONCLUSION

How great a treasure Romans is for a Christian counselor! Why, when there is such material as this in the Bible, would anyone turn elsewhere? It is almost unthinkable. But, if you are convinced of this after reading this far, let me make a couple of suggestions that may help you use more fully the material found here. First, why not skim through the book once more looking at any underlined passages or otherwise noted sections and list these on the inside back cover of the volume? Add any other principles that you may not have previously noted. Jot down the page(s) where a discussion of these may be found. Secondly, under these, list all the aphorisms you have located in Romans (I have pointed out a few; not all of them), learn them by memory, and begin to use them in counseling. Lastly, memorize what content is in each chapter so that you can say "chapter 1 = the decline of the nations into evil; chapter 2 = the condemnation of the Jews along with the Gentiles," etc. Then you will know exactly where to turn when you need help.

Introduction to PHILIPPIANS

The Book of Philippians is the warmest of Paul's letters. Though not free from the controversies that dogged his steps and plagued his infant churches, nevertheless the tone, in contrast to Galatians, let us say, is altogether different. Here was a church, unique among the congregations, that Paul allowed to send him support. Indeed, part of the reason for the writing of Philippians was to thank the church for the generous gift they sent to assist Paul during his first imprisonment in Rome. In those days, prisoners were granted only the slightest sustenance. If they wanted care, others had to provide it. The Philippian church had sent not only money, but one of their own members to minister to Paul. He, Epaphroditus, had become ill during this time. Paul also wanted the church to know that Epaphroditus was now well.

The letter is chocked full of helpful information for counselors. Its wide-ranging interests cover many concerns that biblical counselors confront every day. It is, therefore, of special interest to those who wish to deal with the needs of many different types of persons in a variety of circumstances. Moreover, it speaks to the needs of the counselor too. Paul, writing from prison, has many useful comments to make about the way that he viewed his incarceration. For those in difficult times, it is instructive to use Philippians to help them to properly evaluate and deal with their circumstances. Paul's own example, incidentally mentioned (as well as overtly referred to), was designed by God's good Spirit to help us to face severe problems in a similar manner. The note of joy that runs through the letter is itself instructive. The joy and peace of the Christian is not dependent on his circumstances; it is a matter of his relationship to God—something that human beings or difficult times cannot shake, a significant insight for you to realize and pass on to counselees.

Of interest, especially to counselors, is the split in the Philippian church, headed up by two women (Ch. 4). That Paul was aware of this division before he sat down to write is obvious; to mend the rent in the Philippian garment was a principal purpose in writing. It is helpful, then, to see how he approaches the matter. Clearly, he waits to broach it openly until chapter four. But, as we shall see, he writes much, from the first chapter on, in a positive way that lays the groundwork for later comments about the split. The whole section from 1:27 through 2:13, dealing with unity, constitutes that groundwork.

Christian Counselor's Commentary

On the whole, then, you will find Philippians a very fruitful study for counseling. It is a book that must be thoroughly understood by every counselor. When he comes to a full knowledge of its contents, he will discover that he will turn to its pages again and again in the counseling process to help erring, suffering and confused counselees out of their difficulties. While it is a book of difficulties, unlike the two letters to the Corinthian church as well as so many of the other epistles, it nowhere even hints at false doctrine in the church. It is problems of pride, of misunderstanding God's ways, of fear and anxiety and the like that Paul handles in the letter. In many ways, then, it is the counselor's book since these are the perpetual concerns faced in the counseling room.

Even in its more negative portions, Philippians is a book that so radiates the joy of Christ in the life of Paul that it is a pleasure to read. You never feel bogged down when studying Philippians, as you might at times when reading other books. It triumphantly moves (I almost wrote "bounces") along from one point to the next. It is the writing of one in prison to those for whom he had the warmest possible love. That is why Philippians is so engaging.

While not finding it necessary to correct doctrinal error among the members of the church, Paul nonetheless carries on doctrinal discussion. He uses doctrine—especially in the great section on the incarnation in chapter 2—in a very practical way, thus guiding the counselor in his own use of doctrine for such purposes. Nor does Paul hesitate to warn about *false* doctrine, as he frequently does in most of his letters.

So, as I indicated, the Book of Philippians is a valuable document for counseling purposes precisely because of the variety of matters discussed and the manner in which the apostle does so. Read it, reread it until you are so well-acquainted with it that you will be able to use it with great freedom in counseling.

Chapter 1

1 Paul and Timothy, slaves of Christ Jesus, to all the saints in Christ Jesus who are at Philippi, together with the overseers and deacons:

Paul writes from prison in Rome. That should never be forgotten when interpreting and applying any portion of the Book of Philippians. Moreover, it is important to remember that the Philippian jailer, a member of this congregation, had himself imprisoned Paul and knew that what he writes in this letter is entirely consistent with the way in which he saw him act on that occasion. He had heard this man sing and praise God after a lashing that laid his back open. He knew that, as Paul is going to tell the congregation, it is entirely possible to rejoice in the Lord *always*.

Paul and Timothy write together. Paul always used a team, whenever possible. And he included their names in the letters that he wrote. It is possible to do team counseling with great profit (for information on this process see my *Competent to Counsel*). Here Paul has no need to stress his official title, "an apostle," as he often does in writing to churches where he found it necessary to assert the authority of an ambassador of Jesus Christ. The Philippians were warm friends. But, because he was in prison, he does make it clear that he is a "slave" of Christ Jesus. A slave had no rights of his own. He was told where to go and what to do by his master. Paul was a slave whom Christ had sent to prison (cf. v. 13).

The letter is addressed to the **saints** (the members of the congregation) and the **overseers and deacons** (the officers of the congregation). The word saints means "those who have been set apart" (from the world to God). Every Christian is a saint. The saints are God's own people. They are saints "in Christ Jesus;" not in themselves. They are reckoned to be "set apart" completely because they are viewed in Christ. The fact is, however, as far as their experience goes, they are *still being* set apart by the Holy Spirit, a process that will continue until death.

There should be **elders and deacons** in every congregation. Though some think the early church was still developing in its form of government, it is clear that there was a well-developed government by the time Paul wrote this letter. It is wrong to think that the apostles failed to organize the churches that they started in a manner that led to good order and functioning. The "bishop" (or "overseer, as that name means) managed the church. He is the same as the "elder" (cf. Acts 20, Titus 1 where the

Christian Counselor's Commentary

two terms are used synonymously). The tasks of the elder are to *rule* and to *teach*. All elders rule (that is their fundamental function as "overseers); some, in addition to ruling, also teach (cf. I Timothy 5:17). The word "elder" speaks of the man and his qualifications; the word "bishop" (overseer) speaks of his office (i.e., his duty or task.).

The other office is the office of **deacon**. Deacons (the word means "waiter, lackey") are those who do the bidding of the elders. The diaconate was formed to relieve the elders of duties that pulled them away from the tasks to which they were called (Acts 6). Deacons, then, serve the Lord by serving the elders. They do not exercise authority, and do not rule. They may teach informally as any other Christian may (cf. Colossians 3:16), but neither is their office a teaching office.

Both deacons and elders are *ordained* to office. Sometimes people become confused about ordination. All ordination is alike in one respect, but ordination differs in another. The ordination of an elder or deacon is the *setting him apart to the work to which he is called* (office) by the laying on of hands (the symbol of imparting the office). In that respect, ordination of both deacons and elders is the same: both are set apart to a work. But their ordinations differ in respect to the particular work (or office) to which they are set apart—the one to the office of ruling and teaching, the other to the office of serving.

To be properly carried out, counseling must be done within the framework of the organized church. That means, counselors will call on the elders and the deacons in their counseling when required. All elders will counsel as a part of their managerial function (I Thessalonians 5:12,13). But counselors, who are counseling as elder representatives of Christ in the church, counsel *officially*—that is to say, by virtue of their office and, therefore, with *authority* (cf. Hebrews 13:17). Counselors, acting as elders, may actually order counselees to *obey*, when they are without question commanding what the Scriptures teach ("You must stop committing fornication"). The use and recognition of authority is a fundamental reason for doing counseling in the church. There is no legitimate counseling authority outside of Christ's church. Ponder that a while. Moreover, in cases where the official aspects of discipline are required (just before formally submitting the case to the church), the elders should always be involved (for more on discipline, see my *Handbook of Church Discipline*). Elders are the fundamental office of rule and order in Christ's church. While there were many other offices ordained by God, the eldership persisted throughout the Old and New Testaments as the one stable, unchanging office. Prophets, priests, kings, seers, scribes, apostles, etc.,

Philippians 1

2 May help and peace from God our Father and from the Lord Jesus Christ be yours.
3 I thank my God every time I remember you,
4 always in every request of mine for all of you, making the request with joy

---

came and went and served their purposes, but the eldership continued, in an unbroken line, right through the Old and into the New Testament periods. The presbyter (Greek word for elder) was, as his name suggests, a mature person (not necessarily in chronological age, but in spiritual maturity). His qualifications are set forth in Titus and I Timothy (q.v.).

When a counselee needs food, clothing, shelter, funds, medical treatment, a job, etc., it is the counselor's privilege to call on the deacons to do whatever they can to meet these needs. The deacons maintain a fund that may be used for such purposes. Deacons also may assist the elder-counselor in ways that, if they did not, would take his time away from counseling. To know that the elders are there to back up counseling with church discipline, and that the deacons are there to assist in material ways and the working out of many of the details of counseling, is a relief to busy counselors who, in talking to those with problems, have enough on their hands. They do not need to become weighed down with details that someone else could do as well or better. That is what the office of deacon is for.

The blessing in verse 2 is not unusual. Both **grace and peace** are needed by all, and the two terms (one the Hebrew greeting, one the Greek), fortuitously coupled together, form a fitting benediction for a New Testament letter. They were not words simply bunged in from the culture, but, placed together, their union is evidence of purposeful intent. Doubtless, Paul wished both God's grace and God's peace to permeate and dominate this church.

A thanksgiving, followed by an explanation of a part of it (vv. 7, 8), comes next in verses 3-6. Something of the warmth Paul felt for the Philippian church immediately appears in verse 3: he thanks God for them *every time he remembers them*. Unlike the remembrance of other congregations, in which there was little to give thanks for, Paul says also that he could pray for them joyfully, no matter what the nature of the request. Those words are evidence, together with what follows, of the great love that existed between Paul and this congregation.

How many pastors can speak this way about their churches? I talk to pastors all the time in conferences. And the dominant note that I hear is

> 5 because you shared in announcing the good news from the first day until now,
> 6 and confident of this, that He who began a good work among you will keep on perfecting it until the Day of Christ Jesus.

the opposite. Indeed, some counselors will discover when counseling pastors that these men *hate* their congregations and would like to be free from them. Now, there was, as I have said, a unique relationship between Paul and the Philippian church. Yet, doesn't it set forth the ideal? Many times, a pastor is not at fault for strains between himself and his congregation. It is hard not to become bitter in such circumstances, though as Paul did in writing to other churches, he must always try to reestablish relationships and bring about a good result. But frequently, bad relationships are primarily the result of bad attitudes on the part of the pastor. Never is a pastor justified in becoming bitter or resentful or harboring hatred toward a congregation. What is revealed to us in verses 3 through 8 is God's ideal toward which all counselors should point pastor-counselees.

One of the things that endeared the Philippians to Paul was their insistence upon "sharing" in the work of announcing the good news from the very first day they became a congregation until the time he wrote this letter (v. 5). Obviously, they must have helped in many ways when he lived in their midst. But, since then, they had faithfully supported him financially, no matter where he was. And, in prison, they had sent not only funds, but Epaphroditus as well, to minister to his needs. This tie that had been formed early and had remained throughout the years meant much to Paul. It is questionable whether he was able to sustain such a relationship to any other church (but more of that in chapter four).

Paul was also confident that the relationship would continue (v. 6). However, he trusted neither himself nor the Philippians, for that. God began the good work in them, and *He* would continue it until the day of Christ (probably, here, until the day when Christ closed the warm relationship between them by calling Paul to himself. If this referred to the second coming—as some always take any phrase that might seem to—it is clear that the hope Paul had for them failed. Where is this church today?).

It is good to know that the Lord Jesus Christ is the One we can depend on to accomplish fruitful and joyous relationships between Christians. It was He who stirred up their hearts to send funds and other help to Paul. And, it is He who would continue to foster that relationship until the

Philippians 1

7 It is right for me to think this about all of you, because I have you in my heart, since both in my bonds and in the defense and confirmation of the good news, you all share grace with me.
8 God is my witness about how I yearn for you with the emotion of Christ Jesus.

---

day He determined to close it out. And, not only would it continue, but, Christ would *perfect* that relationship (make it more and more complete) throughout the years.

That is the outlook that you must communicate to tired, discouraged pastors that you see in counseling. They need to cement better relationships with their people, and by prayer and concern, foster a growingly better relationship throughout the days ahead. Good relations don't come all at once, as Paul's words plainly indicate; they must be perfected over time. Some counselees want it all over night. But, as we read the letters of the New Testament, we do not see good relationships springing full-blown from the head of Zeus! They must be cultivated, often through hard and difficult work. Here, the relationship had been good and was continuing to grow better.

That is Paul's thanksgiving. He now appends a word of explanation for some of the things that he expressed in it (vv. 7, 8). He knew that his words were full of warmth. But he wants to explain why. **I think this way** about your church, he says, **because I have you in my heart.** He could not get away from it; the Philippian church brought joy to his heart. Both in prison and without, they had continually sent their love-gifts to him (v. 7). And, as a result, the Lord confirmed the work he was doing both to him and to them. What Paul says is "Let me tell you, these are not words of mush; God knows—I call Him to **witness** to what I am saying. He knows that I **yearn** to see and fellowship with you and minister to you with the same kind of emotion that led Christ to give His life for us! I truly care!"

Well, that is a unique thanksgiving with a unique explanation. How deeply does your love for your counselees go? Could you say anything even approximating verse 8 about your love and concern? Once again, we see that there can (ought to) be a warm, filial relationship between the counselor and his counselees, and not the white-coated supposedly professional attitude that some counselors affect. Nothing could be farther from the ideal and finest practice of New Testament ministry.

In verses 9-11, Paul prays for the Philippian church. "The love you

Christian Counselor's Commentary

9 This is what I pray: that your love may abound more and more in full knowledge and clear perception,
10 so that by testing them you may discriminate between things that differ, in order that you may be pure and free from impediments for the Day of Christ,

---

have I pray may increase." How typical of the apostle. He never let's up. If they show love, good. If there is more they could show, let them do so. He wants the very best for them. There is no settling for some lesser goal or attainment. Some counselors will settle for far too little. No, not only does he commend them for what is good, but *on the very basis of that commendation,* prays that they will do even better. Since you are on a roll, don't quit. Just gain more momentum!

This **love** of which Paul is writing is not amorphous goo; it is love that exhibits itself in action ("God so loved the world that he *gave...*"). Moreover, it is love that grows out of a knowledge and clear perception of the will of God. Don't let counselees speak abstractly about love. It must be exhibited by giving (cf. Gal. 2:20, Eph. 5:25, etc.), and it must be occasioned by knowledge and understanding of what it is that pleases God. It is both intelligent and active. See comments on I Corinthians 13 for a more detailed explanation of the biblical concept of love.

This love must be tested in actual life situations (v. 10) in order to know **how to discriminate between things that differ.** Life is full of choices. Those choices should be made on the basis of what it means to love God and neighbor rather than self. In the crunch, that is not always easy to determine. But as one gains greater knowledge and clearer perception, by **testing** his best conclusions against actual situations that arise, he may soon know what is worth doing and what is not.

Legalistically minded counselees want it all spelled out for them—whether or not to wear a tie, and, if so, what color. God doesn't operate that way. He gives us many specific answers, it is true, but He also gives us many larger principles that must be applied to specific situations. These are the ones that must be **tested.** But, these answers grow out of knowledge and perception of His will as it is found in Scripture alone. The testing of one's conclusions, then, like the testing of medals by fire, takes place in the milieu of real life situations. Counselees must be taught this fact. By **learning to discriminate between the worthwhile and the worthless** they will be purified and freed from **impediments** to love when the Lord Jesus determines to take them to Himself (cf. comments on v. 6).

Philippians 1

11 filled with the fruit of righteousness that grows through Jesus Christ, to God's glory and praise.

12 Now I want you to know, brothers, that what has happened to me has served rather to advance the good news,

---

And their lives will be filled with the fruit of righteousness that, in turn, will redound to Christ's glory and praise.

Now we come to the letter proper. There was a problem with which the Philippian church was grappling. They loved Paul and so appreciated his ministry that they could not understand how God could allow him to remain in prison for over two years. At first he was in his own rented quarters; now he had been thrown into prison and was chained by the hand to a guard day and night. What was wrong? Had God goofed? Where was the providence of God? How could it be that the greatest missionary of all was now shelved—socked away in prison? Thoughts like these must have been going through their minds. They couldn't understand why God had allowed the preaching and the spreading of the gospel to be so radically curtailed.

Immediately, as the first matter of business in this letter, Paul addresses the question. Paul is deeply concerned to straighten this out. So he says, **I want you to know...** What was it they needed to know? That what had happened to him (his imprisonment) had not curtailed the progress of the gospel, that God had not goofed, that His providence was very much at work in the imprisonment. How so? Paul says, what has happened to me had happened **rather** (the key term in the verse) to *further* the gospel.

That is quite a claim, but it was true. Paul backs up his statement in verse 12 with these two proofs: the gospel has been preached to **the entire praetorian guard** (at that time, 16,000 men assigned to the emperor's palace) and to **everyone else** (the cooks, shoemakers, grooms, stable hands, etc., etc.). God had given Paul a ministry to those in Caesar's palace! And, as a result, there were already saints in the emperor's household.

The second piece of evidence that supports Paul's claim for a providential ministry at the palace is the fact that **many of the brothers** who, before, said "let Paul do it," were now coming out of the woodwork and preaching. So that there were many more than previously who were proclaiming salvation (v. 14). They saw the need, now that Paul could not travel freely, for some of them to preach. Moreover, they thought, "If Paul

Christian Counselor's Commentary

> 13 so that it has become evident to the entire Praetorian Guard, and to everyone else, that I am in bonds because of Christ.
> 14 Most of the brothers in the Lord, gaining confidence by my bonds, have become far more daring in fearlessly speaking God's Word.

can preach while in prison, surely, I who am not in jail can do so." So, Paul's example led to new courage on the part of many.

What is important for the counselee to know, is precisely what Paul wanted the Philippians to know—God often advances His gospel through trouble. Instead of complaining, whining, getting angry or going to pieces when trouble comes, the counselee should be taught to find the ways in which the gospel may be **advanced** by their trouble. Perhaps in a hospital, during a financial reverse or in a marriage crisis.

Here is how Paul saw it. First, he recognized that God is in the trouble. Paul claimed that his bonds were **the bonds of Christ** (v. 13). It was neither the Jews nor the Romans who imprisoned him; it was His Lord. What a different thing trouble seems when one recognizes that fact. To help counselees see this is, in itself, helpful. Indeed, in the midst of trouble it ought to add a note of anticipation—even excitement and adventure! They are not alone. God is there. He is behind the trouble.

Secondly, God is up to something. Trouble is not meaningless; it has a purpose. How important that fact is! One may not be able to see His purpose right away; but at length it will, in part, become clear. As with Joseph, who eventually could say "You meant it to me for evil, but God meant it for good," so too could Paul at length see how, in his trouble, God intended it for good. When counselees can get hold of that principle, it will make all the difference.

Finally, Paul looked for an opportunity to become involved in what God was doing. When Joseph was thrown into the pit or, later, into prison, he could not foresee that God was at work to make him the ruler of Egypt in order to save the people of God alive. But, he believed God was in his troubles and, instead of complaining, remained faithful. When Paul was taken to prison, he did not know that there would be an opportunity to spread the gospel among 30,000 to 50,000 people at Caesar's palace. He did not know that there was a place that would be called America in which his letter to the Philippians would prove a blessing to distraught counselees. He could see in part, in time; the rest he never knew in this life. But he too remained faithful.

Instead of complaining about his sore wrist to which the manacle

Philippians 1

15 Some, indeed, preach Christ out of envy and strife, but others out of good will.
16 The latter are motivated by love, knowing that I have been placed here for the defense of the good news.

---

was fitted, Paul looked down the chain to the opportunity on the other end. There was a man. You can imagine Paul thinking, "Captive audience!" To him, and to others, Paul must have preached the gospel. Some must have believed, saw to it that they were able to return again and again for instruction, and after a while, themselves became preachers to their fellow soldiers. From them and those who heard, the gospel spread like fire across the palace population until Paul could say that they had all heard! What a new mission field! And some of those very 16,000 troops were shortly sent to Europe where they carried the gospel to some of our ancestors.

Paul's imprisonment, Paul's trouble, it turned out, was for the good of all. Counselees must be reassured that God has not goofed, when trouble comes their way. Rather, He is up to something—something good for all involved. But it may take time to see it. When your nose is right up against the trouble it is hard to see; when the tears fill your eyes, it is most difficult. Usually you must get off and gain a little perspective. Yet, in it all, you must not lose faith, but, instead, remain faithful waiting for God to show you what he is doing—in His time—and become involved in whatever small ways that are apparent at the moment. Look down the chain; don't miss the opportunity on the other end! The passage provides counselors with heavy ammunition for assailing the complaining, whining attitude that many counselees exhibit in the face of trouble.

But there was a fly in the ointment: not all of the brothers who set out to preach Christ did so from the most altruistic motives. Some, as Paul pointed out, were **motivated by envy** and wanted to cause **strife** and division. They were glad enough to see Paul in prison; perhaps, they thought, they could enter into territories Paul had not yet traversed and beat him to the punch. Others, it seems, wanted to stir up trouble and strife in the churches he planted, perhaps trying to take over the leadership of these congregations themselves. Happily, they were not all of this sort (v. 15^b). Some were **motivated by love** (v. 16). They understood what Paul wants your counselee to understand, that Paul's trouble happened in order to give him an opportunity to present and defend the gospel (v. 16). The first group had a **spirit of rivalry**. They did not see themselves in cooperation

Christian Counselor's Commentary

> 17 The former proclaim Christ from a spirit of rivalry, not sincerely, thinking that they can add affliction to my bonds.
> 18 So what! The key thing is that in every way, whether in pretense or in truth, Christ is proclaimed, and I am glad about it.
> And, as a matter of fact, I shall continue to be glad,

---

with Paul and his team, but in rivalry with it. And they were glad when anything they did caused him pain because they wanted to **add affliction** to his bonds (vs. 17).

There are always persons like that. In the midst of trouble, they will take the opportunity to kick the one who is down. Your counselee must be shown that this is nothing unique, but rather, is to be expected. By observing that such treatment is *not* unique, that even the apostle Paul was subjected to it, they should take heart. Knowing that others have undergone the same or similar trials also helps (cf. I Corinthians 10:13). Moreover, if you can "prep" them to the fact that this might take place, before it actually does, you can help in that way as well. What you *expect* rarely comes as such a shock. Like a good physician, tell them what symptoms to anticipate after the operation.

It is sad, but people, even Christian people—and preachers at that—do have rivalries among themselves. Counselees, caught up in these or noticing them for the first time with dismay, must be awakened anew to the fact that there is no one who is perfect. How did Paul treat those who were thus preaching Christ out of this alien spirit? In verse 18 he tells us: he is **delighted that Christ is being preached!** Here, perhaps, as plainly as anywhere, the magnanimous heart of Paul can be seen. Let me be pained, let them add affliction to my bonds. **So what? The key thing is that Christ is preached.** That's what makes me happy. I am rejoicing in the fact and, indeed, will **continue** to do so (v. 18).

Here is the goal for you to set forth for the counselee who complains about unfair treatment. If others in any way are furthering the message about Jesus Christ, rejoice in that—regardless of what they do or say to you. In other words, Christ and His church must come before yourself. That is a hard pill for many counselees to swallow because of their pride, because according to self-love doctrine, they have been taught that they are to care about themselves first of all. Yet, it is an altogether important lesson to learn: you do not come before Christ and His kingdom.

Now, Paul was not letting these preachers motivated by rivalry and strife off the hook. Obviously, they had the right message; that was not the

Philippians 1

19 because I know that this will result in my deliverance through your requests and the resulting provision given by the Spirit of Jesus Christ,
20 in keeping with my eager expectation and hope that I shall not be put to shame by anything, but rather with all boldness (now also as always before) Christ will be exalted in my body, whether I live or die.
21 To me, to live is Christ, and to die is gain.

---

problem. It was their personal attitudes and behavior that was in question. His words condemn them. But, whether they were, in time, disciplined by the church (perhaps in the manner mentioned in I Timothy 5:19, 20) or dealt with by God Himself (or both), we don't know. Paul drops the point here, because to go on would not serve his immediate purpose. But, if and when they were faced with their sin, that matter must be separated from Paul's response, which is the enlightening fact taught here. He rejoiced that Christ was preached—*even at his own expense*! Surely, you can find plenty in all of this to help your counselees, can't you?

Now, in verse 19, he turns to the fact that, having served his time as a missionary to the emperor's palace, he would be freed once again to take up his other work. But that freedom would come only as he successfully endured the trial before Nero, that monster of the ancient world. I am certain that I will be **delivered** (lit., "saved") from the evil machinations of the emperor when I appear before him because of **the supply of the Spirit that God will give me in that hour in answer to your prayers** for me. It will not be easy. It would be simple to deny the Lord Jesus and walk out a free man. But Paul could not do that. He must give the presentation and defense of the gospel before the emperor of the fourth kingdom just as Daniel did before the rulers of the first two world-kingdoms. And, it was of deep concern to him to do a good job of it (v. 20). "And, whether I am freed or executed, I want to maintain the former boldness that I have always known in times past when faced with difficult circumstances. In this, the most important of all trials I have to face, I want to honor, not disgrace, my Lord."

What an attitude! Overwhelming concern to honor Jesus. That is the note to strive for in all your counseling. In contrast to man-centered systems of counseling (and many are presented even within the pale of the church today) throughout your counseling, you must keep the focus not on the counselee, but on the Lord. The best end result for the counselee, of course, always comes from honoring the Lord; but that is a by-product.

The philosophy that underlay Paul's ability to put Christ before him-

22 Now if to live in the flesh means fruitful work for me, I don't know what I will choose.
23 So I am hard pressed by two things: having a desire to depart and be with Christ (which is far better),
24 but knowing that to remain in the flesh is more necessary for you.
25 I am convinced of this and I know that I shall remain and continue with you all for the progress and the joy of your faith,
26 so that your pride about me in Christ Jesus may overflow because of my coming once more to you.

---

self is tersely expressed in verse 21. **To live is Christ; to die is gain.** His reward would follow. His present concern is to live for Christ. I shall leave the latter to God, which I know is **gain** (all the care, suffering, tension and pain will be gone and I shall see Christ and remain with him forever) and I shall concentrate all my efforts on living for Christ here and now. Seen in the light of counseling, not merely as a verse taken out of context, you can understand how this philosophy was able to undergird Paul in the midst of any and all trouble. It is the philosophy for your counselee to adopt. It is not a bad verse for him to memorize. It is crisp, yet powerful in content. It sums up everything.

"If it were mine to choose whether I would live or die, that would be a hard choice to make (vv. 22-26). Especially, if **to live in the flesh** means to go back to fruitful missionary work (v. 22). After all, with this beaten and bruised body, with the heartaches all around and, most of all, **absent from the Lord** Jesus Whom I long to see, there is a tremendous heavenly tug on me. But, knowing that you yet need my earthly ministry, I am sure Christ will free me and allow me the joy of ministering to you so that your faith may progress and grow (v. 25). And the 'pride' you have expressed in becoming so intimate a part of my ministry will overflow by a ministry in your midst in the future (v. 26)."

Obviously, here is a man dedicated heart and soul to the Lord and to His church. He is torn between the two. But accepts that which is less advantageous to him. To die is gain; it is **far better** for him (vv. 21, 23) and he desires it with all his being. But fruitful ministry is far better for others, so he **chooses** to **remain**.

To raise counselees to the point where they are interested in the welfare of others above their own is a part of most counseling. Certainly, if that attitude is not present in your counselee, then it is essential to work toward it. To put the welfare of Christ's Name and His church before one's own is the corollary to that attitude. Can you think of a passage in which these points are made more clearly? If so, use it. If not, then use this passage to the full to enforce the truths contained in it. And, as you do, you may find it helpful to observe that the one who was talking this way was in a dismal prison, chained to a guard.

The fact that I mention all of these elements should alert you to the need to fully exposit a passage that you are using to make your points. It is not enough for you to understand what the passage means and how it may be used, if you have not conveyed that meaning to the counselee as well. Clearly, in emergencies, you are not able to sit down and give a full explanation, but you can mention in passing that you want to at a more appropriate time. Then, when that time comes, or in non-emergency situations, do so. Why? Because your counselee needs to understand that what you are saying is not merely an idea of yours, perhaps triggered by the passage, but is a direct application of the teaching of the Scriptures to his situation. Why that? Because he must be shown that this is *God's* word to him.

Just as you must always keep the eyes of the counselee focused on pleasing God, so too must you keep his attention on what it is that God says pleases Him. Enough, then, for this section. It is not only very valuable counseling material, but it provides much of the underlying philosophy of life, death and the life to come that every Christian must adopt.

If I had my way (which obviously I don't), I'd change a number of the chapter headings in the Bible. Among the first I'd tamper with would be chapter two of Philippians, which ought, by any reasonable reading of the text, to begin with what is now verse 27 of chapter one. The thought begun there is carried on throughout the first 13 verses of chapter two, making a total of 15 verses in all. The subject matter is important, and it should not be divided unnaturally by an uninspired chapter heading that suddenly interrupts the flow of the discussion in the middle. I am, therefore, going to close chapter one at this point, stopping with verse 26, and begin chapter two with verse 27.

Christian Counselor's Commentary

> **27** Let me emphasize one thing: live as a citizen of God's empire in a manner that is appropriate to the good news about Christ, so that whether I come and see you or continue to be absent, I may hear this sort of thing about you—that you are standing firm in one spirit, struggling shoulder to shoulder with one soul for the faith of the good news,

As I explained in the last paragraph of the previous chapter, chapter two ought to begin with what is now chapter one, verse 27. So, in order to avoid breaking into the middle of a discussion that runs from 1:27 through 2:13, I have chosen to include the last four verses of chapter one in this chapter.

In a very positive manner, Paul begins to develop some important thoughts on the question of unity in the church. There was (as we shall discover in chapter 4) a division in the Philippian congregation. Tactfully, Paul approaches the subject here yet mentions nothing about the division or the parties involved. Only when he reaches the fourth chapter, having thoroughly spoken about the importance of and the elements that bring about and maintain unity, does he mention the split. That is one (not the only) way to deal with problems. Knowing the sensitivity of the Philippians, and how they would react, Paul chose to approach the problem gradually. His choice also may have had to do with the fact that he had opportunity to do so. In I Corinthians, on the contrary, he brought up the matter of the sectarian division in that church at the very outset. Probably, until that was disposed of, he could hardly deal with any of the several other problems that I Corinthians addresses. Here, there was but one problem in the church; that meant he could take time to allow the discussion to move from positive considerations to negative ones in its own natural, you might even say meandering, way.

Counselors will not deal with all counselees in the same way. Persons in the Galatian churches had to be handled one way, in the Corinthian and the Philippian churches in other ways. The counselor who employs a canned approach makes a dreadful mistake. It is probably safe to say, however, that whenever there is time to do so (it not being an emergency situation as in Galatia or a basket full of problems spilling all over as at Corinth) ordinarily it is best to approach matters as Paul does here. When one has the opportunity to measure his life over against the standard, set forth unemotionally beforehand in a positive manner, then he can more readily acknowledge how far from it his deviant behavior is.

Beginning his discussion of unity in the church, Paul stresses the

Philippians 1

importance of living **as a citizen of God's empire in a manner that is appropriate to the good news about Christ.** Philippi was a Roman colony, the citizens of which were aware of the value of their Roman citizenship. To be a good citizen of God's kingdom was a greater privilege of far greater import. How should one live so as to be a worthy citizen of the colony of heaven? In ways that are consistent with the gospel. The gospel tells us that Jesus did for us what we could not do for ourselves. That means that, to be saved, one has to be utterly dependent on Him. To live as a good citizen of His kingdom simply means to continue depending on Him.

Sometimes, counselees forget that their sanctification, leading to the solution to the problems they bring into the counseling room, is as dependent on Jesus Christ as was their justification. Good citizens of heaven must take directions from Him as well as find power to follow them from His Spirit. That, counselees need to know, is how to live in a manner **appropriate to the gospel of Christ.**

Glum, angry, depressed, frustrated, whining counselees hardly exhibit attitudes consistent with the most glorious news ever heard—the gospel. There is something wrong if the counselee is not basically a joyful person. That does not mean that he has to go around all the time with a cheshire-cat grin on his face. But it does mean that there is a basic satisfaction and well-being that dominates and characterizes his life. Counselees who claim that their depression, anger, etc., is consistent with the Christian life should be reminded that they are to live in a manner that exhibits the great truth that they have become citizens of heaven by the best news ever spoken by a human tongue. The inconsistency of their non-Christian attitudes with these facts ought to stand out so sharply that they are impelled to admit that something is quite wrong and needs fixing. The note of joy runs throughout this letter.

In particular, what the Philippians must do to live appropriately in their situation was to **stand firm in one spirit, struggling shoulder to shoulder with one soul for the faith of the good news.** That is to say, they must unitedly defend and promote the faith (note the numerous terms that denote unity). And Paul wants to know that this is indeed the case whether he is able to come and see for himself or whether he hears about it in reports from others. What a verse for the counselee who is having problems with other believers in his church! "God wants unity. Unity is essential to the proper propagation of the truth. Let's see it in you! Your growth in this counseling session will have something to do with the growth of your church. And it may even mean the salvation of souls."

Christian Counselor's Commentary

28 and not terrified by anything that your enemies may do. This is to them evidence of their destruction but of your salvation—and that it comes from God!

Often, counselees forget the way the world looks at a divided, squabbling church. Indeed, sometimes a believer has been known to appeal to unsaved persons to take his part in a controversy with others within the church. I Corinthians 6 makes it clear how disgraceful that is; how it smears the Name of the Lord. All matters between believers must be settled within the church. Tomorrow, I shall meet with a pastor and members of his church to attempt to bring about unity within the congregation. Counselors are obligated to stress unity in the church of Christ. One of the principal concerns that they should have in all their counseling, therefore, is bring about this unity. There are counselors, nevertheless, who by the things they say, the sides that they take and the ways in which they counsel, actually promote disharmony. All such counseling is destructive and unbiblical.

About what am I speaking? Well, all sorts of things: speaking against the elders in a congregation, advising divorce on unbiblical grounds, urging counselees to leave a congregation when there are matters that remain unsettled, etc. The counselor, instead, must be a paragon of those concerned to do things biblically. When he does, what he does will promote unity.

Verse 28 makes it clear that unity helps one in his relationships with unbelievers, even with those who persecute. And, when counselees stand in unison to face trouble from their **enemies**, they are thereby strengthened by that unity. It was the unity between Latimer and Ridley that enabled them to face burning at the stake. When your counselee expresses unity, moreover, it becomes clear that the enemy is in the wrong and deserves punishment and that the counselee is right and is in the way of **salvation**. There is great strength and comfort in unity based on God's truth. Your counselee, weak in the faith, needs the support of others to enable him to face the enemy in ways that glorify God. If he is miserable to live with, then he must change his ways so that he may be able to draw close to others. Drawing near to others through a change of attitude and behavior, is an element in promoting unity, just as the achieving of unity also strengthens the counselee in becoming a more likable person. Each feeds the other. It is possible, therefore, to break into the circle at either point.

29 You were given the privilege, for Christ's sake, not only to believe in Him, but also to suffer for His sake,
30 having the same struggle that you saw and now hear to be mine.

CHAPTER 2

1 So then, if there is any encouragement in Christ, if there is motivating power in love, if there is any fellowship that comes from the Spirit, if there are any feelings of affection and compassion,
2 then make my joy complete by thinking alike, having mutual love, being united in soul, thinking as one.

In verse 29, Paul makes it plain that believers should not expect to escape persecution. How important, then, if persecution of some sort or another is inevitable, to have others with whom he can stand. The sort of thing that we saw happening to Paul, we can expect to see happening to us as well. Therefore, unity is a high priority. In times of trouble, there is nothing more important than the comfort that Christ brings through other members of His church. Paul experienced that in prison. Counselees must not only appropriate this comfort for themselves, but also offer it to others.

Chapter Two

We come now to verse 1 of the second chapter in which the concern for unity continues. **So then**, writes Paul. Obviously, he is continuing the first part of a discussion he began in the last chapter and is now reaching a conclusion to that aspect of unity. "If love for me has any power to motivate you (and since he knew his readership, he was sure it did), if the words of Christ are an encouragement that moves you (and of course they were), if you recognize any kinship with one another and with me because we possess the same Spirit that has made us brothers and sisters in Christ (and they did), if you have any feeling of compassion for me in my imprisonment (and there was every evidence of it)—then," Paul says, **Make my joy complete by thinking alike, having mutual love, being united in soul, thinking as one** (v. 2).

What a powerful appeal. In it Paul has garnered and compiled every sort of motivation to appeal to the Philippians. Look at the phrases for unity, strung out in 2^b. Think of the fact that their disunity is painful to Paul who here begs them to **complete** his **joy**. He is happy about the Philippian church in general; this one thing—the spat between two women

Christian Counselor's Commentary

> 3 Do nothing out of selfishness or vanity, but rather in humility consider others better than yourselves.

and their followers—marred it. Do you see anything of import for counselors in this?

If you don't, then you are blind! You too must learn how to appeal to counselees. Pile motive on motive that you believe will reach them. Even make a personal appeal, whenever that might be appropriate. Talk about the joy that their compliance with biblical injunctions will occasion in you or others. Emotional appeal will sometimes reach an emotionally-oriented counselee. Paul's example makes it plain that it is not wrong to use strong appeals, when they are earnest and true to the facts. Some counselors, who have respect only for a clinical approach, would think such a practice unseemly. Unseemly or not, in grand profusion, the apostle Paul, writing under the inspiration of the Spirit, uses it—perhaps as effectively as anyone could. Clinical types need to rethink their own practices, it would seem.

Emotion, however, is not enough. The counselee must understand and follow those principles that lead to unity. Paul is about to set forth two fundamental principles of unity in the two verses that follow. The first: **Do nothing out of selfishness or vanity, but rather in humility consider others better than yourselves** (v. 3). You are not left with vague, uncertain advice to give your counselee. Here is explicit direction about how to achieve and maintain unity. The counselee must learn to stop putting himself first. He must cast aside selfish ways and leave vanity behind. Instead, he must concentrate on how he may promote the good of his fellow Christians. Looking not for their faults (most counselees are adept at that), he must learn how to discover their excellencies (he may not be very sharp at this; you may need to train him to do so through multiple assignments). And, whenever he does, he must put them forward instead of himself. This must not be done as a gimmick; the endeavor must be sincere. But like every new thing, the counselee may, at first, find it difficult and awkward. That will change as he earnestly persists in following this biblical command. He will soon find that he is becoming a very different person. Nothing draws two people together like helping one another to become more proficient, or find new avenues of service, in areas in which they already excel. And it will soon be true that bitterness and rancor will be replaced by love and concern for others. Conversely, selfish behavior coupled with the demeaning of others in order to make one's self look better,

Philippians 2

4   Each of you should not only look out for his own interests but also the interests of others.

5   You must think about yourselves what Christ Jesus thought about Himself.

---

turns out to achieve just the opposite. One soon learns to steer away from such persons. Thus unity is broken.

The second principle appears in verse 4. And Paul considers it so vital that he develops it in the remainder of the verses in this section. The principle is to *put the concerns of others above your own.* That may be easy enough when Joe is sick. You lay aside your interests and go to see him in the hospital. You pray for him. But what about when all is going well with Joe—perhaps, you even think, *too* well! Can you still be friendly and give thanks when Joe gets the raise his family needs—even when you didn't get one? Are you willing to take off a Saturday and help Bill move when you could be mowing your own lawn and, now, it will mean you must take several late evenings to do the work? Putting the affairs of others before yourself doesn't mean neglecting your own family; it means sacrificing some of your own interests. Counselees who reach out to others in a proper, biblical way rarely find themselves at odds with those others whom they serve. Notice, I said "in a proper biblical way." You can get into a peck of trouble if you are looking for it! If you seek to serve with a jaundiced eye you will soon see things that are wrong with your neighbor: "he wasn't grateful; he didn't thank me" or "he needs help less than I do." Your attitude must be to please Christ, regardless of what your neighbor does or doesn't do. Bottom line: *God* is the One you are serving. Your attitude toward your neighbor will be more compassionate, more loving when you serve, not to get some return, but out of gratitude to Christ for what He has done for you.

In verse 5, Paul says, **Have this mind in you that was in Christ Jesus.** That is to say, "Think the way Jesus does." Now this is not some philosophical idea that Paul is inserting here, out of context. No. He is still addressing the problem of unity in view of the split in the Church. The material that follows, though based on profound theological reflection about the nature of the incarnation, nevertheless, is used in an extremely practical way. That is something that every counselor must learn. He must know his doctrine well. But it is not doctrine that he learns for doctrine's sake, as some watery-eyed intellectual in a seminary may learn it. It is doctrine-*cum*-application that he should learn. Every doctrine has practi-

> 6 He, while existing in the form of God, didn't consider His equality with God something to be graspingly held on to at all costs,
> 7 but, instead he emptied Himself, taking the form of a slave, becoming like a human being.
> 8 Being found in human appearance, He humbled Himself, becoming obedient even to the point of death—death by a cross!

cal applications to life. There is no abstract doctrine in the Scriptures. While one may learn the fine points of doctrine in an abstract manner, it is imperative that he take the next step and discover what implications those doctrines have for life. As we look at the next few verses we shall see how Paul did just that.

What then does it mean to think the way Christ did? It means to think in such a way that your actions follow His. Paul is enlarging on the second point of unity—putting others before one's self. *That is what Christ did in the incarnation.* That is the import of his statement. Like Christ—who is the greatest Example of one Who put the interests of others before His own—you should do so. He who enjoyed all the privileges of heaven, exemplified by the manifestation of His deity in glory and honor, laid that aside as He emptied Himself of it (not of His deity, but of its manifestation) and took upon Himself the form of a man. But not only of a man. He humbled Himself to become a slave. But not just a slave. He further humbled Himself to the point of death. But not only of death. He humbled Himself to die the ignominious death of the worst sort of criminal. That is how far Christ went in order to save you!

Now, having explained what it meant for Christ to take on the form of a human being and become one of us (vv. 6-8), how far He went in humbling Himself for you, Paul says, "Have the same mind that He did." Think about the interests of others as He did. In other words, be willing to go every bit as far as you can, the way He did, for others. He did what He did for you, putting your interests before His own; you do the same for one another at Philippi.

This is a powerful passage to use in humbling counselees who think that others should do everything for them, while they do nothing for others. What makes it so powerful is the heavy theological content in it. It is powerful because while it teaches what Christ—the holy, harmless, Son of God—did for wretched sinners, it condemns any others who think they are above putting themselves out for another. Theology is essential to good counseling. Everything one does in counseling has theological

Philippians 2

9   As a result, God highly exalted Him and gave to Him the name above all names,
10 so that at this name that He gave Jesus **every knee** of heavenly beings and earthly beings and beings under the earth **should bend**,
11 and every tongue should confess that Jesus Christ is LORD to the glory of God the Father.

---

implications. All of the counseling material that you encounter in my books grows out of theology—the theology that I believe the Bible teaches. And, at every point in developing principles and practices of counseling I have tested them against the theological understanding of Scripture that I hold. It is my goal to say nothing about counseling that is inconsistent with my theology, and, at the same time, to discover as many of the implications and applications of that theology for counseling that I can. Because the Bible is a Book that has theological teaching everywhere behind every statement, even when it is not explicitly spelled out as it is here, all that one does in counseling is theological. It is those who do not realize this who, unwittingly, accept all sorts of pagan counseling principles and practices that are inconsistent with biblical theology, thinking that they are doing no harm by this.

Verse 6 says that Christ didn't consider that His privileges must be **graspingly held on to at all costs.** What a perfect characterization of those in counseling who stubbornly cling to their own interests instead of putting the interests of others first. It is a vivid description of selfishness. The selflessness of the Lord Jesus, in contrast, is the model for us. If, in situations where counselees manifest strong, selfish willfulness, you turn to this discussion by Paul, you will be able to stop them in their tracks. Why not make the point by asking, "If Christ thought the way you are thinking, would you ever have been saved?" That fact, pressed to its full upon a true believer, ought to bring him to repentance and soften his hard heart. If it does not, there may be real question whether his profession of faith in Christ is credible.

Verses 9 through 11 tell us that because of Jesus' willingness to humble Himself, **God highly exalted Him** above every other man, giving Him (as man) the title **Lord**. And, the prerogatives that go with that title were handed over to Him (as man) as well: verses 10 and 11.

God recognizes those who, in this life, put others' interests before their own. They will be rewarded even as Christ was (that is the obvious import of vv. 9-11). And when counselees object, as some do, "It is hard

Christian Counselor's Commentary

> 12 So then, my dear friends, just as you have always obeyed before (not only when I am present, but even more so when I am absent), work out your own solution to the problem with fear and trembling.
> 13 since it is God Who is producing in you both the willingness and the ability to do the things that please Him.

to wait for recognition and reward till the life to come," you may observe, again with theological precision and power, that even Jesus had to wait till beyond His earthly life for this. Why should we think we are entitled to more than He?

Theology, as I said, is essential. I suggest that, if you do not already own it, you should obtain a copy of Louis Berkhof's *Systematic Theology* and familiarize yourself with it from stem to stern. It will serve you well not only as a corrective to incorporating practices that are out of accord with biblical theology, but in thinking through biblical approaches that are backed with solid theology, to use in responding to counselees. Paul's use of theology in a practical way, as we have seen it here, is exemplary of much of what a counselor should do. Note, in passing, that when you so use theology, you not only address the counselee's thinking and behavior in a powerful manner, but, at the same time, you teach facts about God, man and the world that every Christian should know anyway. Such a use, thereby, has a double effect for good.

Verses 12 and 13 complete the section begun at 1:27. The words, **so then**, with which verse 12 begins, indicate that Paul has been arguing a point throughout and that he is now about to draw a conclusion to his argument. The rest of the verse, in which he speaks of obeying whether he is present or not corresponds to the beginning of the section in which there is very similar language. What Paul is trying to do is to make such a powerful argument for unity that it will be effected whether he, personally, is able to come and see that it occurs or not. In any case, it is not likely that he would be able to come prior to the reception of this letter, so, he wants unity to occur without having to superintend the process. So, his appeal is **work out the solution** to the problem of the split on your own. Obviously, Paul is not saying save yourselves; he was writing to "saints" who were already saved. Nor is he saying (according to the cutesy little sayings of some), "work out what God has worked in" or "bring to bloom the flower that God formed," or anything like that. This verse has been grossly misinterpreted. He is concluding an argument for unity. He says, "I want you to solve the problem of disunity on your own according to the

Philippians 2

14 Do everything without grumbling or arguing,

---

principles I have just finished enunciating to you. Listen to what I say, not only as you do when I am present with you, but even more so since I cannot be there to help. On your own—that is, without my help—work out your own salvation (deliverance, solution to your problem)." Already, in verse 19 of the first chapter of the letter, he used the word **salvation** to mean getting through a difficult problem successfully; here he does the same.

There comes a time when every counselee has to be thrown back on his own resources. He cannot go on forever allowing the counselor to call the shots. To begin with, the counselor may ride herd heavily to see that biblical practices are followed. But, at length, the counselee must be turned loose. That is when he must obey biblical injunctions his counselor taught him even more than before. Good counselors, like Paul, emphasize this.

"But you said he must be turned loose to rely on his own resources. Is that right? Should a Christian ever rely on *himself*?" I didn't say that. What are his resources? Verse 13 tells us: God, Who, in the Person of the Holy Spirit dwelling within, gives both the incentive and the power to accomplish whatever He has required in His Word. Your counselee is never really alone. The Spirit dwells within. In harmony with His Word, He works within to enable him to do what is necessary. Counselees must be taught to rely on their resources—the very resources of God.

When we turn to the next 5 verses, we have something of a unit that, while not a part of the above plea for unity, nevertheless grows out of it and is appropriate to it. Of course, in bringing about unity it is important not to **grumble and argue**. But the problem exists even where basic unity prevails. God loves a cheerful worker; not one who does what is required, but grumps about it and causes trouble for others when he does get around to doing it. Counselees must make a commitment at some point in counseling not only to do what God wants them to do but also to do it in the spirit of willingness, attempting to maintain good relationships with those who are involved. These two problems—grumbling and arguing—are characteristic of many counselees, perhaps most. The counselor, therefore, must be on guard for the problem and address it early on in the sessions.

Christian Counselor's Commentary

> 15 so that you may be blameless and upright, God's spotless children in the midst of a crooked and perverted generation, among whom you shine like stars in the world,

How does one stop **grumbling**? Not by a mere effort of will. Rather, he must learn gratitude. If Christ was willing to bear the cross, surely he can bear some difficulty of far less magnitude. The emphasis should not be on the problem, or on the counselee but on Jesus Christ. The task to be performed, about which one is likely to grumble, may not be a pleasant one. The counselee does not have to work up some sort of artificial enthusiasm for it. What he must do, however, is to recognize that he is working for Christ (not for a boss or a husband, etc.). And he must become enthusiastic about pleasing Him, even if it means to do so he must engage in some onerous task. His enthusiasm must be *for the Lord!*

What is it that makes the difference between a believer and an unbeliever? Just this—the believer is always cheerful—even rejoices (as Paul says)—when working at tasks. The unbeliever doesn't understand this, because he works for that ungrateful boss or that lazy husband. But, as we said, the believer works for the Lord. That is how work should be done; how it was done before the fall and how it is done by grateful believers now. The world, however, has twisted and warped attitudes toward work as well as attitudes toward everything else. So, when a Christian joyfully engages in his work, he stands out in a world that cares only about paychecks, overtime and retirement. He, being **spotless, blameless and upright** in all that he does day by day, bears a significant testimony to those who are lost. In a world of workaday darkness, he **shines like a star** (v. 15).

Shining like a star in the darkness that pervades most workplaces is an ideal to hold out to counselees. It may be something they have never thought about. Well, if not, it is about time. We shall say more about work when coming to the passage in Colossians 3 that so powerfully addresses the subject, but here, the idea of purity and joy at work over against the darkness of the generation in which ones pursues his work, is an ideal not to be missed. Problems at work are among the most frequent that are brought to the counselor. Because of this, the counselor ought at all times to have this section of Scripture ready to bring up short those who incessantly complain and get into arguments with others at work.

How does one keep from **arguing**? Well, not all argument is wrong, of course. There is a time and place for productive argument. But heated

Christian Counselor's Commentary

> 16 holding out the Word of life, so that in Christ's Day I may be able to boast that I didn't run in vain or labor in vain.
> 17 But even if I am poured out as a drink offering on the sacrifice and service of your faith, I am glad, and glad together with all of you.
> 18 Similarly, you should be glad, and be glad with me.

argument—which is what this passage doubtless is talking about—is another thing. One must learn to use the soft answer to turn away wrath. He must also remember that his testimony before the lost is at stake (as the next verse intimates). And he must, at all times, remember that it is the Lord for whom he is working. If he cannot convince others that he is right, surely the Lord can do so. He must not necessarily win every argument. He has a resource to which to turn, in cases where he can't, that the world does not know about. He can take the entire problem to the Lord in prayer. Then, having done all he can in a proper and kindly (non-argumentative) way, he can leave the problem with the Lord to solve in His own time and way. That is the way closure often comes for the Christian.

When he lives a joyful life at work, not complaining or arguing, he is able to **hold forth the Word** (message) that, when believed, brings life. Others will listen to the gospel when he presents it. If they can see what the faith has done for him, they will, in times of need or crisis, be likely to turn to him for help. And, says Paul, in the day when I see Christ, I will be able to say my efforts were not in vain. Again, the personal note in a letter in which Paul felt close to those to whom he was writing. See above.

And, says Paul, even if I die at the hand of Nero, I shall rejoice in this, that I served you faithfully in the process. And, I want you not to mourn, but to **be glad along with me** (vv. 17, 18). So, learn to be happy, learn to be glad, learn to rejoice no matter what happens. It's all in the Lord's hands. This attitude toward work and toward life in general (in the last two verses Paul broadens his scope of thought) is precisely the one needed by most counselees. Many take themselves too seriously. The world will cave in if they should not get their way. The fact is, Paul says, if I die, that too should be a joyful experience for us since Christ does all things well in His providential working. Even Paul didn't think of himself as indispensable. If Counselees can be brought to the place where they see that God will go on running His world His way whether or not their desires are fulfilled, they will begin to acquire an attitude of rejoicing in whatever comes to pass. This is not easy, it does not mean forsaking con-

Christian Counselor's Commentary

> **19** Now I hope in the Lord Jesus to sent Timothy to you shortly so that I may be cheered by knowing the facts about you.
> 20 I have nobody else who shares my attitude, who genuinely cares about your interests.
> 21 All the others pursue their own interests, not the interests of Christ Jesus.
> 22 But you know his character, that he has served with me to spread the good news like a child works with a father.

victions or failure to work toward goals, but it does mean that, ultimately, we must learn to rejoice in the will of God—whatever that may be!

In the remainder of the chapter, two persons are singled out and discussed. One is Timothy, whom Paul expected to send to Philippi in the near future, probably as a follow-up to this letter. The other is Epaphroditus, who was a representative of the Philippian church, sent to minister to Paul. He too was returning to Philippi, and may have been the bearer of this epistle. What Paul says of these two men is instructive of how well he worked with others and what he thought was necessary to a profitable ministry that honored Christ and was a blessing to churches. He holds both men in high esteem. Consequently, the counselor, Himself, may learn from Paul's incidental comments what God approves in those who minister in His Name.

Timothy was going to Philippi soon, and Paul hoped that he would send back word about what he found there that would cheer him. This was a hint that he expected the church to take heed to his letter and change the things that needed to be changed. He wanted Timothy to find a church that had worked out its own solution to the problem of disunity. But just in case matters had not improved, or had gotten worse, Paul assures them that Timothy has not only full authority to minister in Paul's name, but that he **shares** Paul's own views and perspectives. He is a man who can be trusted. He will not undermine his ministry, but will support it at all points. There is too much rivalry going on in the church of Christ among those who serve Him. And undermining is a large part of how that rivalry is expressed. But, like Paul, Timothy is outgoing, concerned about others more than about himself. He is an example, lesser than the Lord, of course, of one who is more concerned about the affairs of others than those pertaining to himself. Others have divided loyalties (v. 21). As a counselor, are you willing to put yourself out for your counselees? Are you more interested in their affairs than in your own? Or is it merely a job for you? The "merely a job" attitude is what permeates the Christian

Philippians 2

23 It is he, then, whom I hope to send just as soon as I see how things turn out for me
24 (and I am confident in the Lord that shortly I myself shall come also).
25 I have considered it necessary to send to you Epaphroditus, my brother and co-worker, and fellow soldier, and your messenger and minister to my need,
26 because he had been longing for all of you and has been distressed because you heard that he was sick.
27 Indeed, he was sick, and came near to death, but God had mercy on him (not on him only, but also on me, lest I should have grief upon grief!).
28 so then, I am all the more eager to send him so that you may be glad over seeing him again, and my grief may be lessened.

---

counseling field today. And, it is destructive to true ministry, which as much as anything else is a giving of one's self to those to whom he ministers. Until you move out of the "job" mode into the ministry mode, you will counsel ineffectively.

The close relationship between Paul and Timothy is mentioned in verse 22. That is the way older and younger ministers of the gospel should pair up. When they do not, there is always strife and strain. As soon as it was clear to Paul whether he would be released from prison or put to death for his faith, he would send Timothy to Philippi. But, release looked favorable. If, indeed, he would be released in the near future, not only would he send Timothy, Paul says "I myself will come too!" (v. 24).

Verses 25 through 30 extol the virtues and faithfulness of **Epaphroditus.** He has been longing to go home to Philippi, so Paul wants to send him back. He is a faithful Christian **brother, co-worker and fellow soldier.** Somehow Epaphroditus had been in the trenches with Paul, fighting side by side for the gospel. We only wish we had more information. He also had a lot to do with the propagation of the gospel in Rome. He had been more than faithful. In Paul's need, Epaphroditus had been sent by the church at Philippi to bring the gift and to minister to Paul. This he had done in an exemplary manner. Paul wanted the Philippian church to know so. In the course of his activities at Rome, however, he had been taken seriously ill (v. 27). People in the church at home learned about this and were concerned. He is OK now, but returning himself would be the best way to confirm the fact. Paul says God was merciful to Epaphroditus and healed him, and that this was a **mercy** to him as well. If he had died, Paul would have only one more **grief** piled on top of the many others he bore. So, he says, I'm glad to send him to you so that you too can rejoice in his

Christian Counselor's Commentary

29 Therefore receive him with all gladness in the Lord, and hold such persons in honor
30 because for Christ's work he came close to death, risking his life to make up for your lack of service to me.

---

healing and so that you can honor him as he deserves. He came close to death because of his ministry for Christ, **risking his life** so that he could make up for the inability of the rest of the congregation to minister to Paul.

Have you ever laid your life on the line for Christ, counselor? Would you, should the occasion arise? Do you deserve to be honored for your work for Him? It may be instructive to read these words from time to time to compare and contrast the ministry that you carry on with that of Paul, Timothy and Epaphroditus.

So ends the second chapter. It is a powerful piece of writing, varying widely in content. There is the appeal stemming from a theological understanding of the incarnation to the evaluation of the faithful ministries of Paul's cohorts. There is much more in the chapter than I can take the time and space here to discuss. But a full study of it will yield many precious truths that are useful for all Christians in general and for Christian counselors in particular. I urge you to make such a study in the near future.

CHAPTER 3

1 Finally, my brothers, be glad in the Lord. To write the same things to you is not in order to bore myself, but it's for your safety.
2 Look out for the dogs, look out for the wicked workers, look out for the slashers!

Chapter 3 begins with an exhortation to gladness—**rejoice *in the Lord.*** There is no reason otherwise to rejoice. Life is hard; the consequences of sin are difficult to bear. Imprisonment, and all that Paul suffered ought to have made him a cynical, miserable person if circumstances were actually the cause of such attitudes. Yet he was anything but. Here he is, in prison, encouraging the Philippians to rejoice. Such rejoicing centers on what God is doing, not what is happening to me. That is how your counselee, in the midst of trials and tribulations can, nevertheless rejoice. God's Name is honored, His Word is spreading regardless of the fact that I am suffering; so rejoice! Thus no one can take your peace and joy from you. Try putting it that way to the next, cynical, complaining counselee and see what happens.

Paul has said these things before. They are not new. He is not repeating them only to **bore** himself! No. He does so for the **safety** of the church. He is concerned about them. So, he does not hesitate to repeat things it is necessary for them to hear over and over again. One of those things is the ever-threatening danger presented by the Judaizing faction that has been dogging his steps, destroying the infant churches he began. They wanted Christians to become Jews before professing faith in Christ and said that Paul's message (the gospel) was incomplete (for details, see the Book of Galatians). They are **dogs**, says Paul, scavengers (the dog was the street cleaner of the day). To call one a dog, then, was a strong insult. Paul doesn't hesitate to use powerful language to describe the errorists who were perverting the gospel. Indeed, he also calls them **wicked workers and mutilators** (literally, **slashers**). They were ever ready with their knives to circumcise gentile Christians in order to lead them into a works-ceremony salvation by attempting to keep the law.

It is not wrong to speak strongly of those who pervert the truth of God's Word—not to be nasty, but for the **safety** of the church. Paul didn't want the Philippians to fall prey to the Judaizers should they appear in Philippi as they had elsewhere. So, he warns them ahead of time. Often, not only heresy, but other ways in which Christians can become prey to

Christian Counselor's Commentary

> 3 We are the circumcision, we who are worshiping God by the Spirit and boasting in Christ Jesus and not putting our confidence in the flesh,
> 4 although I have reason for confidence in the flesh. If anybody else thinks that he has reason for putting confidence in the flesh, I have more:
> 5 circumcised the eighth day, from the race of Israel, the tribe of Benjamin, a Hebrew from Hebrew lineage; with reference to the law, a Pharisee;
> 6 with reference to zeal, a persecutor of the church; with reference to righteousness, by the law blameless.
> 7 But, whatever was gain to me I have counted loss for Christ's sake.

nefarious influences, must be mentioned before they encounter the problem. To be safe, counselors must warn counselees about the many pitfalls into which they may fall in attempting to carry out an assignment. For instance, a counselor may say, "Now when you go back and confess your sin and ask for forgiveness, don't mention anything wrong that the one *you* wronged did. Focus on your sin alone. Otherwise, the two may be confused and you will do more harm than good." Keeping an eye out for all such pitfalls that relate to particular problems and solutions is not only prudent but necessary if you plan to carry on effective counseling. And, it doesn't hurt a bit to repeat one's self about these pitfalls from time to time in counseling.

After all, who is it that represents **the circumcision** anyway? The true circumcision is in Christ. All those who worship Him by means of the Spirit Who has made that possible, are the circumcision. As everything else that happened in the life of Christ is attributed to those who believe in Him (His death, burial, resurrection, seated in the heavenlies, etc.) so too is His circumcision. If you are in Christ, you are counted before God as having lived His life and, therefore, having been circumcised in Him. It is a spiritual circumcision, of which Paul speaks—not a fleshly one that has no power, and in which he would not place his confidence (for more details, see Colossians 2, where circumcision in Christ is more fully discussed). The circumcision party boasted in the number of Christians they could get to submit to physical circumcision; Paul says he boasts in Christ.

Now, says Paul, if anyone ever had reason to place his **confidence** in physical circumcision for salvation, it would be I. Indeed, I can outclass these slashers if it comes to that. Listen to my pedigree (which he recites in vv. 5, 6). I have all the credentials they seek, and then some. After all, I was even more **zealous** than they, **persecuting the church** of Jesus Christ. And, in terms of doing what the Pharisees required, I was **blame-**

Philippians 3

8   Indeed, to put it even more accurately, I count everything as loss compared to the priceless privilege of knowing Christ Jesus my Lord, for Whose sake I have suffered total loss, and count what I have lost garbage, in order that I may gain Christ
9   and be found in Him, not having a righteousness of my own that stems from the law but, instead, that which comes through faith in Christ, the righteousness from God based upon faith,

---

less. But all to no avail; righteousness does not come by the law, but by grace.

But now, he says, **whatever was gain to me I have counted loss for Christ's sake**. In that statement you find the spirit of the true Christian who realizes that he is nothing, has nothing to offer to God to commend himself and is wholly dependent on Jesus for life and godliness. It is a statement that ought often to be repeated to counselees who think that because of their "exemplary" lifestyle, God should exempt them from difficulties. Anything, and everything of one's own doing must be **counted loss** as you compare what is on the other side of the ledger: Jesus Christ. Indeed, Paul goes on to say, in even more dramatic terms, I count *everything* loss when compared to **the priceless privilege of knowing Christ**. And, as a matter of fact, all that I had I did lose—totally. But I count all those things that I trusted in before, which could never save, but dung, **garbage**. So, why be concerned if I have lost them?

I am interested in gaining Christ in all His fullness, found to be in Him, **having a righteousness** that He has provided, rather than my own, a righteousness based not on works of the law but on faith in Jesus (vv. 7-9). Here, in these verses, Paul speaks as if he were an accountant figuring up gains and losses. In laying aside all the supposed virtues of my past, he figures, I have lost nothing worthwhile and in trusting in Christ, I have gained the greatest possible wealth. It is a mighty good trade! Does your counselee think this way about gaining the righteousness of Christ? Do you? If you have the same spirit of faith that the apostle evidences here, doubtless, you will communicate it to your counselees. Make sure that you do rather than putting yourself on a pedestal. It is all too easy for a counselor, upon whom people depend for help to develop an attitude about his own ability and value. If he is successful, as most biblical counselors are, the temptation to boast in and depend on one's own merits is even greater. Watch out for this subtle trap. Be wary every time anyone praises you for the help you have given. Remember, anything worthwhile

Christian Counselor's Commentary

> 10 and in order that I may know Him and the power of His resurrection and participation in His sufferings, being conformed to His death,
> 11 that I might somehow be in a condition of resurrection from the dead.
> **12** Not that I have already received all of this or that I have already been made perfect, but I pursue it in the hope of laying hold of it, since I was laid hold of by Christ Jesus for this.
> 13 Brothers, I do not consider myself to have laid hold of it yet, but there is one thing I am doing: forgetting the things that are behind and stretching forward toward the things that are before me,

---

that you have imparted to another is only because you first received it from Christ. He is the One to Whom all glory must be given. Paul's attitude in this place is of importance; read it over and over again every time you are tempted to get a big head!

Indeed, Paul wanted to go farther. He wanted to know Christ so well that he could experience the **power** that raised Him from the dead and even understand what the **sufferings** of Christ were like by participating in the same kind of sufferings Christ endured. If he was **conformed** to Christ's death (i.e., all that led to it) he would be satisfied, because then, he could be able to experience a **resurrection** like His.

It is hard to know all that Paul meant in these verses, but one thing stands out. He was not satisfied, even though he had suffered many things for Christ's sake; there was more to be experienced (cf. v. 12). He knows he has many failings—he is not yet perfect. He is no sinless perfectionist! He, therefore, doesn't know fully what it is like to be raised to fullness of life. So, he **pursues** the goal with vigor in expectation of attaining it some day when he goes to be with Christ. Then, he will **lay hold of it**; after all, he was laid hold of for this very reason. Counselees who think they are pretty hot stuff, and all others in their purview are not so good, need a good dose of the third chapter of Philippians. Verse 12, in particular, is useful for exposing the pitiful amount of spiritual progress they have made. If Paul, who served so faithfully and accomplished so much, could write this way about himself, how much more so should we recognize the great distance we are from laying hold of all there is in Christ!

Then, having recognized one's distance from the goal, verse 13 becomes pertinent. Even though we are so far off from the goal of perfection, there is no reason to give up. With Paul, **forgetting** the accomplishments of our past (they were worthless anyway as Paul says), we must make it our highest priority ("one thing I am doing") to **stretch forward to the things that are before me**. The picture is of a runner racing toward

Philippians 3

14 I pursue the goal, for the prize of God's high calling in Christ Jesus.

15 So then, as many of us as are mature must think this, and if you think otherwise about anything, God will reveal this to you also.

16 Nevertheless let us walk on the same level that we have attained.

---

the goal, stretching every muscle to attain it. Paul has not given up the race. Nor should you or your counselee. It is all too easy to become discouraged. Counseling is not very pleasant at times. Difficult things must be done; hard decisions must be made. Often things must get worse before they get better. But you are both in the race. Therefore, no matter how much the muscles may ache, stretch them forth to attain the goal. Run for all you are worth!

There is a prize at the end (v. 14) for those who finish the race. The Savior Himself will give it to you as He summons you up to the highest point in the stadium where He sits. Keep the finish line in view, but also think about the prize that awaits beyond it. The goal and the prize; that is what Paul is running for. The goal is to know Christ in all His fullness; the prize is to hear His word "Well done, you good and faithful servant." With the goal and the prize before you, it will be possible to endure all that counseling involves—for both the counselee *and the counselor!*

Moving to the next section (vv. 15-21), verse 15 is transitional. If you haven't been of a mind to **think** this way, if you have any growth in Christ, if you consider yourself mature, then, says Paul, start thinking like this. This is not simply for me; it is for you too. And, if it isn't yet clear what I am talking about, God will make it clear in time (15^b). That is a wonderful promise: that God will clarify those things that are not yet plain. But, of course, if you do not read the Bible as you should (in an in-depth manner) this will not happen. God gives no special revelation today; His Word has been given to enlighten you about what you need to know. He will work through that Word to teach you those things you need to understand. That is a marvelous promise. It is an encouragement for every believer to read the Scriptures and to faithfully attend a church where the Bible is expounded and applied to his life. Every time a counselor takes on a counseling case, he should early on insist that the counselee engage in regular Bible study and be faithful in attendance on the preaching of the Word. That is minimal background for the counseling that is done. "But," says your counselee, "I don't think God has revealed to me everything yet." Well, that is no excuse. Tell him, "You must live up to what you have learned" (v. 16). The counselee is to walk according to the knowledge he

Christian Counselor's Commentary

> 17 Brothers, together become imitators of me, and take notice of those who also are walking as you have an example in us;
> 18 there are many of whom I told you often (and now again I tell you weeping), who walk as enemies of Christ's cross.
> 19 Their end is destruction, their god is their stomach, and their glory is in their shame; they are those who think only about earthly things.

does have; not that which he doesn't. The level of understanding of God's will and the level of obedience in his lifestyle should not vary. But, of course, they do. None of us lives even according to the meager light he has. Well, then, there is still plenty of room for growth. Check out the understanding the counselee possesses and hold him to that as his standard of life, while teaching him to grow beyond it.

Having mentioned the Christian's **walk** (his manner, or style of life) Paul develops that thought in verses 17 and 18. First, he suggests that there is much that can be learned not only from the teaching one receives, but also from the implementation of that teaching as it is exhibited in the lives of others who are faithfully walking (conducting their lives) in the truth. Paul says, you can imitate me, and it will be well for you to take notice of others who are walking in ways committed to Christ (v. 17). Biblical writers never tire of talking about the force of **example**. After all, that is largely how the Bible itself is written—as teaching given in connection with the lives of the saints. But, there is also the opportunity to learn from those who are **enemies** of Christ; those whose lifestyles are antithetical to Paul's. This is important: "I have stressed it before, but now, again, I tell you (while weeping for what they have done to destroy the church and disgrace the Name of our Lord) there are many such persons. Be on your guard."

These persons are enemies of **the cross**. Their interests are in themselves; they do not eat to live, they live to eat. **Their god is their stomach!** They **glory** in the very things of which they ought to be ashamed. Their focus is on this life alone and what they can attain in it. They have no thought about the life to come. Many counselees either fit this description or run with those who do. You will never hear a word about glorying in Christ from them; their interests are solely in what they can obtain here in this earthly life. Some may not be Christians at all (as these enemies of Christ's cross surely were not). Others may be very worldly Christians. If they are of the former sort, apart from the gospel, there is no hope for them: **their end is destruction**. They live for this life only, and when it

20 But our citizenship is in the heavens, from which country we await the coming of a Savior, the Lord Jesus Christ,
21 Who will transform our degraded bodies, making them conform to his glorious body, by the power that enables Him to subject all things to Himself.

---

comes to an end, all they lived for also ends.

Warn those who claim to be Christians if they are living purely for physical satisfaction that they are perilously close to destruction. Some may need to reconsider the genuineness of their salvation. People like this ordinarily do not trust in Christ but in their own efforts; they are enemies of grace, and therefore of His cross. Check out their faith in the cross, their recognition of grace as the impetus for their salvation and their concern to live for the Lord out of gratitude.

These people think only of earthly things; the true Christian is a **citizen of heaven** (v. 20) with all its joys and privileges. His mind rises to think of heaven often during the day; he looks forward to the coming of Christ Who now dwells in the heavenly **country** and Who will **come** from there to take him home. He is looking forward to the day when Christ will transform the **bodies** we now have, ravaged by sin, and habituated to act in sinful ways. At His second coming the Lord will give us **glorious bodies** that will conform to His glorified body (presumably with all the abilities of that post-resurrection body that could pass through walls, etc.). He has power to do this. He will **subject** sin and its effects, now so prevalent and so obvious to us, to himself, eliminating it and all its nefarious effects from us forever!

That is a glorious hope. Persons ill, disadvantaged physically, crippled, and the like can have no greater one. It must be mentioned again and again in counseling them. But it is a glorious fact for all true Christians—one that keeps them from fixing on this world alone and helping them to transfix their attention on the Savior and the world to come.

Christian Counselor's Commentary

CHAPTER 4

> 1 So, my brothers whom I hold dear and greatly desire to see, my joy and winner's wreath, stand firm in the Lord, dear friends.
> 2 I urge Euodia and Syntyche to think alike in the Lord.

We turn now to the last chapter of this interesting letter. In it, perhaps, is the passage to which counselors will turn most frequently—the section on worry. But first, there is also other important material. Finally, Paul comes out and openly challenges the women who were the heads of two factions in the church that, among other matters, occasioned the writing of this letter. We have seen how Paul tactfully approached the problem of division in a positive manner, stressing the need for unity and the principles and practices which, if accepted and followed, would bring it off. Now, he openly names names.

Disunity was causing instability in the congregation. Paul urges each member to **stand firm in the Lord** (they could not in their own wisdom and strength). He did not want this church to come apart at the seams. He loved them dearly. Notice how this affection for the members of the Philippian church emerges from time to time in the letter. Here, he calls them not only **brothers**, but **my joy and winners wreath**. Like the valuable prize won at an Olympic event, the Philippian church was a crown to the great apostle. They were a constant source of joy to him. And they were **dear friends**. It is hard to imagine the impact of these words as they were read to the congregation on the first occasion after the receipt of the letter. There was the warmth, but immediately following, there is straight talk as well. Picture Euodia and Syntyche sitting there, glaring at one another over whatever trifles had separated them. The first verse of the fourth chapter is read. Then the congregation hears, **I urge Euodia**... Can you see Syntyche look at her with a sneer ("Paul is going to tell her off")? But the reader continues, **and Syntyche**... Now Euodia is looking at her! They are equally at fault, and must equally hear this exhortation which pertains to both. There is no order of preference; as in English, he simply refers to them in alphabetical order.

How important it is to get down to brass tacks. You cannot skirt around the facts of a counseling case. There are real people involved. They must be singled out and dealt with specifically. Abstractions and generalizations will solve few problems. Yet, it is quite important to set

Philippians 4

3 Yes, I also ask you, who have shown yourself to be genuine in bearing the yoke together with me, to help these women, who struggled together with me for the good news, along with Clement and the rest of my co-workers whose names are in the Book of Life.

---

the stage for direct confrontation. That is where prior generalizations are of significance. In his discussion of unity, Paul did just that. When he told them they would have to work out the solution to the problem of disunity in their church, he was addressing the entire congregation, because they would all have to play a part in doing so. However, it is now time to address the two ringleaders of the factions (we don't know how large they were) themselves.

And, it is also a matter of some importance to call on the teaching elder of the church to become involved in settling the dispute. He is not named, but is identified as one who has shown himself in the past to be genuine in **bearing the yoke together with me** (i.e., in carrying out the ministry of the Word as I do). Paul knows what kind of man he is and has high hopes that he will be able to help. Presumably, for whatever reason (perhaps fear that he would do more harm than good), up until the present he had played too meager a part in dealing with the problem. It was his task and responsibility to **help these women**.

Obviously, here is a call for counseling. It is not enough for ministers of the gospel to preach the truth, they must enforce it as well. But, at least in the early stages of that enforcement, it is their duty to bring **help** to those who are going astray. There are ministers who will tell you that their "strength is in preaching, not in counseling." In most cases, the claim can be fairly disputed. The two tasks go together (cf. Acts 20:20; see especially Calvin's commentary on this verse). It is doubtful whether any preaching that is not coupled with the individual and practical application of Scripture in counseling is effective—no matter how informative it may prove otherwise. And the converse is true too.

At any rate, the pastor of the Philippian church was to help the two warring women, so that once again they would be able to carry out work for the Lord as they had in the past. Interesting, isn't it, that they had been faithful workers together with Paul in times past: they **struggled together with me for the good news.** Paul has not forgotten. He recalls the former days as an incentive to unity and more of the same in the future. What he is specifically referring to is unknown to us, but clearly known to them; it is the work done in conjunction with the efforts of Clement and the other

Christian Counselor's Commentary

> **4** Be glad in the Lord always; I shall say it again, be glad!
> 5 Let your leniency be known to everybody. The Lord is near.

co-workers in Christ who are true believers and destined for eternal life.

Perhaps it is among those who have worked the hardest that most problems arise. Apathetic Christians are not so likely to tangle with one another. After all, they care less, have fewer "convictions!" As counselors, do not be surprised when you discover that those who come are often of this sort. If they are not doing something for the Lord, there is little likelihood that they will get in one another's way. Pastors must constantly keep things on an even keel in the church as they *work with workers*.

Those three opening verses in the chapter are quite enough. Paul now turns to other things. Verses 4 and 5 seem transitional. Though there are difficulties, don't worry. Instead—rejoice in the Lord (not in what men do or say)—always. There is no situation, no matter how bleak, in which you cannot rejoice, since you know that all things work together for good to those who love Christ. Even as this split was occurring, God was at work, bringing good out of evil: this tremendous letter, for instance, would not have been written—or at least written as we have it—if the split had not taken place. Consequently, we would be at a loss for such profound teaching on unity as we have in it. So, in spite of all, **be glad**! (v. 4)

God has not forsaken you, says Paul; Christ is near to help (cf.; 2:13), So, let's not have a Donnybrook over this problem. Solve it amiably, and in doing so, let's see **leniency**, not severity (v. 5). But the church must have been concerned about what effect the news of their division would have on the apostle in his extremity. He does not want them to **worry**. So, just as he gave them a rather full discourse on unity and how to effect it, so here he writes about worry and how to overcome it.

What does he say? Let's consider it carefully, since you will find yourself turning to this passage again and again as you help counselees overcome this most American of problems, worry.

First, notice that worry is sin (the word translated "anxiety" in many versions ought to be translated **worry**. It means, literally, "the sort of concern that tears you apart." How do we come to the conclusion that worry is sin and of what importance is it to do so? Take the second question first. It is absolutely crucial to recognize worry as sin. In sermons I have asked, "How many of you have problems with worry?" Hands go up all over the congregation. Then I ask, "How many have trouble with lying, adulterous thoughts, etc.?" Few, if any, are raised. Why is that? Because worry is the

Philippians 4

6   Don't worry about anything, but instead in everything by prayer and by petition with thanksgiving make your requests known to God,

---

acceptable sin. People don't really believe it is sin, or they would be ashamed of it as they are of these other sins.

It is important to realize that worry is sin since until it is recognized as such, counselees will not become serious about eliminating it. They will go on grinning about it as if it were inevitable, and nothing can be done about it. But, once convinced that it is a sin against God, the matter takes on a different complexion. It must go. It is a sin, because, as Matthew 6 (the other important passage on the subject) says, it is lack of trust in a loving, caring heavenly Father. If He cares for the lilies of the field and the birds of the air, he will care for you. But worrying Christians give evidence that they disbelieve this.

How may the counselor convince his counselee that worry is sin? Verse 6 is all he needs to do so. It contains two absolutes. Absolutes are not frequently encountered, but whenever they are, they should cause one to utter a sigh of relief. You don't have to decide when you may worry or when you can't; you may *never* do so, but you must *always* **pray instead**. That is the import of the words in verse 6. And this is put in the form of a *command*: "Don't worry...but instead...make your requests known to God." The matter is not optional; God expects His commands to be *obeyed*. Disobedience to God's commands is sin.

But, when you read verses 6 and 7, you will find that counselees often break in and say something like this: "I tried that but it didn't work. I prayed but I didn't get **peace**." Now, God's promises don't fail; so I know that the problem is in the counselee, not in the Bible. That means as a counselor, it is my job to discover where the counselee has failed, point this out to him and help him to rectify it.

I would begin by stressing that verse 6 is complex, not simple. It has a number of prayer requirements. First that **prayer** must always replace worry. Next, that it must be **fervent, specific and accompanied by thanksgiving.** If anywhere, it is common for counselees to go wrong by failing to give thanks for the problem. Not that you thank God for the pain or sorrow itself, of course, but for what He is accomplishing through it. If that note is not present, then prayer is one-sided. It becomes little more than a plea to remove difficulties, rather than the prayer that God's will be done in the circumstance to His glory and to the ultimate benefit of counselees and the Church. Now, it is not always easy to give thanks when one

Christian Counselor's Commentary

> 7   and God's peace that goes beyond all understanding like a sentinel will guard your hearts and your thoughts in Christ Jesus.

is in fear or pain. Often, one's nose is too close to the problem to gain any perspective on it. But there is always the fact, which every counselee should know, that God (as we saw in chapter one) is in our troubles at work bringing about something good. For that—even though it is not apparent at the moment—one may always give thanks.

You ask the counselee, "Well, did you pray?" Yes. "Did you pray fervently and specifically (as the words in v. 6 require)?" Yes. "Did you thank God for whatever it is that He is doing through the trouble?" Yes. Suppose there is no problem there; the counselee has fulfilled all the requirements of verse six. He even comments, "My pastor preached on these verses recently, and did a better job of explaining them than you are doing. And I have been trying to follow them to the nth degree. Yet, I have not received **peace** of heart or mind. What is wrong?"

Well, if there is no problem in his fulfillment of verse 6 (often there is), then you may continue as follows: "Then, how about the rest of the verses?" Huh? "I said, what about the rest of the verses that have to do with gaining peace?" I didn't know that there were any other verses. Ah! You have discovered the problem. He has been infected by the Christian disease. I discovered it, so I get to name it. I call it plaquitis (it has nothing to do with your teeth). It is the spiritual sickness that comes from reading Scripture from wall plaques!

Verses 6 and 7 are typical of the kind of verses that are ripped out of context, placed on wall plaques and never again read from the Bible. There are more verses in the context that pertain to peace: notice verse 9 is still talking about peace (**the God of peace will be with you**).

Now, there are enough Christians out of work already. We don't want to put the wall plaque people out of business. So, I have the idea; if you have the money, we can go into business making context plaques. These will hang next to the verse plaques and will contain the context from which the verses have been taken. They will have a hole the size and the shape of the verses taken out of context so that you can recognize that they fit there. We can sell them for more than the verse plaques since they are usually longer! Now, some of you are thinking of Bible wallpaper—but that's too much context!

I hope that the message in the foolishness of the previous paragraphs gets through. Many fail because they use the Bible wrongly, taking verses

Philippians 4

8 Finally, brothers, whatever is true, whatever is serious, whatever is just, whatever is pure, whatever is lovely, whatever is of good repute, if there is anything morally excellent and if there is anything praiseworthy, focus your thinking on these things.

---

out of context. This is a place in which that problem is notorious. Let's see what has been missed.

It is not enough to pray instead of worry. To empty your concerns on God is good; but that leaves the mind empty. Other worries or other sinful thoughts will rush in to fill up the space if you do not purposefully refill it yourself. Verse eight tells you how to repackage your mind. It gives criteria for determining the kinds of things upon which you ought to concentrate **your thinking**. There is no space here to develop each word, nor is there need to do so. The exegetical commentaries do that quite well. Here, the important matter is to see that one must learn to **focus his thinking** on these sorts of things. In that injunction you have God's leash law for the mind. He does not want you to allow your mind to wander all over the neighborhood, poking its nose into every garbage can that might be open.

You must train your mind so that you can control it. But that is part of the problem. Counselees will tell you that they don't know how to train or control their minds. You probably will have to help them with this. I always suggest that "one way to begin is to make a Philippians 4:8 think list to carry with you. Whenever you find your mind wandering into the wrong places, whip out your list and start thinking about the next item on the list. These should be mind-engaging items that accord with the categories in verse 8." Some counselees will tell you that they don't even know what to put on the list. So, I hand them a slip of paper and a pencil and tell them "Number lines from one to twenty. Now I will give you the first item as a freebie. Write this out under number one: 'Things to put on my Philippians 4:8 think list.' If you start thinking about that, it will get you the other 19!"

Do you really give such specific directions as that? You'd better believe it. Counselees are confused, and often not very creative. You must help them with "How to" material. It is not enough to give them the "What tos" alone.

Well, one must pray, casting all his cares on Christ, knowing (as Peter says) that He cares for you. Then, he must repackage his mind with proper thinking. Is that all? No, there is more to obtaining **the peace that passes all understanding**. Verse 9 says, those things learned by precept

Christian Counselor's Commentary

> 9   Whatever you have learned and received and heard and seen in me practice, and the God of peace will be with you.
>
> **10**   I was very happy in the Lord that now at length you have renewed your thoughts about me. You indeed did think about me, but you had no opportunity to do anything about it.

and by example that God expects you to do about your problem, must be **practiced**. "Do?" your counselee asks. "What do you mean 'do'? I prayed about it. What then must I do?" Many counselees think that prayer is punting. They pray, the ball is in God's hands; now it's up to Him to act. But God has given directions about what He wants done concerning problems. That is why we have a Bible. Sometimes, you will have to convince the counselee that he must act; especially if his mind has been filled with quietistic theology that teaches God must do it for you instead of you. I often put it this way; "You've prayed the Lord's prayer, haven't you?" Yes. "Well, have you prayed 'Give us this day our daily bread?'" Yes. "Then what you did was sit around and wait for a loaf to fall out of heaven?" Well, ...no. "Why not? You prayed, didn't you?" Yes, but there's something over in Thessalonians that says if you don't work you shouldn't eat. "Then it isn't wrong to work as well as pray?" Well, I guess not.

Notice that the verb in verse 9 is not "do" but "practice." Don't expect peace to arrive after the first attempt. When your lifestyle has begun to change with practice, then you can expect to find peace. And this peace comes not automatically, but from **God**, Who is its Source. So it does not depend on circumstances, etc., but on the proper relationship of the counselee with God.

While I shall reserve a full discussion of the last verse of Matthew 6 for the commentary on Matthew, it is significant to note here that worry is a proper concern focused on the wrong day—tomorrow instead of today. When one worries about tomorrow, he can do nothing about it. Today's problems can be faced and dealt with. Therefore, the concern should be focused on today.

Paul turns now to a discussion of the last item that occasioned the letter: the gift the Philippian church had sent to him. He wants to thank them for it, while at the same time letting them know that, ultimately, he is dependent on God alone, Who provides for every need and Who enables him to face plenty or want. He tells of his **happiness** over the concern of the church in sending him a gift to provide for his needs while in prison

Philippians 4

11 Not that I say this because of need; since I have learned, whatever condition I may be in, how to be content in doing for myself.
12 I know both how to be humbled and I know how to abound; I have learned the secret of contentment in every and all circumstances, when filled and when hungry, when in abundance or in need.
13 I can do all these things by Him Who strengthens me.
  14 Nevertheless, you did well in sharing my affliction.
15 You Philippians know too that at the beginning of the good news, when I went out from Macedonia, not a single church shared with me in this matter of giving and receiving except you alone;

(v. 10). On the first opportunity, they did so; prior to that, he realizes, they couldn't. It wasn't possible—for whatever reason there may have been. He doesn't want them to think he is criticizing them for not doing something before this. And, he doesn't want them to think that he is hinting for more. Paul is always very careful about how he deals with financial matters.

God has taught him (perhaps the hard way), and he has learned, **to be content** in whatever situation he may find himself. It is interesting that he calls this a *learning* process. Counselors can take heart in this. Even Paul had to learn. And counselees, as well as Paul, can learn. Notice, he is independent (under God: **in doing for myself**). That is important to realize: one can become independent when it is necessary to do so. He often made tents to carry on his work. He had no regular support from the churches. So counselees can learn to care for their own needs, when necessary.

Yet, according to verse 12, the learning process was difficult. It involved the **humbling** of the apostle, as well as the handling of affluence. Which is the greater temptation to sin is debatable. Both have their problems, and counselors must make it clear that neither state is desirable over the other; neither automatically makes it easier not to sin.

He **learned** (there is that word again; biblical lifestyles do not come about overnight) **the secret of contentment in every and all circumstances** —when **hungry**, when **in abundance**, when **in need**. It is contentment that your counselee seeks. He will never find it until he is able to rejoice in all things! What is the secret of content, worry-free, rejoicing? Drawing on the **strength** of Christ (v. 13). The verse doesn't say that one can do anything he wants, but that he can do the things that Paul discusses in his epistle through the strength that Christ provides. How does He provide it? Through the acceptance and practice of biblical truth.

Christian Counselor's Commentary

16 indeed, even when I was in Thessalonica more than once you sent me something to meet my needs.

17 (Not that I seek the gift, but I seek the fruit that is added to your account.)

18 Now I have all I need and more. I have been filled, having received from Epaphroditus the things that come from you, which are a fragrant perfume, an acceptable sacrifice that is pleasing to God.

19 My God will supply you with everything that you need, in keeping with His riches in glory in Christ Jesus.

20 Now to our God and Father be glory forever and ever. Amen.

21 Greet every saint in Christ Jesus. The brothers who are with me greet you.

22 All the saints greet you (especially those from Caesar's household!).

23 May help from the Lord Jesus Christ be with your spirit.

But Paul is not ungrateful for what they did (v. 14). They did well in sharing their substance with him when he was in need. That this wasn't the only time they did so is clear from verse 15. Indeed, this was the only church that supported him. As a matter of fact, they had given to Paul again and again (he remembers and mentions specific instances; v. 16). Don't get me wrong, he says, I am not as much interested in money as in those who give it (v.17). I want you to receive the blessing that will be yours from such giving. And, this is no hint to do more; I have **all I need—and more**! What you sent with Epaphroditus was a sweet smelling sacrifice, pleasing to God. And, you can be sure, that just as He has supplied all my needs, God will do the same for you (v.19). The richness of His supply is unimaginable.

Then comes the final benediction, a greeting to the saints (there were too many to name them all). And the saints here in Rome greet you—especially those who are converts from Caesar's household. The grace of Christ be with your spirit.

As you have seen, Philippians is a tremendous letter, varied in content, filled with instruction for both counselor and counselee alike. Use it often in counseling and you will not go astray.

Introduction to
I THESSALONIANS

The letter that we know as I Thessalonians is possibly Paul's first letter. The Book is full of helpful and interesting material. Counselors, especially, will find it of use. Teachers, purporting to represent Paul, had already been promulgating heretical views among the members of this fledgling congregation. Paul did not know who they were, but they taught that no Christian would die before the second coming of Christ. Much of the clarification of this teaching emerges in II Thessalonians, by the time of which writing Paul had additional information; yet, already, Paul is dealing with the issue. That is why, in various places, he stresses **hope**. Hope is a dominant note in this letter, one that counselees as well need to hear. Without hope (which in the Bible doesn't mean "hope so", but *expectation* or *anticipation* of something certain that God will do, but just hasn't done *yet*}, counselees (and counselors) will give up when the going gets tough. Hope depends on the promises of God. That is why it is energizing. That is why it forms the basis for all counseling. If you learn nothing else from this fine letter, learn something about how to use the Bible to instill hope in counselees who are discouraged and despairing.

Paul is pleased with the progress of the Thessalonian church. Despite immediate persecution, they had done well so far; therefore, he exhorts them to do even better! Now that the ball is rolling give it an even harder shove. That is the idea (which he continues into the second letter to this congregation). Obviously, that is also a policy that ought to be adopted by every counselor. Commend honest advance, but never allow the counselee to settle back. "Now that you have momentum," tell him, keep it going.

In this letter discover what sorts of things Paul told the members of newly-spawned congregations. Remember, he had been in Thessalonica only three or four weeks. By his allusions to what he taught when there you can learn something about the wealth of material he gave them in that short period, much of which, today, some think ought to be held back until a later time. Paul is always surprising. A good study of this book should lead many to correct their thinking in this regard. Paul covered every aspect of life it seems, making sure that from the beginning Christians would learn of the need to examine and change their lives across the board.

There were some lazy busybodies in the church to whom he alludes in this letter, and whom he deals with in much more detail in the second.

Christian Counselor's Commentary

They may have acquired this posture from the misapprehension that Christ was about to return in the immediate future. What he says about calling others to work is important for counselors as well.

Thessalonica was a seaport town of great importance to southern Europe. From this city many went forth into all parts of the Mediterranean world. And many came here for trading purposes. It was a key place, then, for preaching the gospel. It would be heard by numbers of people who, in turn, would carry it to other places. Because the Thessalonian church had such a vital witness, that is just what was happening. Everything we know about the founding of the church is found in Acts 17:1-10. Before you enter into the study of these two books, read that passage again. The congregation probably was begun sometime during the late fall of the year 51 A.D. For details, see Lenski's commentary, pages 214, 215. Silas (or Silvanus) and Timothy are included as co-writers with Paul because they (especially Silas) were prominent in the founding of the church.

All in all, I think that you are going to be pleased as you study the two Thessalonian letters in the light of counseling principles and practices.

CHAPTER 1

1 Paul and Silvanus and Timothy to the church of the Thessalonians in God the Father and the Lord Jesus Christ: Help to you and peace.
2 We thank God for all of you, regularly mentioning you in our prayers,

---

Paul, Silvanus and Timothy, writing to the **church** at Thessalonica, refer to the fact that it is a church **in God the Father and in the Lord Jesus Christ**. It is apparent that, from the outset, Paul taught new converts about the deity of Christ. This introductory phrase proves it. He writes these words without a syllable of explanation. But it would be utterly impossible to think of coupling anyone else's name with the name of the Father. They appear together because they belong together. Equally, as Those in whom the Church exists, they are the united source of its authority, power and very being. But, notice, it is the *Lord* **Jesus Christ** to Whom Paul refers. This is a church of the One Who died, rose, ascended, was crowned "Lord" and was seated in power and authority at the right hand of the Father. This is a church ordained from the heavenly throne itself!

Grace and peace is precisely what every church (and every member in it) needs in this world. The believer cannot live the Christian life without **grace** (here, that means the assistance or help from the Spirit that God provides to know and to do His will). And, because sin creates so many disturbances both within and without, **peace** is equally needed. Perhaps no two more important items could be listed in the greeting.

Your counselee also needs grace and peace. But he will receive peace only when he avails himself of the grace that is given. All things necessary to life and godliness have been provided for his spiritual growth. They are his for the taking. He may never complain about a lack or paucity of help, direction or peace. If he fails to avail himself of it, neither the Father nor the Son may be blamed.

In verse 2, Paul utters a prayer of **thanksgiving** for the church. As you will discover, this is a church to be commended. Throughout the letter, as well as throughout the second one, Paul has much good to say and little that is bad. And when he comes to the latter, it is *some* who are the trouble; not all.

Even those, however, are persons for whom Paul gives thanks: **We thank God for *all* of you** (v. 2). And, he is able to pray joyfully as he

Christian Counselor's Commentary

> 3   remembering your work that comes from faith, and labor that comes from love, and endurance that comes from hope in our Lord Jesus Christ, in the presence of our God and Father.

---

prays regularly for them. How regular is your prayer for your counselees? Not all counselees are pleasant to work with. Perhaps, per capita, they are the most disagreeable persons in the church to deal with. Yet, they, like the Thessalonians, need your joyful prayers; God must do a work in their hearts through you. Pray that He will be pleased to do so.

What made Paul so happy about the Thessalonian church was **their work that comes from faith, their labor that comes from love and their endurance that comes from hope.** Here we meet Paul's famous trinity of graces. In I Corinthians 13, however, the order is different: beginning with faith, he moves next to hope, then, finally, to love. Here, it is faith, then love, then hope. In Corinth, the need was for love. There were unloving divisions, unloving attitudes at the Lord's table, unloving use of the gifts, etc. The Thessalonians needed hope because of the false teaching about the Lord's return that has affected some in the church. The graces that most fitted the needs of the churches, it seems, were mentioned last, as forming a sort of climax.

Notice the genitives ("of"): they indicate source. Work comes from faith, labor from love and endurance from hope. The Thessalonians needed endurance. The church was born in controversy and persecution from unconverted Jews. There had been and, presumably, would continue to be much to bear. So far they had done well.

Here is a verse every counselor should deeply appreciate. It tells him what to stress if he wants a certain result. If he wants **work** out of his counselee, then he should not stress work, but **faith**. It is faith that leads to work (as James also points out). If your counselee's faith is weak, you can lay out workplans and urge and exhort him to get to work till the cows come home and he will not produce. What he needs is to *believe* with greater intensity. To believe that what he must do is pleasing to Christ, that the Savior really does want him to do this and that this is what will make the difference.

The same is true of **labor** (the word here means work that one does to the point of fatigue). You can beat a person into working hard, but that will last only so long. He will work till fatigue, and then some, however, *on his own*, when he does so out of love. A man may work from 8 to 4 in order to earn his paycheck—with his eye on the clock. But a woman will

4 We know, brothers, that God loves you and has chosen you.

---

labor from dawn till setting sun (and after) for a family that she loves.

Endurance does not eventuate from an insistence upon it. As I Corinthians 10:13 indicates, when one can see beyond the problem to its solution, when he can know that there is an end and that it will be for his good, he can endure. That is to say, if he has **hope**, he can **endure**. Ask, urge, wheedle—or whatever—you can never get a counselee to hang in there when the going gets tough (and it usually does at least at one point in each case); to do so, you must give him hope. Hope in the Bible means certainty of expectation (cf. "the blessed hope"). It is, therefore, the promises of God in the Scriptures that bring hope. If your counselee lacks hope, turn to them (cf. Romans 14:13, 4—read these verses in that order).

How is it that the Scriptures generate hope? Well, it is They that point to the Lord Jesus and the Father as the Source and Guarantors of the promises made therein. It is the Scriptures that disclose the trustworthy character of the Father and the Son whose promises can be believed. This hope, then, is **in the Lord Jesus Christ,** Whose promises were made **in the presence of our God and Father.** That, of course, is why they cannot fail. Insist that the promises of God are true (note how Paul does this in I Corinthians 10:13 "God is faithful Who...") Scriptural promises have behind them the faithfulness of God Himself. If they should fail, God would be proven unfaithful—an impossibility.

Because of their willingness to endure so far, Paul says **We know, brothers, that God loves you and has chosen you.** That is the reassurance every believing counselee needs to hear from time to time during the course of counseling sessions. He is loved by God and has been chosen by Him. Surely, then, God will take care of him—even in the immediate problem, no matter how grave it may be. If he is God's child *forever* (one of the those **chosen** to spend eternity with Him), surely He will care for him *now*. The love of God for His children is also a powerful motive for counseling. But, don't sling around the phrase "God loves you" in a flippant way—as some misguided Christians do. Rather, show how that love was manifested in the terrible act of love of the cross. Picture love as difficult and strong, the Father crucifying His Son for His chosen ones. Avoid all sentimental ideas of love from the first. Anchor all discussion of God's love in the cross. Every other manifestation of that love (and there are many others) is based on, and grows out of, the love that flows from the

> 5   Our good news came to you not only in word, but also in power and in the Holy Spirit and with complete certainty, just as you know what we were like among you for your sakes,
> 6   and you became imitators of us and of the Lord, welcoming the Word in the midst of much affliction, with joy from the Holy Spirit,

cross.

In verse 5, Paul recalls that the good news that he preached came to the Thessalonians **not only in word, but also in power and in the Holy Spirit and with complete certainty**. What is he saying by those words? He is remembering the days when he and his friends first preached the message of life in the city. What happened was not simply preaching, but results, powerful results! The Holy Spirit used the words Paul and his co-workers proclaimed to bring many to faith in Christ. It was an outstanding beginning for a church. There were people who believed who, though they were persecuted for their faith, continued to believe with **complete certainty**; they did not doubt as many might have under such circumstances. They imitated the faith of the founders, and found strength to endure: **just as you know what we were like among you for your sakes.** Paul never wavered when persecution from the Jews was intense. They followed his example. In other ways, later in the letter, Paul would exhort some who needed to imitate his behavior. Perhaps the greatest teaching tool of all is example. In considering an example, you not only get to understand a principle that the exemplar is exhibiting, but you see how it may be put into practice. That is what the Thessalonians had in the example of Paul and his associates as they saw them handle persecution and suffering with complete certainty in what they believed and taught. There was no vacillation. They did not see preachers who taught one thing but did another. Even if you cannot demonstrate what you want your counselee to know, at least you can tell him about instances in your past that do. Or, you may point to the example of someone that he knows for the same purpose.

Because they imitated Paul, who himself was only imitating the Lord Jesus (v. 6), in a secondhand, but true way, they too were imitating Jesus. Not only did these extraordinary Thessalonians **welcome the Word** Paul preached, but they did so with **joy**—even **in the midst of much affliction**! What an encouragement they must have been to Paul in his early ministry.

Your counselee should hear about that. There can be joy in the midst

I Thessalonians 1

7   with the result that you became a model for all those in Macedonia and in Achaia who believe.

---

of great suffering. Many counselees will say things like "Well, I have a reason to be upset, don't I?" or "How can you expect me to carry on cheerfully in circumstances like this?" While there is no attempt to minimize the severity of the affliction, Paul points to the underlying joy they had while suffering for Christ's sake. Here were people suffering ostracism, physical injury, etc., for their newfound faith, yet enduring **with joy**. If they can, surely your counselees can too.

The joy was **in the midst of** much affliction. It was not when they emerged from the persecution that they became joyful, but they were able to maintain joy during the very time when they suffered. How could they do that? Joy and peace do not depend on what others do; only on what God has done. They focused on the love and mercy of God toward them rather than on the affliction. When that is done, anyone—with Paul—can speak of the most intense suffering as "temporary light afflictions," since he is contrasting those with "the eternal weight of glory" that would be his in days to come (cf. II Corinthians 4: 17, 18. Note what he was looking at: the *unseen*, not the seen world). That is how the Thessalonian church was able to maintain joy.

Because they were faithful, spoke the word to many who put in at their Mediterranean port, and doubtless, led a number of them to faith in Christ, they also **became a model** for believers elsewhere (v. 7). Christ's example was the model for Paul. Paul's modeling of Christ was a model for the Thessalonians, who, in turn, through the word that was carried out of the city to Christians elsewhere, became a model to them. Young Christians need not wait to become a model to others. They may begin right away—so long as they welcome the word in **joy** and with **complete certainty.** Your counselee should look not only to his own problems and their solutions, as too many do, but to becoming an example for others. The self-centeredness that one encounters among many counselees must be countered. One way of doing that is to focus on how their lives affect other Christians. Husbands ought to be concerned how their lives affect their wives, wives how they affect their children, and all three how they affect others in the church.

Because it was the center of trade for southern Europe, Thessalonica's port teemed with people going and coming. Word of what God had accomplished in this port city, therefore, was soon carried all over the

Christian Counselor's Commentary

> 8 Now the Lord's Word sounded out from you not only in Macedonia and Achaia, but in every place where your faith in God has become known, so that we don't need to say anything about it.
> 9 Indeed, they themselves tell us about the amazing sort of entrance that we had into your midst, and how you turned to God from idols to serve the living and genuine God,

---

place (v. 8). Indeed, their **faith**, in face of persecution, was so well spoken of that Paul had no need to tell anyone about it. It was as if a great voice **sounded out** the facts. Wherever he went, word of their faith had preceded him. People were telling *Paul* about the **amazing** reception that the Thessalonians gave him and his comrades. They talked to him about the way they had forsaken the foolish **idols** they once worshipped **to serve the living and true God.** And to wait for His Son Who would come **from the heavens**: Jesus, Whom He **raised from the dead** and would deliver them from **the coming wrath** of God (vv. 9, 10).

That was quite a hope. And, it was precisely on that hope that the evil one focused his attention. They had been attacked at the very point of their strength. Someone was telling them that no Christians would die before Christ returned. Presumably, some of their faithful loved ones were dying, or had died, and this caused some confusion. We shall have more to say about this at a later point. But, notice, often the wicked one will attack your counselee (or you, for that matter) at the very point of his strength, seeking to cause both confusion and consternation. Watch out for that. Indeed, it might even be proper to *warn* about this possibility. You will do well for your counselees if you keep this strategy of the devil in mind. You are to be aware of his devices (II Corinthians 2:11). The importance of anticipating problems cannot be too strongly stressed. Yet, this must always be done in the proper manner; don't go around causing unnecessary concern or giving counselees "ideas" that *they* will turn into realities. Warn in ways calculated to show that Christ has provided more than adequately for them to withstand whatever attacks may come upon them.

The great fact that by the death and resurrection of Christ we have been delivered from the eternal wrath of God is something to emphasize as well. No greater suffering can be imagined than everlasting punishment. Because we have been delivered from that with certainty, we can take whatever is thrown at us here and now. And, the good news includes not only the death, but also the resurrection of Jesus Christ. Because He

I Thessalonians 1

10 and to wait for His Son from the heavens Whom He raised from the dead, Jesus, Who delivers us from the wrath that is coming.

---

rose from the dead, we too can wait for Him to return from the heavens (as the apostles saw Him leave). And, at that time He will put down all enemies and give to His own the joy of eternal rest. All of those elements ought to be present somewhere in the discussions that take place in a counseling room. Many counselors, who call themselves Christian counselors, but are so in name only, avoid doctrinal discussion of this sort. Nothing could be more foolhardy. People need to hear again and again the basis for their faith, so that the complete certainty that the Holy Spirit brings to them through His Word may enable them to proceed properly in the midst of much affliction. Lace your counseling sessions, then, with much biblical teaching.

CHAPTER 2

1 Now you yourselves know, brothers, that our entrance into your midst wasn't a waste of time,
2 but after we had suffered and had been treated violently at Philippi, as you know, yet God gave us boldness to speak the good news to you in the midst of much struggle.

The Thessalonian church was bearing a great witness: from them the Lord's Word sounded out like a trumpet reverberating in all parts of the Mediterranean world. Paul wanted this witness not only to grow but to increase. Much of what he says in the second chapter is calculated to bring that about.

He reminds them of his visit, how that his **entrance into their midst wasn't a waste of time**. This they knew very well. Indeed, it had been a howling success. The verse is, of course, an understatement. The account of the work done at Philippi, and its results, may be found in Acts 16:16ff. Paul refers to it in this passage. He mentions having **suffered violent treatment** there. But, as he continues, he observes that he and his companions were able to preach **the gospel boldly** to them in spite of the struggle they underwent. Others, after such treatment, might have held back, trimmed their sails or fudged in one way or another. Not Paul and his associates. What made the difference? Paul tells us in the verses that follow. Essentially, these facts: God gave them boldness (the original word means "the ability to speak without the fear of consequences") because He **approved** what they were doing and how they were doing it (cf. v. 4). Of what did He approve? Their methods and their message were pure (v. 3), they were self-giving (v. 8), they worked hard (v. 9), they were genuine (v. 10) and tender, showing loving concern (vv. 7, 11).

There is every bit as much need for boldness in counseling as there is in preaching. Indeed, it is often easier to speak boldly to a crowd than to speak to one or two individuals who are eyeballing you across a desk—especially if one of those individuals is the son of a leading elder in the congregation! Yet, God can give all the grace necessary even for that.

Boldness is necessary for effective ministry, as Paul made clear in Ephesians 6: 19, 20. It is the way one **ought to speak**. In Acts 4, you have an account of the minister's prayer—a prayer for boldness (see, vv. 29-31), and throughout the book of Acts, Luke refers again and again to the boldness of New Testament preachers. Indeed, the Book of Acts ends on

I Thessalonians 2

3 Our appeal didn't come from error or uncleanness or fraud;

---

the note that Paul was in Rome in his own rented quarters preaching boldly to all who would listen.

If the Christian counselor lacks courage to tell the truth, his counselees will suffer. In the church, as well as without, there are all too few who will give others an honest reading about themselves. If, in counseling, where the counselee presumably has asked the counselor to be utterly frank, that fails to happen, chances are that he will never get such a reading from anyone. And yet, that is exactly what most counselees need. Counselees should be told, "You know, John, I have been listening to you talk for several sessions now, and I continually hear one thing over and over—self pity. I am certain that is one of the principal reasons you did what you did. I doubt that anyone could move in that direction if he hadn't talked himself into it through gobs and gobs of self-pity." Do you ever talk like that? If you don't when it is necessary—but instead hold back—you are doing a great disservice to the counselee.

If you have problems with being as bold as counseling requires, then take a closer look at the next few verses, beginning with verse 3. Notice, carefully, the *motivation* behind Paul's ministry: **Our appeal didn't come from error or uncleanness or fraud**. It was an appeal to believe the gospel that stemmed from pure motives. If your heart isn't right, all else will be wrong. The three things mentioned in verse 3 are the characteristics of false teachers. They must not be a part of your ministry—even in a minimal way.

Error is fundamental to undercutting boldness. God is not going to encourage those who propagate error by granting them boldness. If those who err often seem bold, closely examined, one will discover that it is not boldness at all but militant arrogance. On the other hand, you, knowing that what you are speaking is the very truth of the Creator, may speak with a confidence that nothing else can give. Where can boldness stem from, if not from God's truth in the Bible? Freud, Rogers, Ellis, Maslow, Skinner do not engender boldness. How can they?

Uncleanness is a temptation for every counselor who counsels women. And, don't say, "Then, I won't counsel women" as some have "conveniently" proposed. That is no answer. If Paul did not expect you to do so, why would he have issued warnings against uncleanness and, here, mentioned that it was something he was aware of in his ministry?

Christian Counselor's Commentary

4 rather, just as we have been approved by God to be entrusted with the good news, so we speak, not to please people but God Who tests our hearts.

Uncleanness includes all those thoughts and practices not explicitly called fornication or covered by direct prohibitions in the Bible. It involves playing around the edge of sexual intercourse—jokes, titillation through detailed discussion of sexual matters, etc. Anything that might lead to adultery of the heart as well as adultery of the body is included in the word. As I have said before, the answer is not to counsel women *alone*. Have an elder trainee present.

Fraud is doing something "with guile;" wanting to put it over on someone in some way or other. People who counsel for money, for advantage, for any personal gain while representing themselves as helpers concerned about their brothers and sisters in Christ, fit this description. In talking to such persons, you can often hear the cash register ringing in their words. If this is the reason for your counseling, stop now, until you purify your motives. Counseling can be lucrative. Keep your eyes off of that fact or, subtly, you may find yourself drifting in the wrong direction.

Those to whom God gives holy boldness are those He **approves** (v. 4). They may or may not have the certification of some accrediting organization—that is irrelevant in the long run. Do they have the approval of God? That is the only real question. Paul's ministry of the gospel was **entrusted to him by God**. Has your ministry been entrusted to you or have you simply taken it up on your own? Of course, Paul had a revelation on the Damascus Road in which that happened. I am not suggesting that is what you must look for. However, as he indicates here, there was an ongoing way in which God continued to entrust him with ministry: **God...tests our hearts**. If he were **pleasing people**, presumably God would withdraw that trust. The question for you is whether your ministry measures up to that which is described in these verses. It is a matter of avoiding the wrong things and including those that Paul deems absolutely necessary to faithful ministry before God. As we continue to work through the passage, you will increasingly learn what is a ministry approved by God, one entrusted to a servant by Him.

Much counseling, especially of a pagan sort, is nothing more than **pleasing people**. People are asked what their goals are in coming and these are accepted at face value as the goals for counseling, whether or not they accord with those God has for the individual. What is done in the sessions themselves is done in ways that will never cross the wishes of the

I Thessalonians 2

5   As you know, at that time we didn't use flattering words, or a pretext for greed (God is witness),
6   and we didn't seek glory from people—either from you or from others,
7   though as apostles of Christ we could have made heavy demands on you. Rather, we were as gentle in your midst as a nurse caring for her children.

---

counselee; indeed, sessions may become little more than a time of catering to his wishes, attempting to help him gain his goal his way. These goals are almost always self-centered. People-pleasing is displeasing to the One Whom you ought to be pleasing. If your counseling isn't aimed at pleasing God, it is wrongly focused. Counseling, like all ministry, must at bottom, be God-centered, not (as Rogers put it) client-centered. That, of course, is why counseling must be **bold**; not everything that pleases God is pleasing to people. As a matter of fact, much of what God says is very displeasing to them. Yet, in spite of that, the truth must be presented. Boldness of presentation, however, does not mean crudeness. It can be most loving and charitable, in spite of the differences involved. You will encounter this in later comments, especially during the study of chapter three. Yet a counselor may not trim his sails (rather, the *Bible's* sails!).

In verse 5 Paul details some of the fraudulent things he avoided. Here are some criteria by which to evaluate your own counseling ministry: **we didn't use flattering words, or a pretext for greed...and we didn't seek glory from people—either you or from others**. It is not necessary to develop these words further. They are self-explanatory. Just let me warn you: every one of the things that Paul has outlawed is a temptation for the counselor. Read them again, evaluate your heart, take every measure necessary to remove them from yourself.

In verse 7, Paul makes a transition to the positive side of his ministry. What did he do? Well, rather than making **heavy demands** on the Thessalonians, **as apostles of Christ** might, he and his coworkers took every precaution to avoid doing so and, indeed, did just the opposite. As apostles, they could well have demanded food, lodging and pay. Instead, they paid their own way (v. 9). In I Corinthians 9, Paul discusses this issue in depth, so we will not here. Just let it suffice to say that he and his companions were bachelors, who could do so without harming a family. You may not be. But, what is your attitude? Are there people you will counsel who could not ever pay you either money or in any other way? Think about that—carefully.

Christian Counselor's Commentary

> 8 We were so concerned for you that we were glad to give you, not only God's good news, but also a part of our very souls—because you became so dear to us.
> 9 Surely you remember, brothers, our labor and toil; we worked night and day that we might not become a burden to any of you while we preached God's good news to you.
> 10 You (and God) are witnesses of how holy and righteous and irreproachable we were in our relationships to you who believe.

How did Paul, in all his boldness, treat those to whom he ministered? He tells you, **we were as gentle in your midst as a nurse caring for her children.** The picture is graphically tender. A loving, tender nursing mother (or wet nurse) is not promoting her own interests; she is concerned only for the welfare of her baby. The word **caring,** in verse 7, is a word that means "warming" (it is used in the LXX of a mother bird warming eggs: Deuteronomy 22:6). Do you tenderly work with counselees in that way, with those attitudes? With some, counseling becomes a matter of smashing eggs or dropping babies on the floor!

The concern that lay behind this treatment of counselees is further described in verse 8 as **giving** not only the message, but **the very souls** of those who preached it. In those words there is none of the take it or leave it attitude that some exhibit! There is no white-coated professionalism either; all is warmly personal. The message and the messenger were equally **given.** Paul willingly put himself out for the sake of others. Is that how you counsel? To what can one attribute such a giving attitude? Paul makes it clear: **because you became so dear to us**. Do you feel that way about your counselees?

He recounts what they remembered so well, how he and his companions **worked night and day,** as they preached, to avoid **becoming a burden** to any. Not everyone can do this, nor should he; **the laborer is worthy of his hire**. But, the spirit of it ought to be there. If it is, there will be so much of the counselor's soul given that a counselee could never pay for it (cf. Acts 18:3).

Now, in verse 10, Paul describes the ministry at Thessalonica in three adverbs: it was carried on **holily, righteously and irreproachably**. These are qualities that (elsewhere in Titus and I Timothy) he requires of all who minister the Word. For further comment, turn to the commentaries on those passages.

Finally, not satisfied with the figure of the nursing mother, Paul also describes the apostolic attitude as one in which, as **a Father dealing with**

I Thessalonians 2

11 You know that like a father dealing with his children, we urged and soothed and charged each one of you
12 to walk in a manner that is worthy of God, Who is calling you into His own empire and glory.

13 Now, for this reason, we also thank God regularly, that when you received God's Word, that you heard from us, you didn't accept it as a human Word but rather, for what it truly is, God's Word, which is at work in you who believe.

---

his children, they urged and encouraged and charged each one to walk in a manner that is worthy of God. These are three activities of the fatherly counselor that you ought to become. To **urge**, exhort or to beg is the meaning of the first rather broad term that means to give assistance of the sort that is necessary in a situation. Surely, you do your share of that if you are counseling biblically! But do you **encourage** *soothingly* (as this word translated **encouragement** implies)? And do you **charge** your counselees as well? To charge someone is to lay a solemn challenge before him in the Name of the Lord. The only kind of charges that some counselors know anything about is charging fees!

Note, in verse 11, how Paul indicates that much of this work was done in counseling. This is clear from his words **each one of you**. His ministry did not consist of merely preaching to crowds; he ministered the Word to individuals (see also Colossians 1:28; Acts 20:31. This was not atypical of the ministry of Paul, but his regular practice). In these chapters Paul is describing a counseling ministry just as surely as he is describing a preaching one. Those who of late have turned against all counseling need to think more clearly about Paul's work.

God is in the process of **calling** his children **into His own empire and glory**. Remember that when you work with counselees. These people—with all the warts they now exhibit—are the citizens of heaven! Though they do not yet measure up to what a citizen should be (neither do you, for that matter), God is in the process of making them over into solid citizens. And, He is using your counsel as a significant part of that making over work. What you are doing, and those for whom you are doing it, is important to God.

Paul now turns from the ministry in Thessalonica to his response to the reports of their faith (v. 13ff.). Because they are God's citizens (**for this reason**), Paul says he **thanks God regularly that upon hearing the Word they received it not as a human word but, for what it truly is, God's Word, which is at work in you who believe.** That is a wonderful

Christian Counselor's Commentary

> 14 You, brothers, became imitators of God's churches in Christ Jesus that are in Judea since you suffered from your own countrymen the same things that they did from the Jews,
> 15 who killed both the Lord Jesus and the prophets, and drove us out. They displease God and oppose all people
> 16 by trying to keep us from speaking to the Gentiles that they may be saved, thereby always filling the cup of their sins to the brim. But wrath has overtaken them at last.

---

mouthful. Notice (I will not expatiate on it any more) that it is the *Word* that is **at work** in those who believe. Apart from the Word of God, that making over process cannot take place. How then can Christian counselors withhold the Word?

In verse 14, there is proof of the working of the Word: **You, brothers, became imitators of God's churches in Christ Jesus that are in Judea.** How? By standing firm in the midst of Jewish persecution of the sort that the Churches in Judea received from their brethren according to the flesh. These Thessalonians had suffered. In mentioning the Jews (of which he was one, though converted) he reminds them that they also crucified the Lord Jesus, after killing the prophets over the years, and have (more recently) driven us out of your town. The envy of the Jews is clearly mentioned in Acts. Paul then expresses a commonly-held view of these apostate Jews: **they oppose all people**. Even Tacitus, a Roman, wrote, "They have an attitude of hostility and hatred toward all others" (*History*, 5:5). Paul adds that they **displease God.** This was no judgment of anti-Semitism on Paul's part—he was a Jew. He loved his countrymen, and tried to win them to the Lord. But, he was a realist who "told it like it is." He had been hounded and persecuted by those Jews who (unlike the ones in Berea) were not so noble.

And, he continues, indicating the punishment that will come to them: a final end of it all since the cup of their sins had filled up, would soon come upon them in the destruction of their temple and city and the terrible time of tribulation they would undergo (cf. Matthew 23:29ff.; 24).

Is Paul simply spewing forth vengeance? Of course not. He is comforting the Thessalonians who were similarly treated. In His time God will right all wrongs. You too must be willing to make this clear in appropriate situations to your counselees. They can endure much when they see an end to it and when they know that God will turn the tables on wicked men.

Paul continues: **because we were forced to be separated from you**

I Thessalonians 2

17 Now, brothers, because we were forced to be torn from you for a brief time (in person, not in heart) we were all the more eager, out of great desire, to see you face to face.
18 Accordingly, we wanted to come to you (indeed, I, Paul, tried again and again), but Satan blocked our way.
19 What is our hope or joy or winner's wreath about which we shall boast? Isn't it you in the presence of our Lord Jesus at His coming?
20 Yes, you are our glory and joy!

---

for a brief time (in person, not in heart) we were all the more eager, out of great desire, to see you face to face. If anything comes through loudly and clearly in this letter, it is the great love that Paul has for his converts and counselees. That is the spirit of *nouthetic counseling*. Certainly not that by which it has been caricatured! Biblical counselors do not beat people over the heads with their Bibles. They are bold, but tender—as you have seen. Paul strikes the needed balance.

So, Paul says, we tried to come to see you, but Satan hindered. The adversary had used his troops to cut off the road to Thessalonica. The term Paul used for **hindered or blocked** is a military term for tearing up the road to keep an advancing enemy from proceeding any farther. We know nothing more of what it was that occasioned these comments, but probably it was unconverted Jews from Thessalonica to whom he was referring as the agents of Satan who accomplished this.

The **winner's wreath,** given to the runner who won the race, is the Thessalonians, says Paul. This is what they will be for him in the day when Christ returns. They are his glory and joy! At the coming of Jesus Christ, they will be his crown! It is certainly not wrong, as anyone can see from this chapter, for a counselor to express his care for his counselees. How one wishes there were more men in counseling who had the pastoral heart of Paul! Of course, in no way does Paul countenance saying endearing words to a woman in counseling. Here we are talking about an attitude toward counselees that was expressed to a congregation of men and women alike. It is how he speaks about those counselees *en masse*.

CHAPTER 3

1 So when we couldn't stand it any longer, we decided that the best thing to do would be to remain in Athens alone,
2 and we sent Timothy, our brother and God's fellow-worker in the good news of Christ, to establish you and to encourage you in your faith,
3 so that none of you might be shaken by these afflictions. After all, you know that we are appointed to this.
4 Even when we were with you, as you know, we told you beforehand that you were going to be afflicted, just as indeed it has happened;

The first verse of the third chapter, as is so often the case, does not introduce a new matter. It is a continuation of material that Paul started to discuss in 2:17. He is once more explaining how that though he didn't come to Thessalonica, he went to every length to find out about them and their welfare. He **remained in Athens alone** because, as he said (speaking hyperbolically), **he couldn't stand it any longer**; he had to **send Timothy** to find out how things were and to help **establish and encourage** the church. The work that Timothy would do there was similar to the work that Titus was left behind to do in Crete. He would **establish** the church by organizing it, by answering questions, by solving problems and by teaching those things that there had not been time to teach before. Timothy would also be an **encouragement** in the affliction they were experiencing. He wanted them to remain firm in affliction, **unshaken** in the midst of trouble (vv. 2, 3) As you assign the reading of this chapter to an afflicted counselee, make it clear that, among other things, the instruction and **encouragement** that you are offering him is calculated to have exactly the same effect.

God often sends trouble to enable us to become well-**established** by learning how to handle it His way. After all, says Paul, you will have to be firm because it is to suffering and affliction that you were **appointed** by God. That is probably a new thought to many counselees (and some counselors as well). Tell them about it. Elsewhere he tells us that all who would live godly in Christ Jesus will suffer persecution. When a counselee accepts the fact that he is **appointed** to suffer for Christ's sake (see the Book of I Peter), that will make all the difference to him. The suffering will take on meaning. He will be able to consider it a part of his earthly mission. And he will be able to endure it in new ways since he recognizes that God has appointed it and, therefore, it has some good pur-

I Thessalonians 3

5   so, it was for this reason when I couldn't stand it any longer that I sent to learn about your faith, lest somehow the tempter had tempted you and our labor would have been in vain.

6 But now Timothy has come back to us from you and has brought us the good news about your faith and love, and that you always have good memories of us, longing to see us just as we also long to see you.

7   For this reason, in all of our distress and affliction, we are encouraged about you brothers because of your faith;

8   indeed, now we live if you stand firm in the Lord!

9   How can we ever thank God adequately for you for all of the joy that we have experienced because of you in the presence of our God?

---

pose. See Philippians 1:12ff. for a deeper discussion of this principle.

In verses 4 and 5, Paul tells us about his ministry at the founding of the church. Already, in the first few weeks of their conversion, he was letting them know that affliction lay ahead (v. 4). That is important. Many of those who win others to Christ fail to warn them of what they may encounter. You will find counselees who are done in by problems simply because no one ever told them. You must do so.

Because he was so concerned that they might have been **tempted** to retreat from their profession of faith, and all he went through in Thessalonica would have been for nothing, he sent Timothy (v. 5). **Temptation by the tempter** often is aimed at those experiencing times of unprovoked trouble. The "unfairness" of it (as it is so often called) is what he plays upon. That it is not unfair at all, but a gracious **appointment** of God, is important for them to learn if they are to withstand the test.

When Timothy returned, he brought the good news that they had remained firm in faith and love and that they still had a warm place in their hearts for Paul, longing as much to see him as he was to see them (v. 6). So, says Paul, because of this good report, **we are encouraged** in our present distress to continue serving the Lord. Every counselor knows that encouragement when he sees the work God has done through him lasting even in the midst of trial and suffering. It, in turn, enables him to persevere in difficult times. As Paul put it: **we now live, if you stand firm in the Lord** (v. 8). For him (and for you?), that is life!

And, he is so overwhelmed at the good news that he asks, **How can we ever thank God adequately for all the joy that we experienced because of you?** Too often, it is not joy, as Paul knew, but distress that we experience in the ministry. But here was a situation that was so different. No wonder he was overwhelmed. When counselees bring joy to your

> 10 Night and day, we pray very earnestly that we may see your face to supply whatever is lacking in your faith.
>
> **11** Now may our God and Father Himself, and our Lord Jesus direct our way to you,
>
> 12 and may the Lord make your love for one another and for all people increase and abound, just as ours does for you,
>
> 13 so that He may establish your hearts irreproachable in holiness before our God and Father at the coming of our Lord Jesus with all His saints.

heart, let them know!

Paul wanted to see them and prayed night and day that he would be able to come in order to help **supply whatever was lacking** in their faith. Indeed, in doxological form, he even prays in the letter that he may be **directed** to them (v. 11). Don't you learn much of the pastoral heart in this letter, as the heart of the great apostle is opened wide? Do you want to know why Paul was so successful? Well, when you have developed a great heart that approximates that of the apostle, a heart of loving concern for those to whom you minister, you will be too. And the love that he had for them, he wishes them to have for others (v. 12). And he prayed for their **love for one another and for all people to increase and abound**. What a concern for this church!

Why? Because **at the coming of the Lord,** he wanted them to be firmly established in **irreproachable holiness** (v. 13). Don't hesitate to hold out before counselees the need for such a life when going to meet the Lord or when He comes for them. The coming of the Lord ought to be a strong incentive to be ready and prepared in heart and life (cf. I John 3:3).

The discussion and commentary on this chapter has been brief, not because it is unimportant or uninteresting, but because it is so critical that, in one way or another, Paul over and over expresses his love and concern for those to whom he ministers. There is but a single, critical focus. If a counselor marinates himself in the words of Paul in the chapter, he will be a far better person and counselor to boot.

Chapter 4

1 Finally, brothers, we ask you and urge you in the Lord Jesus, as you learned from us how you ought to walk and please God (even as you are walking), that you continue to do so even more and more.
2 you know what authoritative instructions we gave you through the Lord Jesus.
3 Now this is God's will: your sanctification. This means that you must abstain from sexual immorality,

---

Now Paul turns to practical matters concerning the Christian's **walk** (lifestyle). In verse 1, he **asks and urges**—the kind of persuasion one uses with friends and those you believe need no stronger means. The urging, however, is not for his own sake, even though he has spoken much about his personal relationship to the Thessalonian church, it is **in (or by) the Lord Jesus**. That is to say, he asks and urges them to a Christian walk because Christ—their Lord—desires it. They may wish to please Paul. That is good. But it must ever remain a subordinate reason; primarily they must obey because it pleases Christ. There are counselors who build such a dependence upon themselves that their counselees will say or do anything to please them. Then, when counseling is over, they revert. Christian counseling makes people dependent only on the Lord and His Word. Secondarily, the church and persons within it help, but their help always should be geared to help counselees depend more and more on Christ.

These young Christians had been taught how **to walk so as to please God.** See comments on Ephesians 4:17ff. about the Christian walk and how it must be taught and brought about. Paul did not insinuate that they were not already walking in a manner pleasing to God; they were. But again, as we saw before, since they were doing well—had the momentum —they should continue to walk farther and farther along the same path. Keep the momentum going! When you see things begin to happen in the life of a counselee, don't settle back and quit (or allow him to do so); push all the harder. That is the lesson Paul wants them (and you) to learn.

Originally, Paul had plainly laid out the authoritative instructions that Christ provided for the walk of the members of His church. They knew them. Now they were to continue to walk according to them. **God's will** for them is their **sanctification** (v. 3). Counseling is a process in which sanctification is assisted by helping the counselee apply God's will recorded in His Word to the counselee's situation. It is the process of leav-

Christian Counselor's Commentary

> 4 that each of you must know how to acquire his own vessel in sanctification and honor
> 5 (not in the passion of desire like Gentiles who don't know God),
> 6 and that you must not go beyond the limits and take advantage of your brother in this matter, because the Lord is the Avenger in all of these things, as, indeed, we previously told you and solemnly declared to you.

ing behind the patterns of the old you while habituating the patterns of the new you in Christ that are according to His authoritative instructions. Paul gives an example of what he is talking about, straight out of the change from paganism to Christianity that they were experiencing. It is the matter of how to obtain a wife.

They must **abstain from sexual immorality,** something not only countenanced in paganism, but promoted by it in temple worship. That command, in itself, was revolutionary. But there is more. In verse 4 he says **each of you must know how to acquire his own vessel** (wife; see I Peter 3:7) **in sanctification and honor**. What is he saying? All of the ways in which pagans acquire a wife, that are contrary to the **instructions** I gave, are now to be eshewed. He doesn't attempt to elucidate on that basic statement, but simply puts everything up for examination over against Christ's authoritative instructions. Getting a girl pregnant in order to obligate her for marriage would obviously be proscribed. Having sexual relations with her before marriage would also be included. The **honorable** way to acquire a wife is through a proposal that is honored before and after marriage. The **passion of desire**, mentioned in verse 5, is the principal way in which one wrongly acquires a wife. It is not romantic or sexual factors that should be uppermost in the matter. **Pagans, who don't know God**, make sexual attraction the basis for marriage—a very shaky one! Christians must not. One wonders if it isn't because Christians have failed to observe this instruction by Paul that so many marriages are falling apart today. Have Christians adopted the very practices that the Bible forbids? Are they now reaping the inevitable consequences? Lust, in whatever form it takes, is the last reason for contracting a marriage.

What verse 6 refers to is not altogether certain. To **go beyond the limits** is to go too far. That much is clear. **In this matter,** seems to refer to the issue just under discussion—acquiring a wife in a sanctified and honorable manner. **Taking advantage of a brother** may have reference to stealing a prospective wife from another or may have reference to the girl's father who may be deceived into allowing his daughter to be

I Thessalonians 4

7   God didn't call us to uncleanness, but rather to sanctification.
8   Consequently, whoever rejects this doesn't reject a human being but God, Who gives His Holy Spirit to you.

9 But you don't need me to write to you about brotherly affection, since you yourselves have been taught by God how to love one another;

"acquired" in some fraudulent manner. Whatever it refers to, it is clear that others besides those contracting the marriage are also to be considered in acquiring a wife. A Christian counselor will do all he can to help all persons in the transaction to act as believers should.

And he should warn that the **Lord** Himself acts as **the Avenger** when these laws are transgressed. All this should be understood by the church because Paul had spelled it out fully when he was with them—and in a **solemn** manner. We do not have knowledge of that teaching other than this oblique reference to it. Whatever is involved, it is better that we do not, since that fact alone should cause us to act with caution and the utmost consideration in every aspect of the matter.

In verse 7, there is a possible explanation: **God didn't call us to uncleanness, but rather to sanctification.** In chapter two, verse 3, I have already had occasion to discuss the word **uncleanness.** See that discussion and apply it to the acquisition of a wife. That is largely what I did in my comments on verse 3 (see above).

Paul expects some to rebel against these teachings so he writes, **Whoever rejects this doesn't reject a human being but God.** Here is another assertion of the inerrancy of the Word that Paul was writing. It is a stern warning to any who would **go too far**. Such persons should be warned by Christian counselors today as well.

After all, there is no need to think that believers cannot control their passions; God, the One Who commanded this not only knows they can, but has provided the assistance of **the Holy Spirit** to help His children, among other things, to restrain their sexual passion. There is no place for "I couldn't help it" thinking. That is what the counselor must contend with so often. Let him be firm in the matter. He may ask, "Are you a Christian?" Answer, "Yes." "Then, you have the Holy Spirit, don't you?" Answer, "Yes." "Then, since the fruit of the Spirit is self-control, you have no excuse. You could control your passions. You just didn't (cf. Galatians 6:16-26)."

While alluding to **brotherly affection**, he says at the same time, they don't need to be exhorted; they already have been **taught by God how to**

10 indeed, you show love toward all the brothers throughout Macedonia. But we urge you, brothers, that you continue to do so even more and more, 11 and that you eagerly aspire to live a quiet life and mind your own business and to work with your hands as we have instructed you,

---

love one another (v. 9). It is interesting that God Himself often teaches His children beyond what they learn from His teachers. That is what he means here. But that teaching must always accord with the Scriptures (in fact, today, He teaches only through them). Indeed, he says, your love is so great that you have been showing love toward Christians throughout **Macedonia**. But again, he urges, never be satisfied with how far you have gone; keep on growing—even in that in which you already excel. That same emphasis appears in this letter over and over again. Mark that fact, and take heed.

There was a problem beginning to raise its ugly head—some were goofing off, minding everyone else's business but their own, failing to work (vv. 11, 12). In the next letter, Paul will be more explicit and more insistent about this matter. We shall reserve most of our comments for that place (II Thessalonians 3:11). Let it be said, however, that the problem became so serious that Paul even contemplated applying church discipline to those involved. Perhaps this attitude was occasioned by the false teaching about an imminent return of Christ that had come their way.

Paul had already instructed them in the matter, so there must have been leanings toward laziness before any such teaching reached them (v. 11^b). He was concerned that such inactivity would affect their **walk**. They were becoming disorderly (lit., "out of line") in their walk. This was a disgrace before **outsiders.** The witness of Christians is an important factor in Paul's eyes. Evidently, some were even becoming dependent on unbelievers. Can't you hear them? "What is this Christianity that you have adopted that has made you of no earthly good?" Unbelievers would not only be repelled, but, as many love to do, would stereotype all Christians by the failure of a few.

Moreover, having time on their hands, they were stirring up trouble by becoming **busybodies**. That meant that the **quiet life** that a Christian should endeavor to lead (v. 11) was being upset. Clearly, there is much here for the Christian counselor. He will encounter more than his share of people who are lazy and don't want to work. He will have to deal with people who stir up trouble because they won't **mind their own business**. And he will have to deal with those whose lives are so troublesome that

I Thessalonians 4

12 so that you may walk decently before outsiders and won't need to be dependent on anyone.

13 Now, we don't want you to be ignorant, brothers, about those who sleep, lest you grieve as others who haven't any hope.

14 If we believe that Jesus died and rose again, in the same way, through Jesus, God also will bring with Him those who sleep.

15 This we say to you by the Lord's Word, that we who remain alive until the coming of the Lord surely will not get ahead of those who are asleep.

---

they are giving Christianity a bad name before unbelievers. Certainly, the exhortations in this passage and in the third chapter of the letter that follows are of great importance in handling each of these types. Notice, however, though there may be only one and not another of these problems in a person's life, if it persists, in time, the rest will likely appear. Indeed, whenever you encounter one, look for the rest. You should remain alert to common problems like these that tend to come in bunches.

At last, he comes to the question of the Lord's return. Surely, Paul had taught them the facts, but since others were beginning to confuse them with faulty teaching about the second coming (the second letter tells us more about that), they needed further instruction. He is interested in facts. Facts help in time of grief. Presumably some of their loved ones had died or were about to die, and this was the reason for the confusion. The false teachers said that no Christian would die before Christ returned. Yet, here were professed believers dying. What was wrong?

In verses 13 through the end of the letter, he reiterates the facts. He would not have them **ignorant** about Christians who **sleep** (that is, have died). The body is what sleeps in the grave (our word "cemetery" means "sleeping place"), not the soul, which goes to be with the Lord. The Christian has a **hope** (expectation), and while he grieves at the loss of a loved one, he does not grieve as those who have no such hope. Paul goes on to describe that hope. The Christian should anticipate the coming of Christ together with **those who sleep.** If they believed the gospel (about the death and resurrection of Christ), they should look for this (v. 14). That is also *our* expectation concerning those who have died in the Lord. And, according to the Word of the Lord Jesus, those who **remain alive** until the coming of Christ will have no advantage over them. Indeed, the bodies of the dead who come with Christ will **rise first** (v. 16). Here's how it will take place:

Christian Counselor's Commentary

> 16 The Lord Himself will descend from the sky with an assembling shout, with the voice of the archangel, and with the trumpet of God, and the dead in Christ will rise first,
> 17 then we who remain alive shall be caught up together with them in the clouds as an escort to welcome the Lord as He comes into the air, and so shall we always be with the Lord.
> 18 Therefore encourage one another with these words.

1. Jesus will **descend from the sky**.
2. He will give **an assembling shout**.
3. The **voice of the archangel** will cry out.
4. The **trumpet of God** will sound.
5. The **dead in Christ will rise first**.
6. Living Christians **will be caught up together with them**.
7. **Together they will welcome Christ as an escort** as He returns to earth.
8. Both will forever be **with the Lord**.

These are facts of which they ought not be ignorant. Nor should we. Why? Because they are comforting, encouraging facts to relate at the death of a loved one. How important to have unquestioned facts with which to meet the situation. Christian ministers should never fudge or act uncertain about death and the coming of Christ; they have been given facts with which to comfort those who have sustained the loss.

That is why Paul concludes this discussion with the exhortation, **Therefore, comfort one another with these words** (v. 18). While there are matters of concern about some aspects of this coming of Christ that ought to be debated, and while this passage plays a prominent role in that debate, nevertheless, that should never be the controlling purpose for which it is used. First, and foremost, it has pastoral, not merely doctrinal, value.

Chapter 5

1 But you don't need me to write to you about the times and the seasons, brothers,
2 since you yourselves know quite well that the Lord's Day will come like a thief at night.
3 When they are saying, "Peace and safety," at that very time sudden destruction will come upon them in the same way that labor pains come upon a pregnant woman, and they certainly will not escape.

Coming to the fifth chapter, once more we encounter the now familiar phenomenon of a continued discussion that is really part of the previous chapter. Paul had been discussing the Lord's return. He continues to do so: **But you don't need me to write to you about the times and the seasons, brothers** (v. 1). The times and seasons of what? Of what he had been talking about—the second coming of the Lord Jesus Christ. The words could refer to nothing else. He is concerned to give them more facts, facts that will counter the false teaching that he knows has been confusing them.

So, what does he say? He had already discussed this matter with them when in Thessalonica (what an amazing number of topics he took up in the short period that they had been Christians!). As a result, they know **quite well that the Lord's Day will come like a thief in the night**, he says. Evidently, they had been told that this coming would be a surprise to many (that is how a thief comes—when he is least expected). He calls the coming of Christ the **Lord's Day**. And, indeed, that is what it will be: the Day in which He will manifest Himself for all He is. It is *His* great Day. Man may have his day now, but the *Lord's* Day will come, a Day *par excellence*! Too often Christians think only of what they will receive on that Day. While those things are true and wonderful, on that event no Christian will be admiring his new body; he will be glorifying His great Savior, Jesus Christ—it is *His* Day!

But should *Christians* be surprised about that Day? No. That is Paul's point. When the *world* **is saying "peace and safety," sudden destruction will come upon *them*.** It will be like unexpected **labor pains** that overtake **a pregnant woman**. And it will be too late for unbelievers; **they certainly will not escape.** That is Paul's description of the event in relationship to the unbelieving world. Warning the unsaved that *now* is the time of salvation, therefore, is important. It will be too late in that unex-

Christian Counselor's Commentary

> 4 But you, brothers, are not in darkness for that Day to surprise you like a thief;
> 5 you all are sons of light and sons of the day. We are not of the night or of darkness.
> 6 So then, let's not sleep like others do, but rather let's be alert and levelheaded.
> 7 Those who sleep, sleep at night and those who get drunk, get drunk at night.
> 8 But since we are of the day, we must be level-headed, putting on a breastplate of faith and love, and for a helmet the hope of salvation.

pected hour of sudden destruction. But what of the believer?

Paul next describes the *Christian's* relationship to that event. In contrast to the world, he says, **But you, brothers, are not in darkness for that Day to surprise you like a thief.** In other words, the Christian should know **the times and the seasons** of the Lord's coming. His relation to the event should involve knowledge and expectancy. He should know the times and the seasons (though he will not know the day or the hour). What sort of times and seasons will prevail? Jesus will return at a time when the world thinks that it has it made. Proudly, the world's leaders will be boasting that at last they have achieved **peace and safety**. Presumably, the United Nations, or some similar organization, at that time may even declare that universal peace has been attained. The return of Christ will not occur at a time when the world is saying, "war" and "more war," as it does now. Darkness is on those who have no inside information as Christians do. In fact, the world doesn't even know that Christ will come again.

Because Christians are **not of the night or of the darkness** (v. 5), they should not **sleep** as others in ignorance do. They should be **alert and levelheaded**. That is to say, they should anticipate Christ's coming when they see the signs of it at hand. And they should always be looking for them. They must never become so absorbed in the things of this world that they forget the coming of Christ, but rather, should look forward to it.

Those who sleep, sleep at night, Paul says. **Those who get drunk, get drunk at night** (v. 7). Those are common enough observations to which most will agree. But, **those who are of the day** must not sleep or get drunk with the wine of worldliness; they must remain **levelheaded** (sensible, clearheaded, keen about what they are doing, prepared for Christ's return).

How do they wait? Armed to withstand the devil's attacks (v. 8).

I Thessalonians 5

9 God didn't appoint us to wrath, but rather to secure salvation through our Lord Jesus Christ,
10 Who died for us so that whether awake or asleep we may live together with Him.
11 Therefore, encourage one another and continue to build each other up, as indeed you have been doing.
12 Now we ask you, brothers, to recognize those who labor among you, and manage you in the Lord, and counsel you.

They must wear **faith and love** for protection, and the **expectation** of ultimate **salvation as a helmet** to guard their heads. God didn't **appoint wrath** for the Christian, but for the unbeliever (v. 9). Christians, in contrast, will be saved eternally. The contrast could not be set forth more clearly than it is here.

Christ died for the believer, so that asleep or awake, he will **live together with Him** everlastingly (v. 10). While disobedient, sleepy Christians will not be commended for their behavior, even if "asleep" when Christ comes, they will be saved. That is a strong assurance for weak Christians. But it must not be used to condone laxity.

What is the practical upshot of these facts? Paul states it in a grand exhortation in verse 11: **Therefore, encourage one another and continue to build each other up, as indeed you have been doing** (don't miss the last phrase; it is another repetition of the reoccurring theme to do better since you are doing so well). There is to be a lay ministry of mutual encouragement and mutual edification. Stress this to your counselee. Unless he is encouraging another Christian and building him up in the faith, he is missing out on the very things that will keep him alert as he anticipates Christ's coming. And, by the way, check him out on whether he is looking for that glorious event. Part of his problem may be that, like an unbeliever, he is sleeping.

In verse 12, another issue is raised. It has to do with authority in the church. Timothy has done his work well. He has organized the church at Thessalonica, and elders have been appointed to rule the congregation. How should the members view them and their work? That is what Paul is about to discuss. And an important matter it is!

The members of Christ's church are to **recognize those who labor** among them (v. 12[a]). That does not mean to be able to identify them on the street. But **to recognize** (lit., "know") them is to recognize their place of authority in the church, to recognize them for what they are as elders. They must, therefore, treat them with the respect and appreciation that

> 13 Think quite highly of them in love because of their work. Be at peace among yourselves.

belongs to those who hold the office. It is not a titular office, but one that requires **labor**. Labor, according to the original term, means *wearisome toil*. The eldership, when properly exercised, is no easy task. To show respect, then, is quite proper. Many counselees are rebels. They show little or no respect for God's authority in the church or for those who have been called to the arduous task of exercising it. As a counselor, who derives his warrant for counseling from that very authority, you must not allow counselees to get away with that. Rather, it is your responsibility to urge them to recognize those who labor and have the rule over them (cf. Hebrews 13:7, 17).

These elders not only labor, but they labor at **managing** the church and **counseling** those over whom they bear rule (v. 12^b). Their two tasks are to manage (rule) and counsel. The word manage means "to be over." The word for counsel is "to confront nouthetically." Nouthetic confrontation has three ideas inherent in it. There is something in the counselee that needs to be changed. This change must take place by verbal confrontation. The confrontation always occurs out of concern for the counselee. Nouthetic counseling, then, is *confrontation* out of *concern* that leads to biblical *change*. The reason I have brought this biblical word over into English is because it expresses, in one term, more of the biblical concept of counseling than any other English word.

There should be an attitude on the part of the members of the church that holds the elder in high esteem **because of his work** (v. 13). Too often that attitude is missing. When counselors work with counselees, they should always attempt to raise the respect level that they have toward the authorities in their congregations. This is a matter of **love**, says Paul. Not only should the officers of the church be loved, but to love them is one way to love God who called and ordained them to their work.

The counselee must be urged to be at peace with his elders. Too often the opposite is true. Now, it is clear that not all elders understand their work. And it is also true that many who do, misuse the office. Nevertheless, the office must be respected because it is an office in which the authority of God is being exercised. Everything possible must be done to build up elders, not to tear them down.

Every member, informally, is to counsel along with the elders who do so formally (authoritatively). Paul **urges** them to **counsel the idle,**

I Thessalonians 5

14 We urge you, brothers, counsel the idle, encourage the timid, support the weak, be patient with everyone.
15 See to it that nobody returns evil for evil, but rather always seek ways of doing good to one another and to all people.

---

encourage the timid, support the weak and be patient with everyone (v. 14). The problem of idleness, mentioned earlier, and in more detail in the second letter, seems to have been a serious problem. There were people who refused to work and who mooched off of others. They needed to be counseled. Interesting, isn't it, that for even such a matter as this, Paul urges mutual **counsel**! How we have departed from becoming responsible for the behavior of our brothers in Christ.

The **timid**, whom they must **encourage**, are (as the original indicates), literally, the "small souled." Can't you picture the small, shriveled up souls in some people, souls that have been starved, that need to be nourished on God's Word? These are people with little get-up-and-go. They have to be pushed and pulled into everything that they do. Yet, as with the idle, we must have **patience** with them. Often, that is hard to do. You want to light a stick of dynamite under them to dislodge them from their spiritual lethargy. But you must not. While never for a second condoning their behavior, yet you must not give up on them. Take heed, counselor. Certainly, if anyone does, you get your share of such persons to work with!

The **weak** must be **supported** (lit, "held on to"). If you don't, they will fall away. Everyone knows these people. They are influenced by every wind of doctrine. They have trouble standing on their own two feet. They drift, they are blown; they change with the weather. That is why you must stand with them, supporting them, hanging on to them, so that they will not be carried away from the church and the strengthening influences of the preaching of the Word and the fellowship of God's people. Here, again, your work is cut out for you, counselor. As in the instances above, here too you are told precisely how to handle the weak. Surely, Paul does not mean to go on supporting them forever. His idea, doubtless, is to continue to patiently support them during the period in which you are attempting to strengthen them. But that period will be difficult. They are not easy to handle because of their propensity to drift with the tide.

Again, Paul is concerned with the mutual relations that exist among the members of the congregation. He reminds them (in words similar to those found in Romans 12), **See to it that no one returns evil for evil,**

16 Always rejoice.
17 Pray regularly.
18 Give thanks in every situation; this is God's will for you in Christ Jesus.

---

but seeks [lit., "pursues" or "tracks down like a hunter"] **ways of doing good to one another and to all people** (v. 15). They are to do good in return for evil not only to Christians, but to unbelievers as well (cf. Romans 12:18).

Here is an assignment appropriate to probably more than two-thirds of your counselees: "This week, seek several ways to do good to [here fill in the name of the person] who has wronged you. Bring in the results next week so we can evaluate what you have done and get you started on a course for doing at least one of them." You will find yourself handing it out again and again. Few things are harder for some counselees to do. But, when you have them **seek for ways** to do good, you will discover who does and who does not wish to overcome his anger and hatred. Because they do not think biblically, many will find it difficult to come up with ways. When this happens, you can point out how desperately they need to change their attitudes. You may need to stress the strong word **seek** (see above). And, you may even have to help some out by giving suggestions, or drawing suggestions out of them with questions (the preferable way of doing so). "Mary, are you a good cook?" "Why, of course, pastor. You've eaten my lemon meringue pie. You know that." "Sure I do. Well, have you ever thought of baking a pie for Jane?" "Hmmmmmmm..."

Much of the Book of Philippians, written by Paul from prison, is a commentary on the short verse 16: **Always rejoice.** Turn to the passages in Philippians 4, for instance, to understand what Paul has in mind. Never forget, your peace and joy don't come from people, from circumstances or from any other source but God. That is why you can rejoice **always**. Counselees don't believe this or understand it. It is your task to present the truth to them persuasively.

In another short verse, Paul says, **Pray regularly**. A survey of his prayers in the introductory passages of his letters might serve as a good example of what he is saying. Notice how the busy apostle did pray regularly for a variety of churches, situations and persons.

In the early church there were prophets (cf. comments on Ephesians 2:20; 3:5). Through them, prior to the completion of the canon of Scripture, God directed the first churches. These **prophecies** were to be heard,

I Thessalonians 5

19 Don't quench the Spirit.
20 Don't dismiss the prophecies as if there were nothing to them;
21 but test all of them and retain those that are good.
22 Abstain from every form of evil.
  23 May the God of peace Himself sanctify you completely; may your entire being—spirit and soul and body—be kept blameless for the coming of our Lord Jesus Christ.
24 The One Who calls you is faithful, and He will accomplish it.

---

held in high regard (**dismiss** in this verse means "express contempt for") and, upon proper **testing**, heeded. We don't know a great deal about the problem that led to despising prophecies, but (obviously) it existed. Nothing that God says is to be despised, but all is to be handled with the utmost respect as a gracious, valuable gift.

Prophecies were to be tested, and those that were good (genuine), retained. That means that there were spurious prophecies. Perhaps that explains the contempt that some might have shown for them. How to test them is a question. Some help on this is found in Deuteronomy 13, I Corinthians 14:29 and I John 4:1. We do not need to know all about the testing procedures since we are not involved today in receiving and evaluating prophecies. All we need has already been evaluated as genuine and placed in the canon of Scripture known as the New Testament.

Verse 22 has been misunderstood and misused. It does not mean to abstain from everything that might *appear* to be evil, but **abstain from every form of evil**. But what does that mean? Truth is single, error is multifaceted. It can take many forms—and does. It comes in all sizes, shapes and colors. Evil is packaged in various ways in different ages. One can only be right one way; he can be wrong in many ways. So, one must be on the lookout for these multifaceted ways in which evil pops up. He must abstain from every sort of evil in whatever shape it takes. You will find people who do not understand this and, consequently, are persecuting themselves unmercifully by the faulty interpretation that is possible from the KJ Version. After all, in some way or other, almost anything one does can be misinterpreted as evil. Help them out.

Now, the final doxology. God is the Source of **peace** (see above on v. 16). Paul calls on Him to shower upon the Thessalonians the sanctifying grace that will bring it. He wants them to know God's **peace** in their **entire being**. There is not a threefold division of man, a view that is wrongly derived from verse 23. Paul is heaping up terms here to indicate **completeness**. For a fuller discussion of this matter see my book, *A The-*

25 Brothers, pray for us.
26 Greet all the brothers with a holy kiss.
27 I solemnly charge you by the Lord to read this letter to all the brothers.
28 May help from our Lord Jesus Christ be with you.

---

ology of Counseling. When Christ comes, Paul wants them to meet Him pure and holy in their entire beings. That is his point. They are incapable of pulling this off. But **the One Who calls is faithful, and He will accomplish it,** says Paul. How encouraging that concluding note is!

His last words: **Brothers, pray for us. Greet all the brothers with a holy (nonsexual) kiss. Read this letter to all the brothers. The grace of the Lord Jesus Christ be with you**. He knew he needed prayer. And he didn't hesitate to ask even new converts to pray for him. He wanted to encourage unity and camaraderie among the saints, so insisted on greeting everyone. And he wanted everyone to know what he had written, so that all would receive the instruction, encouragement and love poured out in it.

CONCLUSION

Well, there it is—I Thessalonians. A marvelous book, chock-full of help for the counselor. Don't fail to consider Paul's love and tenderness, yet in the setting of an unwillingness to compromise with sin. The balance here is remarkable; perhaps unique in all of literature. Read the letter in its entirety, over and over again in order to appreciate and soak up something of the remarkable balance with which he wrote; that is the way to gain some of it.

Counseling is hard work, as Paul says in this last chapter. But it has its compensations. Think of the joy, the love, the closeness of Paul and this church. Something of that happens in counseling too, when people obey God's Word and their lives are transformed. Every counselor knows this, and, on balance, that makes all the difficult and discouraging cases seem worthwhile. When you are wondering if you should give up counseling, my advice is to reread I Thessalonians. If you do, aright, you won't quit!

Introduction to
II THESSALONIANS

II Thessalonians is a follow-up to the first letter. It more clearly delineates some of the strengths and the weaknesses mentioned there. Further time and information allowed Paul to respond more directly to the problems concerning the time of the coming of Christ and the difficulty of busybodies who were acting in an irresponsible, idle manner. On the positive side, the encouragement, love and deep concern that Paul had for the congregation, and that they returned in kind, persists. Paul is still at the business of telling them how well they are doing, and that this means they ought to do even better. The if-you-have-it-moving-don't-let-it-stop idea is still with us. Of course, other matters are dealt with as well.

The great eschatological passage in chapter two is a challenge to every interpreter. Because much of it is yet to be fulfilled, it is impossible to identify the character who is the subject of it. Some of it is cloaked in general language, perhaps to avoid direct understanding by those who might use this information in a detrimental fashion in regard to the church. That, too, makes interpretation difficult. The spirit of the passage, however, along with the exhortations that accompany it, are plain and of great value to us today—even when we do not understand every reference. Indeed, it is the very elements that the Christian counselor should extract from the passage that are clearest. So, lack of understanding of the referents in all cases will by no means hinder our use of the verses concerned as we endeavor to understand counseling attitudes, principles and practices.

CHAPTER 1

1 Paul and Silvanus and Timothy to the church of the Thessalonians in God our Father and the Lord Jesus Christ.
2 May help and peace from God the Father and the Lord Jesus Christ be yours.
3 We ought always to thank God for you, brothers, as is appropriate, because your faith is growing so well and the love that every one of you has for one another is increasing so much
4 that we ourselves boast about you among God's churches for your endurance and faith in all your persecutions and in the afflictions that you put up with.

The same three writers are identified as in the first letter (v. 1). See the commentary and introduction to I Thessalonians for more information. The church also is similarly identified, along with the desire that they receive **grace and peace from the Lord Jesus Christ**. I shall begin my comments, therefore, with verse 3.

Paul expresses the personal obligation he believes that he has (it is not an external compulsion) to thank God always for the Church at Thessalonica. After all, they had brought such joy to him (cf. I Thessalonians 3:9) that, as he attempted in the first letter, he found himself almost incapable of expressing it. And, in addition, his prayers for them (I Thessalonians 3:10, 12) had been answered in a remarkable way. The members of the congregation were experiencing vigorous spiritual **growth** (in **faith**) and their **love for one another** was **increasing so much** (overflowing) that thanksgiving to God, Who had protected and nourished their new-found faith, was entirely **appropriate**. When you see such results from your prayerful help of counselees, like the apostle are you likewise driven to thanksgiving? Or does your pride swell? The answer to that question should tell you much about yourself and your counseling.

Paul was proud about the church (v. 2) and even **boasted**. But, notice, it was about what God had done among them—he thanked *God* for them. He was thankful for **their endurance and faith** in the midst of **persecution, and in the afflictions** (sufferings, etc.) that t**hey put up with** (v. 4). This is something that he told other **churches** about in order to encourage them to do so too. The good work of one counselee can be a stimulus for others to follow. It would be helpful, at times, to bring in someone who has successfully gone through affliction and suffering to

5 This is a clear indication of God's righteous judgment that you may be considered worthy of God's empire, for which indeed you are suffering,
6 since it is just for God to repay affliction to those who are afflicting you,

---

speak to counselees who wonder whether it is possible to do so. And the fact that Paul's use of "boast" in the original is intensified ("strongly boast") suggests that he considered this a good thing to do and that he believed it ought to have powerful effects. Explore ways of using the example of people who have been helped significantly through difficult times, when counseling others.

To some, suffering such as the young church bore would be an indication that God was not with them. You can hear certain counselees right now, can't you?—"What did I do to bring this on?" "Maybe God doesn't love me after all."—And so on. But Paul didn't think so. The way in which they grew in persecution, **put up with** it, etc.—and the very fact of persecution itself (cf. I Thessalonians 3:3,4)—were, to him, **a clear indication of God's righteous judgment** (v. 5). That is to say, they were but a clear sign of what God's judgment (to be mentioned later in the chapter) will be like. He also saw their suffering as a sign that, in Christ (surely not in themselves), God considered them **worthy** to be included in His **empire**. If they were able to suffer for Him, they could be called His citizens. After all, it was for that empire (to further it) that they were suffering. If they had not suffered, under the kind of circumstances in which this congregation was born, there might have been serious doubt about the genuineness of their profession of faith.

Probably not one counselee in a dozen thinks that way. Again, counseling means, to begin with, changing ideas and views to conform more closely to those in the Bible. The Bible everywhere indicates, as it does here, that the perseverance of the saints (cf. the word "remain" [KJ= "abide"] in John's writings) is an evidence of God at work in a life.

Now, what of that judgment that Paul says the perseverance of the Thessalonians during persecution foreshadowed? He is speaking of the judgment to come at the return of His Son, Jesus Christ. In verse 6 God says that, in that Day, He will turn the tables (a powerful modern picture of the table with the chess board being turned around so that the winning one is now losing) so that in His holy justice He will **repay affliction** to those who are afflicting His people (v. 6). The affliction they now receive is but a meager indication of how much their oppressors will receive in

II Thessalonians 1

7   and give rest to you who are being afflicted (and to us) at the revelation of the Lord Jesus from the sky with His mighty angels
8   in flaming fire, taking vengeance on those who don't know God and who don't pay attention to the good news of our Lord Jesus.

---

that great, everlasting affliction of the second death—the lake of fire! And on that Day the Christian will no longer suffer affliction, but will receive everlasting **rest** together with the apostle and his comrades (note the "us" in v. 7). They were as sure of that fact as anyone could be sure of anything. What a wonderful promise! Believers, regardless of their present state of turmoil due to sin and its consequences in this life, will receive rest. Think of it: rest from all the troubles that bring people into counseling! You can detail them for yourself, beginning with the last six cases. And you, counselor, like the apostle Paul, have the privilege of ministering that revealed truth to them. Where, then, is the place for complaining, for giving up, for throwing in the towel? Obviously, there is none.

When will this happen? **At the revelation of Jesus Christ from the sky with His mighty angels.** On that **Day**, though neither you nor your counselees have seen Him (cf. I Peter 1:8, 9), you will see Him for the first time not as the suffering Servant of Isaiah 53, about Whom there was nothing to make Him desirable, but as the great God and Savior Who comes as the King of kings and Lord of lords. You will see Him in all His power, splendor and glory!

Accompanied by those **angels** who did not rebel, **mighty** beings who are capable of putting down every power on earth that opposes, He will bring **flaming fire** upon those **who don't know God and who don't pay attention to the good news**. Then, God will take the **vengeance** He promised in Romans 12:19. Since at times you will be questioned about whether the heathen are lost, it is informative to note that Paul says **vengeance** will come upon those who reject the gospel—that much many will accept—but also on those *who do not know God.* People sometimes have a more difficult time with this. Yet, there it is, in black and white. In a day such as ours, when people who report near death experiences (they never really died) in which they imagine seeing a being of light (regardless of their belief in the true God), it is hard to get people to believe in any kind of vengeance. **Vengeance**, indeed, is a word hardly ever encountered any more, and on those rare occasions on which you do, it is in a no-no context. Even in some supposedly Bible-believing churches the idea of God taking vengeance is repugnant. No wonder, then, that there is so little

Christian Counselor's Commentary

9 They will pay the penalty of eternal ruin and separation from the presence of the Lord and from the glory of His might
10 when He comes to be glorified by His saints and to be admired by all those who have believed (because our testimony to you was believed) on that Day.

---

comfort among those who are afflicted by the wicked; they see no righting of wrongs, they do not believe in God's justice. To worship a god who will not exercise judgment (including the pouring out of His avenging wrath in judgment) is to worship a god different from the One presented in the New Testament.

Of what does this vengeance consist? Listen to verse 9: **They will pay the penalty of eternal ruin and separation from the presence of the Lord and the glory of His might**. In other words, they will receive the opposite of everything to which the Christian is looking forward. The phrase **pay the penalty** refers to the execution of a judgment from the point of view of the Judge. The term translated **ruin** means the loss of everything that is worthwhile. And **separation from the presence** (lit., "face") **of the Lord** is the greatest tragedy of all. They will never know what it is to enter into eternal **rest** (see Hebrews 4), where believers will bask **in the glory** of the Lord's **might**. Think of it. While now one may not be a Christian and yet be on the winning side, when Christ comes, those who are now winning will lose, and lose big! And Christians at that time will at last be seen to be on the winning side, and winning big! Counselees impatient with their present lot need to be reminded (and often shamed in doing so) of these future facts.

According to verse 10, at His coming Christ **will be glorified by His saints**. How marvelous to be able to sing His praises in that Day. It will be *His* Day, not yours. He will return to this world that rejected, despised and crucified Him as the Lord of glory. He will put down all opposition and assert His true claims once and for all, demonstrating to all the universe Who He really is. And as you see Him you will **admire** Him. In that Day, when you see Him, your mouth will hang open at His astounding glory. It will far surpass the stunning glory that briefly shone on the Mount of Transfiguration. Yet manifested there was the first glimpse of what He will be like in that Day.

When Paul thought about these things he could do no less than pray for them, that **God will consider them worthy** (i.e., "to be made right or fitting for something") **of His call** and that they will **fulfill all their good**

II Thessalonians 1

11 Indeed, we always pray this about you, that our God may consider you worthy of His call, and may fulfill every good intention and every faithful deed of yours by His power,
12 so that the Name of our Lord Jesus may be glorified by you, and you by Him, in keeping with the grace of our God and the Lord Jesus Christ.

---

intentions (resolves prompted by goodness) **and faithful deeds** (activity inspired by faith; resolve that is followed by action). Of course, not in their own wisdom and strength, but **by His power**. That is God's way of preparing His sons for glory, never by self-help. But, on the other hand, His power is manifested, as this whole chapter indicates, by God-enabled obedience to His Word, not by some quietistic stance in which one settles back and says, "Let go and let God."

Paul wants them to be worthy so that Jesus' **Name is glorified** by them, **as they are by Him, in keeping with the help** (grace) that the Father and the Son supply. In Hebrew thought, the Name was associated with one's person and character. We also speak of having a good (or bad) name, meaning a good or bad reputation. That is a closely related idea. When a counselee is concerned about what kind of name he will have if he admits his sin, for instance, he is asking about what others will think. The only one about whom he ought to be concerned is the One with Whom he ultimately has to do. It really doesn't matter what others think or say, so long as the Name of Christ is held high. Again, the balance— avoiding self-help and quietism—is set forth as the Biblical center. We glorify His *Name* by His *grace*.

Chapter 2

1 Now we ask you, brothers, concerning the coming of our Lord Jesus Christ and our assembling to meet Him,
2 not to be quickly shaken out of your senses or disturbed, either by a spirit or by a word or by a letter supposedly from us, saying that the Lord's Day has come.

Without a doubt, the second chapter of this book is difficult. But, as I said in the introduction, the things that are certain are the very things most profitable to us from a counseling perspective. There is a parallel here between Revelation 20:7ff. and this chapter. See my book, *The Time is at Hand* for details. I shall mention some of the similarities only in passing. To begin, it is interesting to notice how the question of the Lord's return broached in the first letter consumes much of the second—almost two chapters of the three! It is of such great importance because of false teaching that was creating confusion. Paul is deeply concerned to root out the error and to establish the truth in its place. That is largely the reason the subject takes up so much space. Of course, the second coming of Christ occupies a key position among the loci of Christian theology, and so is an important matter *in itself*—it is not *only* because of the error that needed to be refuted that it merits detailed discussion. But, doubtless, so much is said because of the problems connected to it in Thessalonica.

If, as I suggested in comments on the first letter, the idleness (which we will meet again in chapter three) was due to a view that the Lord's return was imminent, as many think, then it is interesting to note how doctrine—even doctrine having to do with eschatology—may have to be dealt with by counselors in order to resolve the practical problems of living that result from them. That means, counselor, you may not settle for least-common-denominator studies; you will have to know something substantial about the *entire* corpus of doctrine. The person who told me that he can counsel from a total of six verses is, obviously, more astute than the apostle Paul who found it necessary to write in detail, at length.

In verse 1, Paul begins with a request (**we ask you, brothers**) that is based on the facts about the coming of Christ and **the assembling** of believers (mentioned in I Thessalonians 4) in response to the shout and the trumpet calling them forth to go out **to meet** the Lord in the sky in order to escort Him on His way back to earth in power and glory. This request shapes up in verse 2: don't **be quickly shaken out of your senses**

or disturbed, either by spirit or word or by a letter supposedly from us, saying that the Lord's Day has come. Clearly, now, as Paul writes this second letter, he more fully understands what the false teaching is; he has acquired additional information after Timothy had an opportunity to confer with the church about it. In any one or more of a variety of ways (Paul doesn't seem to know exactly how—by spirit, word or letter) this error has been introduced.

Paul's teaching had been misrepresented. Have you ever been misrepresented, counselor? If you haven't, you haven't done much counseling. People misrepresent others regularly from misunderstanding, a desire to bend facts to their advantage, superficial study of what you said or wrote, etc. In my first book, *Competent to Counsel*, published in 1970, I plainly said that sickness and trouble do not necessarily come from the sin of those who are afflicted by them. I even cited the cases of Job and the man born blind (John 9) and developed that theme at some length. Yet to this day there are people going around saying that I teach every problem and every sickness is the result of that person's sin.

Well, Paul deals with the misrepresentation at length. It was even possible, he thought, that his name had been attached to a letter that contained this error, purporting to be from him. In other words, some holding this view might have been using his authority with the congregation to muscle in their view. You will even find people today doing similar things. Don't let these misrepresentations of your teaching—or something that you have said to or about a counselee—slide by unanswered. It is not that Paul had to vindicate himself, but he was concerned about truth and its impact on the thinking and living of his new converts. You too must be concerned to correct misrepresentations for the same reason.

Evidently, from the language used in verse 2, the church had been greatly impacted by these errors. He urges them not to let the false teaching affect them too much. Error can throw your counselee off track. It can **disturb** his spiritual progress. Help him get back on by countering it with truth.

What was the error? That **the Lord's Day has come** (v. 2^b). This simply wasn't true. As Paul goes on to observe, it couldn't be true since two important events must occur first: **the apostasy** (about which, presumably, he had already told them) and the appearance of **the lawless person** (also someone whom he had described while with them). Why do I say that he had previously taught them these things? Because the way he refers to them indicates that he is referring to familiar items. He has no need to explain these references.

Christian Counselor's Commentary

> 3 Don't let anyone deceive you in any way; you see, that Day won't come until first the apostasy takes place and then the lawless person is revealed—the son of destruction—
> 4 who opposes and exalts himself above everything that is said to be god or that is an object of worship, so that he even takes a seat in the temple of God, demonstrating that he himself is a god.
> 5 Don't you remember that when I was yet with you I used to tell you these things?

The **apostasy** (lit., a "standing off from") refers to a great turning from the teachings of Christianity by those who have grown up in the church and still (though falsely) claim to be Christians. This term is often used in a military context of those who defect to the enemy. Here, of course, it is religious defection that Paul has in mind.

And the **revelation of the lawless person** would also have to happen prior to the coming of Christ. He is also called by Paul **the son of** (i.e., one prepared for) perdition (or **destruction**). He is connected with this great apostasy from the pure gospel. Plainly, then, since neither the apostasy nor the revelation had yet occurred, the Lord could not have come. This coming and apostasy are somehow connected with what we have seen in I Thessalonians 5. This person and this event will bring about a time of worldwide "peace" during which people will think they are "safe." But, contrary to that false assurance, they will receive "sudden destruction" at Christ's unexpected coming like a thief. It is when the world, presumably under the leadership and rule of this lawless person, thinks that it has it made that the Lord will return. It is easy to deceive people about the Lord's return; Paul's warns against allowing this to happen (v. 3).

In verse 4 Paul describes the lawless person who will eventually head up the apostasy. He opposes every god worshipped in the world, and exalts himself far above those gods. He even **sits** (or "makes his seat") in the **inner temple of God** (the *naos*), **displaying himself as god**. In other words, he demands self-worship in place of all other worship. In nearly every age, people have attempted to identify this personage with someone on the scene. But when he comes and the times in which he appears should be so clear to Christians who have I and II Thessalonians as their guide that they will not mistake him.

During the time when he was with them Paul had been telling them about this occurrence (v. 5). And he had given them rather detailed information: **you know what is holding him back at the present time so that he may be revealed at his time. The present time** (Paul's, that is) was

II Thessalonians 2

6 You know what is holding him back at the present time so that he may be revealed at his time.
7 The secret of lawlessness is working already; only the one who now holds him back will do so until he arises out of the midst.
8 At that time the lawless one will be revealed, whom the Lord Jesus will do away with by the breath from His mouth and will destroy by the brilliant splendor of His coming.
9 The coming of the lawless one will be motivated by Satan with all sorts of lying powers and signs and wonders,

---

not the time for Christ to return, though even at that early date **the secret of lawlessness was at work** (v. 7). **The one who holds the lawless person back** would continue to do so until he (the lawless person) **arises out of the midst** [of the apostasy]. Literally, Paul writes "he will become out of the midst." It is as if Satan is holding his man in the wings till the right moment, when the force and the person prohibiting his coming ceases to do so, and then, out of the growing apostasy, he sends him forth on the world stage (see v. 9).

That the lawless one has not yet arrived on the scene of world history is apparent because he will be slain at the second coming by Christ (v. 8). The lawless one will be Satan-motivated and will come offering every sort of false miracle (v. 9). And these unrighteous deceptions will be accepted by those who are lost and who have rejected the truth (v. 10). Because of their rejection, God will cause them to believe the lie (v. 11). And they will be condemned because they love error rather than truth (v. 12). Now what can we make of this passage?

Well, I can't tell you who the man of lawlessness is. He has not yet appeared, but the mystery (secret) of lawlessness, in which the rejection of God's law is the prominent factor, was already at work in Paul's time. So whatever this was, and whoever (and whatever) was holding back the revelation of this preeminently evil person, has been at work from then until now. It involves, as it did at the beginning, in the garden, an assault on the Word of God. That is clear. We have yet to look forward to the denouement of this lawlessness, however, in an apostasy **out of the midst** of which the lawless individual **will arise**. That is about all I can tell you for sure. The standard Protestant interpretation since the Reformation is that the apostasy is the coming into being of the Roman Catholic Church; the mystery of lawlessness already at work is the early seeds of that apostasy. Certainly, nothing has been with us over so long a period as the apos-

Christian Counselor's Commentary

> 10 and with all sorts of unrighteous deceptions for those who are perishing because they refused to love the truth for their salvation.
> 11 So, for this reason, God will send them an error that will cause them to believe the lie,
> 12 that all may be condemned who did not believe the truth but rather took pleasure in unrighteousness.

tasy that developed out of sacerdotalism. That some future pope will be the lawless man is also altogether possible. Coupled with some international body such as the U.N., which has gained power in recent years, it could affect much of what is predicted here—especially if the declarations of the popes over the years are ever taken seriously by the world in general. For interesting material in this regard see John Leahy, *The Roman Antichrist,* published by The National Union of Protestants (Ireland).

But notice some things that we *are* able to learn. First, truth rejected, and lies accepted, are a judgment of God. And the very name of the individual, "the lawless man," indicates what he thinks of the Scriptures; above all else that characterizes him is the fact that he rejects God's law. Moreover, the evil one loves to receive the worship that belongs to God alone. He revels in the fact that lying wonders can bring the world's population into submission to a false god through whom he receives the honor of unbelieving men. Truth, then, rather than error, is of great importance.

God hardens those who refuse to accept the truth. Notice how Paul puts it in verses 11 and 12: **So, for this reason [because they refused to love the truth; v. 10], God will send them an error that will cause them to believe a lie that all may be condemned who did not believe the truth but rather took pleasure in unrighteousness**. Those are powerful words. Because they took pleasure in unrighteous activities that became rampant as the apostasy grew in intensity, they were subject to the working of error so that they believed a lie.

Counselees may wonder why unsaved spouses or loved ones don't come to Christ. One reason may be their pleasure in unrighteousness that leads to God hardening their hearts and directing them into error and lies. While we can never declare another person reprobate before death, and must seek to win all to Christ, it is altogether possible that *in God's sight* he is reprobate. The fact is, however, you and I do not possess God's sight!

Paul moves on. Again, he expresses his **thanks to God** for the church at Thessalonica—a constant theme of these two letters. Why?

II Thessalonians 2

13 But we ought always to thank God for you, brothers dear to the Lord, because God chose you from the beginning for salvation by the Spirit's sanctification and by faith in the truth,
14 to which He called you by means of our good news that you might secure for yourselves the glory of our Lord Jesus Christ.

Because, he says, **God chose you from the beginning for salvation by the Spirit's sanctification and by faith in the truth, to which He called you by means of our good news** (vv. 13, 14^a). We have said enough about Paul's love for the members of this congregation and his utter gratitude to God for the church they were forming. But note, he also gives thanks for God's election (**choosing**) of them **from the beginning**. Paul was grateful for the plan and purpose of God from the beginning of the world that had actually come to pass in time. When you and your counselee can rejoice over **God's election** of individuals in a congregation—some of whom may not be very pleasant to live with—you will have gone far toward dealing with the problems that you face with them. If they are God's chosen ones, who are you, counselee, to rail at them? How dare you judge another man's servant? It is important to understand that God chose people from the beginning, not because they were delightful people, but out of grace. He is in the process of turning them into more pleasant people. But, sometimes, it does not happen as rapidly as it did with the Thessalonians.

The **Spirit** set them aside (the use of the word **sanctification** here does not refer to the process but, as it sometimes does, to the act of separating the chosen ones out of the mass of mankind). But this always happens through the means—never apart from it. They had to hear and believe the gospel message (**by faith in the truth**). That is how the Spirit set them apart as God's elect (v. 13).

The internal **call** of the Spirit, by which he gave life to believe, coincided with the external call of the preaching of the good news by Paul and his associates. When they believed, they **secured for themselves** (not *by* themselves) the eternal **glory** that awaits all of those who will stand with Christ some day sharing His own glory. What a wonderful truth! Don't fail, when things look utterly glum in counseling, to bring out the glory of the future that awaits God's own. Glory is a word to be used frequently by counselors. There isn't much glory here in this life of sin and its consequences. So people need to hear about the glory to come. It can only brighten and enlighten those otherwise grimy and sordid sessions filled

Christian Counselor's Commentary

> 15 So then, brothers, stand firm and hold on to the traditions that you were taught by us either by word or by letter.
> 16 Now, may our Lord Jesus Christ Himself, and God our Father, Who loved us and by grace gave us eternal encouragement and good hope,
> 17 encourage your hearts and support you in every good work and word.

with the rotten things that so often are trucked into counseling.

Verse 15 says it all, by way of conclusion: **So then, brothers, stand firm and hold on to the traditions that you were taught by us either by word or by letter**. It is important not to be turned aside by falsehood and error. The apostolic message came two ways: **by word and by letter**. All that was of importance for the church of the future was ultimately incorporated into the writings of the New Testament. But at that time, the New Testament was not completed. So the apostolic word possessed by the churches was still largely verbal. The word **tradition** used in this verse means simply, "that which is handed over." It could be handed over, says Paul, in either of two ways.

The Thessalonians were suffering for their faith. Paul, therefore, exhorts them to **stand firm and to hold on to** their present beliefs. Such exhortations are not without point. Do you give them to those suffering for Christ?

Lastly, in this chapter, comes the benediction. In it, Paul calls on the Father and the Son, **who loved us and by grace gave us eternal encouragement and good hope, to encourage their hearts and support them in every good work and word**. A wonderful benediction, appropriate to every one of us. Many need to be encouraged. The **good hope** of eternal life and the heavenly inheritance and the hope of glory will itself **encourage** the heart if and when adequately understood. But more than that, Paul prays that they may be supported by God in every good work in which they engaged and every good word they spoke. Surely, you can do no less. Some counselors only scold and whip counselees. That is wrong. They need encouragement. Much of what the two letters to this church are all about is encouragement—giving those facts that would instill hope and reassurance that will encourage the reader. That is an essential part of all good counseling.

CHAPTER 3

> 1 Finally, brothers, pray for us that the Lord's Word may run freely and be glorified as indeed it was with you,
> 2 and that we may be delivered from eccentric and evil persons, because not everyone has faith.

In chapter three, Paul turns from a discussion of the second coming to a variety of matters, in particular, to the problem of those who were living in a disorderly fashion. He begins, however, requesting prayer for himself and his companions (vv. 1, 2). He is concerned about two things: first, **that the Lord's Word may run freely and be glorified** as it was with them, and second **that they may be delivered from eccentric and evil person**s who, it seems were the cause of some kind of interference that kept the Word from running unhindered. It is a pleasant figure to see the Word of God running, as in a race, across the Mediterranean world. It is not so pleasant to hear about eccentric and evil persons. The devil uses all kinds to hinder the Lord's work. It is not only those who are obviously or intentionally evil—there is a fair share of them in the way of every minister—but it is also those who want to take up time and energy over crazy ideas and problems manufactured by themselves, where there is no problem after all. Every counselor might with Paul, ask his constituency to pray to be delivered from the latter as well as the former. Perhaps, if anyone, counselors are the ones who tend to run into a larger than ordinary proportion of these eccentric types. They are the ones who come out of left field, who are always troubled about some unusual or weird difficulty that should trouble no one. They can waste much of your time if you allow them.

And these are people who do not have faith. Sometimes those who are eccentric seem only to be unusual, yet many of them develop their eccentric ways as a result of not knowing Christ. Biblical teaching tends to level out one's life. It doesn't bring utter sameness or hinder individual expression, but it does keep one from the excesses. No Christian should be far out. If he is, chances are he doesn't have faith—or has just become a Christian. The individual attitudes and ways of Christians, which might be of interest, are always within the broad parameters of what is genuinely Christian. Within those parameters is plenty of room for movement and individuality.

Counselor, the utterly eccentric must be questioned about their faith;

Christian Counselor's Commentary

> 3 But the Lord is faithful Who will support you and guard you from the evil one.
> 4 We are convinced in the Lord that you are following and will follow those authoritative instructions that we are giving you.
> 5 May the Lord direct your hearts into God's love and into Christ's patience.

---

that is the message Paul is delivering in verse 2^b. The word translated "eccentric" is, literally, "out of place, odd." It speaks of those who hinder in strange ways. That one might suspect this of those who show markedly **evil** tendencies is much clearer. Christians ought to question anyone who takes glee in evil about his profession of faith. That simply doesn't compute.

Those who are afflicted by the **evil one**, nevertheless, are also supported by the Holy One (v. 3). He **guards** them and keeps them from falling. It is the Lord Himself that makes one stable, firm. Counselors only minister the Word through which He brings this about. There is nothing they can do to make another stable or firm. But God promises He will. Counselees who affirm the opposite are calling God a liar. And that is serious business. Be sure to warn them about doubt as you continue to assert the truths of this verse. Show counselees how the promise depends on God's **faithfulness**. Doubt doesn't cast a shadow on *your* promise when you assert the guarding and supporting power of God, but, at bottom, it is a challenge to the **faithfulness** of *God*.

Having been with them when the Word of God was received with such a welcome, and having heard from Timothy how they are now doing, Paul is confident that they are **following and will continue to follow those authoritative instructions that he is giving** them. That is a fine assurance to have about a counselee. Only too frequently you will have to say that you are not **convinced**. In such cases, why not read this verse to a counselee and ask, "When am I going to be able to say that about you?" It might startle him into thinking about his failure. At the least, it will give him a goal toward which to move.

In verse 5, Paul expresses a prayer-wish. He wants God to direct (not only their feet, but) their hearts into God's love and into Christ's patience. He wants love and patience to become a thing of the heart—an inner reality. It is interesting to notice the combination. Endurance in the face of trial need not harden one; he may use the experience to deepen his love. But it is God's love and Christ's patience, not some human counterfeit of

II Thessalonians 3

6 Now we authoritatively instruct you, brothers, in the Name of the Lord Jesus Christ to withdraw from every brother who is living in idleness and not in keeping with the tradition that you received from us.
7 You yourselves know how you ought to imitate us, because we were not idle among you,
8 nor did we eat anyone's bread as a gift, but rather, night and day by labor and struggle we worked so that we might not be a burden to any of you.

---

that. God must work this love and patience in the believer; it is not naturally there. It comes from Him. And it is like the patience and love of Christ that He once lived before us. His example with Him as the Source is what every counselee needs.

Now comes a longer section, with which Paul concludes (vv. 6-15). In this section, Paul discusses the disorderly way in which some idle persons in their midst are living and what to do about them if they do not heed his call to change. In every way, this passage is crucial for counselors because it deals with the latter stage of church discipline that every counselor must understand if he is to counsel effectively. For detailed direction about the entire question of Church Discipline see my book, *The Handbook of Church Discipline*.

Throughout these two letters Paul has been giving **authoritative instructions** that he expected them to obey (the word was used of an authority issuing a summons). He begins this section, therefore, with one such **instruction: withdraw from every brother who is living in idleness and not keeping the tradition that he received**. The word "withdraw" is a nautical term meaning "to furl sails." The idea is that as when sails are folded up and stowed away out of sight, so should one take much the same action. He should withdraw from brothers living in idleness. This withdrawal didn't mean total absence from the brother, but it means the withdrawal of Christian fellowship. Presently we shall see what he is to do instead.

Paul gives them no excuse for such idleness; they had a perfect example of industry in Paul and his companions, who worked rather than remain idle when they were with them (see earlier discussions of this and of their example in I Thessalonians). He details what they did in verse 8: **they didn't eat anyone's bread as a gift (they didn't sponge off anyone), but rather, night and day by labor and struggle we worked so that we would not be a burden to any of you,** he says. Tent making (cf. Acts 18:3) was exhausting toil, and it didn't pay well. Yet Paul was not

Christian Counselor's Commentary

9 This was not because we didn't have the authority to do so, but that we ourselves might become models for you so that you may imitate us.
10 Indeed, even when we were with you, we gave you this authoritative instruction: "Whoever won't work shouldn't eat."
11 We hear that some among you are living in a totally unstructured way, and busy at nothing except being busybodies!
12 Now, such persons we authoritatively instruct and urge in the Lord Jesus Christ to work with quietness that they may eat their own bread.

---

ashamed to work at it, nor was he too lazy to do so. He had the right to ask for sustenance as a servant of Christ, but he waived his God-given right to do so in order to become an example for the Church. Did he detect the spirit of laziness in some of them from the outset? At any rate, he became a model, set a pattern for the church. Surely there must have been at least an inkling of the problem since when he was with them he gave them this authoritative instruction: **Whoever won't work shouldn't eat**. That is surely a pertinent instruction for counselors to use in a day of government handouts and people lazier than they ever have been in this land. The authority behind this instruction is *God's* authority—don't ever forget to emphasize that.

Timothy had reported: the problem hasn't been solved. After what you wrote and all I said, there still are **some who are living in a totally unstructured way.** There is a very important insight for every counselor. Most people who are in trouble because of their own failures, in one way or another, lived unstructured lives. They need structure: discipline, regularity, etc. Here, because they didn't work, they roamed around among the rest **busy at nothing but being busybodies**. Clearly, if one will not fill his day with those things that God has called him to do, he will fill it with those things He forbids. The military term **unstructured** sometimes has the idea of being out of step or not standing by one's post. That is precisely what happens to those who have no structure in life. Your task, counselor, is to help counselees develop structure by instruction, laying out proper courses for their lives, and by riding herd on them until they have developed the structure necessary.

Again, in verse 12, speaking now to those who were disobeying, he commands and **urges in the Lord Jesus** (that is, by His authority) **to work with quietness that they may eat their own bread**. Evidently their idle gossip was stirring up trouble. Instead, they should live the **quiet** life (one in which they brought rest and peace to people who lived in their surroundings) of one who works hard. And they are not to do this for a brief

II Thessalonians 3

13 You, brothers, don't give up on well-doing.

14 Now, whoever doesn't obey what we say in this letter, mark that person and don't mix with him so that he may become ashamed of himself.

15 And yet, don't regard him as an enemy, but rather counsel him as a brother.

16 May the Lord of peace give you His peace always in every way. The Lord be with all of you.

---

period of time, but to continue, not becoming **weary in well-doing** (v. 13; cf. Galatians 6:9). Now, there is a problem. So many counselees start out well, but in a short time find that work is hard. They want to quit because they are becoming weary of the labor, the boredom, the routine, etc. That is not the way a Christian should operate. When he works for Christ, the most laborious or wearisome job and the most boring one can become a pleasant challenge. A job is not just what the company or the boss makes it; preeminently, it is what *you* make of it.

Now the part about church discipline. If when a matter comes to the officers of the church (the elders; v. 14) they instruct a member to obey a command of God and he or she refuses, the elders are to **mark** ("identify") that person for the rest of the congregation and they are to cease **mixing with him so that he may become ashamed** of himself and repent. Normal relations must be suspended. There is a **withdrawal** of fellowship (v. 6). What does this withdrawal or cessation of mixing mean? Sally calls Sue. She says, let's go round to the flea markets this Saturday (something they both enjoyed doing in the past). Sue says, "I'd sure love to. But, you see, things aren't right. You are under discipline and I can't fellowship with you as if nothing were wrong." Is that the end of it? No. In verse 15, Paul continues, **yet, don't regard him as an enemy, but rather, counsel him as a brother**. Here is Sue's obligation and opportunity. She ought to continue, in words something like this: "We can't simply ignore your problem. I'll tell you what—instead of shopping, let's spend that time talking about it." She offers counsel. In the process of discipline, counseling moves from one on one to two or three on one, to the elders, to the congregation in an ever-widening inclusion of persons who are willing to help.

Now Paul closes the letter. That Paul does not use salutations and closing benedictions in some inane, mindless, stereotyped manner is clear when you look at this one where he enlarges on his usual wish for peace (v. 16). He says that he wishes them **peace in every way** they can think of. And they will receive it if, as he also wishes, **the Lord is with** them.

Christian Counselor's Commentary

17 I (Paul) write this greeting with my own hand, and this is the indication in every letter that I have written it.
18 May help from our Lord Jesus Christ be with all of you.

Why? Because peace comes from Him; He is **the Lord of peace**. In verse 17 he alludes to his practice of writing the last words of a letter in his own hand. There had possibly been forgeries, as he indicated earlier in the letter. They could determine an authentic Pauline letter by the writing at the conclusion. Finally he wishes, in addition, **grace** (help) from the Lord Jesus for **all** of them. In that little word was hope for the disorderly ones as well as for the rest.

www.ingramcontent.com/pod-product-compliance
Lightning Source LLC
Chambersburg PA
CBHW060509100426
42743CB00009B/1261